Teaching and You

Teaching and You

Committing, Preparing, and Succeeding

- **Jack M. Evans**
  Central Michigan University

- **Martha M. Brueckner**
  Earle Brown Elementary School
  Brooklyn Center, Minnesota

Allyn and Bacon
Boston London Toronto Sydney Tokyo Singapore

Series Editor: *Sean W. Wakely*
Series Editorial Assistant: *Carol L. Chernaik*
Production Administrator: *Annette Joseph*
Production Coordinator: *Susan Freese*
Editorial-Production Service: *TKM Productions*
Design/Composition: *Denise Hoffman*
Manufacturing Buyer: *Louise Richardson*
Cover Administrator: *Linda K. Dickinson*
Cover Designer: *Suzanne Harbison*

Copyright (c) 1992 by Allyn and Bacon
A Division of Simon & Schuster, Inc.
160 Gould Street
Needham Heights, Massachusetts 02194

Library of Congress Cataloging-in-Publication Data

Evans, Jack M.
  Teaching and you : committing, preparing, and succeeding / Jack M.
Evans, Martha M. Brueckner.
    p.   cm.
  Includes bibliographical references and index.
  ISBN 0-205-13248-0
    1. Teaching—Vocational guidance—United States.   I. Brueckner,
Martha M.   II. Title.
  LB1775.2.E93   1992   91-30632
  371.1'0023—dc20   CIP

Printed in the United States of America

10 9 8 7 6 5 4 3 2 1   96 95 94 93 92 91

Photo Credit: Pages 84, 89, and 191 (c) Frank Siteman 1990.

To
Ruth Evans
and
Louis Pichette

■ ■ ■ Brief Contents _____

■ **Unit One   So You Want to Be a Teacher!**

   1   **The Profession of Teaching**   1

   2   **Programs in Education**   35

   3   **Specialized Knowledge**   51

   4   **Observing Teachers and Students in Classrooms**   77

■ **Unit Two   Becoming a Teacher**

   5   **Should I Become a Teacher?**   107

   6   **Becoming a Teacher**   137

   7   **Marketing Your Teaching Skills**   155

■ **Unit Three   What Does the Future Hold?**

   8   **Looking Ahead**   175

   9   **Social Issues Affecting the Teaching Profession**   191

  10   **The Real World**   211

■ ▪ ■ Contents _____

Preface   **xv**

■ **Unit One   So You Want to Be a Teacher!**

1   **The Profession
of Teaching**   **1**

The Profession of Teaching   3

Ethics   8

Defining *Teaching*   9

The Changing Role of Teachers   11

Parent and Community Perspectives   15

School Organization   17
  The Community   18
  The Board of Education   19
  The Superintendent   20
  The Assistant Superintendent   20
  Student Support Services Team   21
  Coordinators   21
  Director of Special Education   23
  Principals   23
  Teachers   26
  Parents and Students   29

Educational Law   30

■ Summary   31

■ The Workshop   32

■ Questions and Thoughts   33

■ Readings and References   34

2   Programs in Education   35

Programs: A Point of View   37
    Chapter I   39
    Elementary and Secondary Education Act (1965)   39
    National Head Start   39
    Open Enrollments   40
    Schools for the Creative and Performing Arts   40
    The Gifted   40
    Magnet Schools   41
    The Boston University–Chelsea Public Schools Project   42
    National Teacher Certification   42
    Multicultural Education   43
    Foreign Language Programs   44
    Educational Cooperative Service Units   44
    Other Programs in Education   44

■ Summary   47

■ The Workshop   47

■ Questions and Thoughts   49

■ Readings and References   49

3   Specialized Knowledge   51

Vocabulary   53
In the Classroom   56
    Left Brain, Right Brain   57
    Learning Modalities   59
    Classroom Management   61
    Classroom Control   64
Why Read Research?   66

■ Summary   69

■ The Workshop   70

■ Questions and Thoughts   75

■ Readings and References   75

**4   Observing Teachers and Students
in Classrooms   77**

The Field Experience   79
Why Visit a Classroom?   81

What to Look For: A Classroom Profile   82
    The Students   83
    The Teacher   88
    The Physical Environment   93
An Observer's Checklist   97
■ Summary   103
■ The Workshop   103
■ Questions and Thoughts   106
■ Readings and References   106

■ Unit Two Becoming a Teacher

5   Should I Become a Teacher?   107

Is Enjoying Children or My Subject Content Really Enough?   109
    The Need to Like Children   110
    Teaching or Playing Games: A Differentiation   113
Factors in Deciding on Teaching as a Profession   115
    Your School-Related Experiences   116
    Interest Inventories and Personality Surveys   118
    Your Commitment   120
    The Specialists: Physical Education, Art, and Music   120
Special Education   126
    Physically Handicapped   126
    General Learning Disability (GLD)   127
    Speech and/or Language Delayed   130
    Reading Specialists   130
    Emotional Behavior Disorders (EBD)   131
■ Summary   132
■ The Workshop   133
■ Questions and Thoughts   135
■ Readings and References   136

6   Becoming a Teacher   137

Curriculum Requirements   139
University Requirements   141
    Admission to the University   141
    Admission to the Teacher Education Program   143
    Student Teaching   146

Majors and Minors   149
    Majors and Minors in Demand   149
    Choosing Majors and Minors   150
■ Summary   152
■ The Workshop   152
■ Questions and Thoughts   153
■ Readings and References   153

7   Marketing Your Teaching Skills   155

Employer Needs   157
Majors and Minors   159
Special Qualities, Training, and Experiences   160
Extracurricular Activities   165
Discovering Elementary and Secondary Education   166
    Elementary Education   167
    Secondary Education   169
■ Summary   172
■ The Workshop   173
■ Questions and Thoughts   173
■ Readings and References   174

■ Unit Three   What Does the Future Hold?

8   Looking Ahead   175

Becoming Certified   177
Maintaining Certification   178
Professional Organizations   179
    Teacher Organizations   179
    Subject Organizations   180
Joining Professional Organizations   181
Tenure   182
Professional Rights and Responsibilities   183
Teacher Accountability   184
    Changing Jobs   185
Obtaining a Master's Degree   187
■ Summary   188

- The Workshop   188
- Questions and Thoughts   188
- Readings and References   189

9   Social Issues Affecting the Teaching Profession   191

Child Abuse and Neglect: The School Component   193
   Identifying Abused Children   194
   Know the Laws   195
   The Support System   196

At-Risk Students: The New Challenge   197
   Effects and Characteristics   198
   Academic Accommodations   198

Multicultural Education   199
   A Definition   199
   In the Classroom   200
   A Matter of Language   201
   Educating All Students   201
   A Changing Student Population   203

Accountability: Who Is Responsible?   205
   Teachers Are Accountable   205
   The Community Is Accountable   207
   Administrators Are Accountable   207
   Parents Are Accountable   207
   Students Are Accountable   208

- Summary   208
- The Workshop   209
- Questions and Thoughts   209
- Readings and References   209

10   The Real World   211

Reality Situations   212
- Summary   221
- The Workshop   221
- Questions and Thoughts   222
- Readings and References   223

Name Index   225

Subject Index   227

■ ■ ■ Preface _____

Teaching and You: Committing, Preparing, and Succeeding serves as a concise introduction to the teaching profession for students who are considering teaching as a career choice. It is designed to assist potential teacher candidates, education students, and nontraditional students in the investigation of teaching as a major course of study as well as a lifelong profession.

The university experience is an exciting, challenging, and enjoyable time for most students. Applying to the various colleges or universities, being accepted for admission, registering for classes, and other activities are all important events in a person's life. Registering for an introductory course in education is one of the important decisions you will make in your college career.

Investigating various professions and careers is an important task; narrowing the choices down to one is prefaced by a number of decisions. What are the requirements and prerequisites for the profession? What are the long-term possibilities for employment and job satisfaction? Who will your colleagues and coworkers be? Will you fit in? These and many other decisions contribute to the inclusion or exclusion of certain careers into the realm of possibilities.

The teaching profession has one big advantage over almost all other career choices: Everyone has been in the system as a participant for a number of years. As a college student, you are continuing your participation in the system in a general way (continuing your education as a student) and in a specific way (considering education as a lifelong profession). *Teaching and You* is designed to help you investigate the teaching profession in very specific ways.

This book is divided into three units. The first four chapters comprise Unit One, "So You Want to Be a Teacher!" Chapter One, "The Profession of Teaching" examines some peripheral aspects of the teaching profession that you will encounter as a teacher. It is helpful to be aware of factors that contribute directly and indirectly to the daily operations of any given profession or career. Chapter Two, "Programs in Education," gives a brief examination of some programs that are operating in our contemporary school systems. Some are mandated by legislation, and others are unique to particular areas.

As a potential teacher, you should be cognizant of these various educational programs.

Every career or profession has a base of special knowledge or information associated with it. Teaching is no exception. Chapter Three, "Specialized Knowledge," presents some of the terminology and classroom information that are helpful for potential teacher candidates to know. One of the most important things for future teachers to realize is what occurs in contemporary classrooms. An efficient way to learn about classroom teaching is to observe students, teachers, children, and the entire school operation. Chapter Four, "Observing Teachers and Students in Classrooms," offers guidelines to help you set up and perform school observations.

There are three chapters in Unit Two, "Becoming a Teacher." Chapter Five, "Should I Become a Teacher?" discusses some feelings, reasons, and influences that lead people to consider teaching as their life's work. It is helpful to identify and think about these things while you are in the process of investigating career possibilities. The various categories of teaching positions for both the elementary and secondary levels are examined.

Investigating a career or profession is an important activity, and deciding to pursue a given career requires specific information that will lead you to that decision in the most direct manner. Chapter Six, "Becoming a Teacher," gives you guidelines for the professional preparations that are necessary to become a certified teacher. Curriculum, state, and university requirements are examined in this chapter. Chapter Seven, "Marketing Your Teaching Skills," discusses the matter of getting a teaching position after you graduate, as well as some additional information regarding which majors and minors can help you become a more employable teacher.

It is always helpful and beneficial to look ahead at your future in a given career or profession. Is it stable? Will there be satisfaction and rewards in this career field? After I am in the profession, what are my responsibilities and commitments? These and other professional responsibilities are examined in Unit Three, "What Does the Future Hold?" Chapter Eight, "Looking Ahead," addresses your future as a teacher. It contains information on certification, professional organizations, professional rights and responsibilities, changing jobs, and future education. Chapter Nine, "Social Issues Affecting the Teaching Profession," discusses emerging social issues and situations that teachers face daily. Chapter Ten, "The Real World," contains some reality situations that describe and discuss some possible reactions to situations that you may face as a teacher.

This book is designed to be a usable, helpful guide for your introduction to the teaching profession. It is directed at both the elementary and secondary levels of education. Each chapter opens with definitions of common educational terminology that you should know, followed by questions to give you focus as you read the chapter. The chapters contain brief spotlights on people who have made significant contributions to education and continue to do so, as well as one or more "Short Shots" that give other information about teaching as a career. Each chapter concludes with "The Workshop," which describes activities to help you learn more about teaching through action, and a listing of recommended readings.

Teaching and You will guide and focus your introduction to the teaching profession. Teaching can be an enjoyable and rewarding career. We wish you the best of luck as you pursue your goal to become an excellent teacher.

Acknowledgments

We gratefully acknowledge the following reviewers of our manuscript: William Matthias, Southern Illinois University; Joseph Clovis Mitchell, University of South Alabama; Morgan Otis, California State University at Sacramento; Janice Streitmatter, University of Arizona; and Kathleen Tominc, Western Wyoming Community College.

Teaching and You

■ ■ ■ Chapter One

The Profession
of Teaching

■ Definitions

Chapter I: This is a federally funded program that helps local school districts educate disadvantaged children.

Clinical Experience: This usually refers to the student-teaching experience, but may also refer to any other experience where the teacher candidate is involved with school or student activities. Examples: student teaching; practicum; lower-, middle-, and upper-tier experiences; pre-student-teaching classroom observations.

Continuing Education: Teachers are required to continue their education beyond the initial four-year degree program. Graduate courses, lectures, seminars, curriculum writing, workshops, and other activities can earn continuing education credits and renewal units for licensing purposes.

Instructional Materials Center (IMC): This is a resource center for teaching materials, media production, reference materials, books, magazines and any other materials that can be used by a teacher or teacher candidate. It may be located at the candidate's university or in the elementary and secondary schools. Other names: materials center, teacher's library, reference room, media center, resource room.

Nontraditional Student: Generally, this refers to students who are returning to college after a period of years following high school graduation, or students who have a college degree and are returning to make a career change.

State Department of Education: Every state has a governing authority that is responsible for the overall control and operation of the educational system of the state. This governance body exercises jurisdiction over finances, teacher certification, school calendar, curriculum, administration, and accreditation. Authority may rest with one person, such as a State Superintendent or Commissioner, or with several persons on a state board. You will need to know the specific title of the governing authority in your state. In this book we will refer to that authority by one of the following common titles: Commissioner of Education, State Board of Education, Superintendent of Public Instruction.

Teacher Candidate: Any student whose curriculum will lead to certification as an elementary, secondary, special education, or special (art, music, etc.) teacher.

Teaching License: The license enables teachers to teach in public and private schools with all due professional privileges. Licenses may be permanent, continuing, or subject to periodic renewal, based on completion of a specified number of years of full-time teaching and required continuing education courses. Other titles: certification, teaching certificate, teaching credential.

Tenure: After a probationary period, usually two or three years, the tenure law guarantees the right of due process related to job security. Tenure places teachers on a continuing contract. Cause has to be shown prior to termination (due process).

■ Focus Questions

The purpose of these questions is to guide you as you read the chapter. Try to answer these questions as you read.

1. What is a *professional?* What are the rights and responsibilities of a professional educator? Remember that all rights carry equal responsibilities; you cannot have one without the other.

2. What are *ethics?* Who determines what is ethical and what is not? What are the consequences for unethical behavior or practices?

3. What is *teaching?* From the elementary viewpoint? From the secondary viewpoint?

4. Describe the changing role of elementary and secondary teachers in schools of the future.

5. What are the roles of parents and the community in the operation of the school?

6. Who is in charge of school organization? What are the specific roles of the administrative staff? What role will your principal play in your professional life? Where do you fit in the organizational structure?

7. How do state and federal laws affect you personally and professionally?

■ Introduction

What is the teaching profession? That is a fundamental question asked by many individuals who are considering education as a career choice. It is a very important question that must be addressed at the beginning of the decision-making process. There are many career fields in education to consider. Some require one or two years of postsecondary training and preparation, some require a four-year college degree, and still others require more professional preparation. Individuals who are interested in teaching should receive as much information as possible about the profession so that all important decisions are made with confidence.

This chapter examines some information about the teaching profession that is helpful in establishing a data base for you. Becoming totally familiar with several aspects and peculiarities of any profession is an important task. Reading educational literature, talking with teachers in the field, and participating in other independent activities are strongly encouraged. Private investigations can help you collect information about teaching realities.

■ ■ ■

The Profession of Teaching

The term *profession* can be described as a special calling or occupation that requires extensive learning. That extensive learning usually begins at the college or university level and continues throughout a person's career. (An

■ Short Shot

What factors led you to choose elementary special education?

I chose elementary special education as a career mainly because I enjoy working with individuals who often have complex emotional and educational needs. Also, the challenge of using Madeline Hunter's effective teaching skills on a daily basis interests me.

Karen Whitehouse
EMR/TMR Resource Teacher

alternative approach is to begin a postsecondary education by obtaining a two-year associate degree at a local community college. It is important to determine that the program will transfer to the university of your choice. Personal circumstances may indicate that this strategy is particularly feasible.)

A profession represents a lifetime commitment to performing special services for others. It demands continual upgrading and refining of the personal skills needed to deliver those services. It encourages and promotes high ethical standards among its members and actively seeks highly qualified persons to enter the field. A profession is characterized by its organizations and associations, which set standards for educational preparation, licensing, and assurance of professional competence. Teacher organizations submit recommendations concerning these areas to state boards for inclusion in licensing policies.

The teaching profession tries to assure that only qualified, dedicated persons enter the field and become licensed to teach. This is done in various ways. Individual teachers recruit students they think can become strong teachers. Teachers who supervise student teachers and interns work diligently to provide classroom experiences that give a true picture of daily professional and instructional responsibilities. Teacher organizations lobby the certification boards, state legislatures, accreditation groups, and university committees to increase or maintain high standards for teacher education programs. The individual university professors, counselors, and advisors are serious professionals who want only the best for U.S. school systems. Their personal dedication to the training and educating of future teachers cannot be overemphasized. The consistently high standards of U.S. educators is a credit to our college and university systems.

Admittance to the college or university of your choice is an important initial step toward becoming a professional teacher. The Teacher Credentialing Office or the Office of Admissions chose to accept you over many other candidates. The system of checks and balances begins here. Personal characteristics, special qualities, previous educational records, employment experiences, and various personal recommendations are examined to find qualified persons who may eventually become teachers. University faculty members and other staff personnel are dedicated to guiding you toward that goal. Your courses and field experiences are designed and planned to prepare you for professional responsibilities. Figure 1.1 graphically shows you what it takes to become a teacher.

Completion of all required professional coursework is necessary. Toward the end of your four- or five-year program, the application of what you have learned is put into practice under the close direction of an experienced professional. This clinical experience is commonly called *student teaching*. (The two-year degree programs also have a variety of pre-student-teaching activities that qualify as clinical experiences.)

The teaching profession places great responsibility and trust in the individuals selected to supervise, direct, guide, and encourage teacher candidates while they develop their teaching skills. This part of the learning process is critical. The Commissioner of Education, the State Superintendent of Public Instruction, the State Board of Teacher Credentialing, and the Dean of Education at your university cannot be in the classrooms of all licensing candidates to observe their teaching. Due to the logistics of the situation, it is

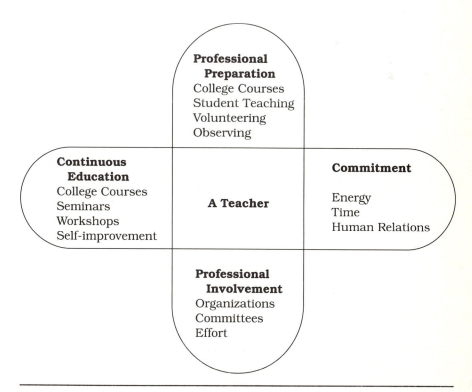

Figure 1.1 Becoming a Teacher: A Continuum

necessary to rely on the ethics, standards, and judgments of other professionals to determine who meets the requirements for certification and licensing. The immediate classroom supervising teacher and the university supervisor are the two people who most directly influence your performance at this point.

Obtaining a high grade-point ratio is an honorable achievement, and certainly the public expects prospective teachers to be good students themselves! However, getting high grades in itself has limited value for licensing purposes if an individual cannot successfully demonstrate the ability to teach children. The clinical experience provides the opportunity to demonstrate your ability to teach and impart your knowledge to others. Performance during the student-teaching period represents the kind of teaching you will do when you have a classroom of your own. A successful experience tells the university that you are ready to teach. In turn, the university will recommend that the state grant you a license to teach all subjects and grades for which you have prepared and trained.

Graduating from a four-year institution with a bachelor's degree and a teaching license is an important step toward becoming a professional educator. Many different types of content courses will be studied, and other personal experiences will lead you to this point. When you obtain a contract to teach for a particular school system, you are viewed as a professional person—a bona fide member of the teaching profession. You will have accomplished much already, but a great deal more is expected of you every year that you remain in the profession.

What are the expectations of the profession? First and foremost, you are expected to give 100 percent of your abilities and talents to teach your students everything that is required. By definition, the profession requires extensive learning. In a special sense, the completion of the four-year degree program is actually just the beginning of a commitment to learning. In a formal sense, continuous learning is realized through the graduate classes and professional seminars and workshops you are required to complete for licensure. In an instructional sense, you will very quickly learn which strategies, methods, and teaching techniques are effective with contemporary students and which ones are not! A professional person is expected to monitor and evaluate his or her own performance in responsible ways. Some of your most significant learning experiences will occur with your own students.

Teachers fulfill their professional duties in both public and private schools, just as physicians establish their practices in offices, clinics, and hospitals. Every school is a distinct entity, with its own unique characteristics, personality, and culture. Whether the school is an elementary or a secondary school, its individuality is evolving and you, the new teacher, are expected to become an integral part of the process.

It is exciting for a school to have a new teacher on the staff. Administrators, teachers, students, parents, and other community members will be eager to meet you. You represent your university as well as the entire educational community. A professional person conducts himself or herself in ways that reflect positively on the system. This is a professional responsibility that should be taken seriously. Personal attire, dedication to the job, and the way you act and react will cause a positive or negative relationship to develop with students, faculty members, and staff.

Becoming a member of the teaching profession requires a commitment to perform the duties of a professional person. Teaching students is your top priority. The profession grows and becomes more vibrant when its members make significant contributions to its growth. Members become more skilled when they help and encourage each other. It is important to learn from the experienced people on the staff; in turn, they are interested in learning from you. Your university coursework, projects, and activities are of great interest to senior-level professionals. They look to new teachers to promote and carry on the traditions and standards they have given a lifetime to develop.

Joining professional organizations is another important way to make a contribution to the profession and your school system. The National Council for the Social Studies, the Association for the Education of Young Children, the National Council for Teachers of Mathematics, and other organizations

■ People in Education

Jean Piaget

Cognitive development and the behavior of children were important areas of research for the noted Swiss psychologist, Jean Piaget. His stage-development theory states that children proceed through four sequential stages in the learning process. Each stage builds upon the previous one(s). These four stages of learning are the sensorimotor (birth to about 2 years), the preoperational thought (2 to 7 years), the period of concrete operations (7 to 11 years), and the period of formal operations (12 to adolescence). Each of these developmental stages is very important for teachers, particularly primary teachers, to understand.

In an effort to teach more content at an earlier age, it is common to see teachers and schools expecting young children to perform academic tasks beyond their capabilities; however, the foundation is not there yet. The stages of development must be considered when teachers plan lessons and activities for children. It is important to set goals that children can reasonably be expected to achieve from a developmental standpoint. *Piaget's Theory of Cognitive Development* by Barry J. Wadsworth (1984) is a good resource for your professional reading program.

offer many opportunities for professional growth and development. The teaching profession expects its newest members to become involved outside the classroom.

The profession grows when its members are assertive, accountable, active, and productive in the schools. School organizations and councils need and actively solicit teacher participation. When teachers make significant contributions to school programs, they reinforce the public image in positive ways. Suggestions and contributions from the professional staff are most effective when given in pleasant, tactful ways.

The teaching profession strives to attract and retain highly qualified people. Persons with an indifferent attitude toward teaching and learning are well advised not to enter the teaching field. Excellent teaching demands a strong commitment, a great deal of energy, and a willingness to constantly learn and grow professionally. Individuals with these characteristics are encouraged to investigate the profession of teaching.

Ethics

Every profession has a code of ethics that governs the behavior and practices of its members. A code of ethics sets the standards and performance objectives for the profession.

What are *ethics?* A combination of definitions would include such things as a philosophy of character, personal and professional conduct, specific duties and obligations, personal and professional principles and integrity, and other specific canons that guide and direct professional behavior.

Professional ethics are the intangible internal directives that lead you to *do* certain things and *not do* others. For example, professionals are expected to lead an exemplary life-style, act as responsible members of the school community, perform their duties at a high degree of competence, and show respect for others. On the other hand, they should not make disparaging remarks about students, parents, school administrators or fellow teachers. They should not accept fees for tutoring students who have extended absences, and they should not use their influence to promote causes for personal financial gain. Professional ethics actually consist of very good commonsense ideas to assist in one's professional growth and development. Individual school systems may have an established code of ethics that all professional staff members must follow.

The National Education Association adopted a Code of Ethics of the Education Profession for its members. The following excerpts show examples of some expectations for professional teachers.

In fulfillment of the obligation to the student, the educator—

1. Shall not unreasonably restrain the student from independent action in the pursuit of learning.

2. Shall not unreasonably deny the student access to varying points of view.
3. Shall not deliberately suppress or distort subject matter relevant to the student's progress.
4. Shall make reasonable effort to protect the student from conditions harmful to learning or to health and safety.
5. Shall not intentionally expose the student to embarrassment or disparagement.
6. Shall not on the basis of race, color, creed, sex, national origin, material status, political or religious beliefs, family, social, or cultural background, or sexual orientation unfairly—
   a. Exclude any student from participation in any program
   b. Deny benefits to any student
   c. Grant any advantage to any student
7. Shall not use professional relationships with students for private advantage.
8. Shall not disclose information about students obtained in the course of professional service, unless disclosure serves a compelling professional purpose or is required by law.

In fulfillment of the obligation to the profession, the educator—

1. Shall not in an application for a professional position deliberately make a false statement or fail to disclose a material fact related to competency and qualifications.
2. Shall not misrepresent his/her professional qualifications.
3. Shall not assist any entry into the profession of a person known to be unqualified in respect to character, education, or other relevant attribute.
4. Shall not knowingly make a false statement concerning the qualifications of a candidate for a professional position.
5. Shall not assist a non-educator in the unauthorized practice of teaching.
6. Shall not disclose information about colleagues obtained in the course of professional service unless disclosure serves a compelling professional purpose or is required by law.
7. Shall not knowingly make false or malicious statements about a colleague.
8. Shall not accept any gratuity, gift, or favor that might impair or appear to influence professional decisions or action. (*Code of Ethics of the Education Profession,* The N.E.A. Handbook 1986–87. Adopted by 1975 Representative Assembly.)

These tenets of a professional code of ethics address student concerns as well as the individual person's conduct relative to the practice of teaching. Ethics is that inner collection of principles that guide and direct one's professional behavior.

Defining *Teaching*

A myriad of images, thoughts, feelings, and ideas come to mind when attempting to define *teaching*. Almost everyone has had a special teacher that had a significant effect on his or her educational experience. Teaching is what that special person did at that time.

■ **Short Shot** _____

Teaching is:

- Committing yourself to lifelong learning and growth
- Respecting children and adolescents
- Sharing one's knowledge
- Guiding, directing, facilitating, nurturing, and planning
- Goal setting for yourself and for your students
- Meeting personal and professional challenges
- Conveying cultural and national values to others
- Creating an awareness of (and appreciation for) your potential

The act of teaching can be described as giving instructions to or sharing one's knowledge with another person. Teaching can be further described as a means for providing students with the knowledge and skills they need to function successfully in the world. In a very practical sense, teaching is diagnosing and prescribing. Teachers diagnose what the specific learning needs (or deficiencies) are, and then prescribe the particular strategies and activities to meet them. This is a very important factor in teaching. The ability to identify student learning needs and to design explicit lessons is what distinguishes the professional teacher from a volunteer, an aide, or any other person who wants to teach.

Teaching content—all the subjects pupils must learn—is what teachers are trained to do. Learning the content and the pedagogy to present it effectively to students is why teachers must be well educated and maintain that level of proficiency over an entire teaching career. In addition to the teaching of content, the teaching of concepts, attitudes, values, and other affective skills is necessary and very valuable. It is easy to mistake teaching with giving long and laborious written assignments, assigning book pages to read, and answering study questions at the end of a unit. Although these things are a part of teaching some of the time, they do not adequately assist in defining what teaching is.

Teaching can be viewed as a very personal interaction between the teacher and the students. The teacher imparts his or her knowledge through individual lessons that are presented to the class. The students receive the knowledge in a whole set or in parts. When that knowledge is internalized, then learning takes place. The teaching and the learning processes flow in a cyclic pattern, as seen in Figure 1.2.

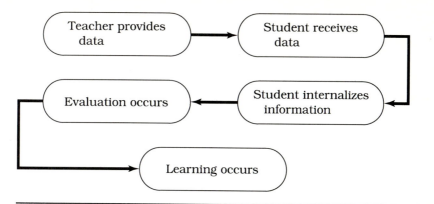

Figure 1.2 The Teaching Process from Beginning to End

The Changing Role of Teachers

To understand the teaching profession adequately, it is helpful to have some basic understandings of the past and present conditions of the profession. Using these understandings, it is possible to forecast the future state of the profession and your role in it.

What was teaching like in the past? What was the teacher's role? In our not-too-distant past, teaching was very different from what it is today. The role of the teacher was largely that of giving information to students. The teacher lectured to the students and they memorized as much as possible or reproduced the information in some way. Oral recitations were viewed as valuable skills. The lessons teachers prepared were primarily expository in nature. Students were at desks or tables and remained there much of the time. Demonstrations or experiments of any kind were performed by the teacher, and manipulative activities were limited.

In the past, teachers were strong authority figures in the students' school experience. They served as an extension of the parents in shaping behaviors, attitudes, values systems, and personal character development. They reinforced the established standards of proper behavior in the community.

At the elementary level, it was common for one teacher (almost always a woman) to have students in more than one grade in her classroom. For example, a primary teacher might have a few kindergartners, a few first-graders, and some second-graders in her room. In retrospect, this was the forerunner of our current multiple-age grouping concept. At the secondary level, teachers were expected to teach several subjects. A social studies teacher could have some freshmen taking the eleventh-grade American history course, and the senior high principal might be teaching classes in addition to performing administrative duties.

Years ago, lessons were taught primarily with a convergent result in mind. The teacher presented certain information and the students were expected to converge toward the right answer. Teaching for convergent thinking was a predominant goal. With this type of teaching, the basic textbook was a primary source of information, along with the information received from the teacher. The teacher appeared to be an authority on all subjects. The process of rote teaching and learning was critical.

The role of contemporary teachers is dramatically different from the formal, somewhat rigid role of the past. Teaching in our present day has evolved into a multidisciplinary, multifaceted profession. Time manager, facilitator of diverse learning activities, behavior manager, expert in several curriculum areas, computer operator, manager of objectives—these are some of the roles teachers now perform.

The information explosion that came with the space age dramatically affected our educational system at both the secondary and the elementary levels. Content and concepts that had traditionally been taught in junior high were to be taught at the elementary level. Some things from the upper-elementary grades were to be introduced at the primary grades. A popular belief among educators was "Anything can be taught to younger children if you teach it at their level."

Teachers have always taught content. However, the importance of teaching process (the *how* of learning) has become very important. We want students of all ages to learn how to think independently, how to seek several methods or ways to do things, and how to become more divergent in their learning skills; teachers are teaching product and process. They use many different strategies, methods, and teaching styles in their classrooms. Students are much more actively involved and responsible for their own learning.

Instruction is branching out of the singular classroom into the media centers, instructional materials centers, learning centers, and other nontraditional places. Schools are undergoing significant organizational modifications to accommodate the new trends in teaching and learning. The effect of educational research is apparent as teachers adapt both their methods and materials to meet the various stages of mental and physical development. The role of contemporary teachers is clearly that of a dynamic agent for change.

What is the future role of elementary and secondary teachers? No one can accurately predict the future, but it is interesting to examine current policies and trends carefully and use them to make conjectures. Obviously, the teachers of the future must continue to be well trained and well educated in all areas for which they are certified. At this time there are states seriously considering making teacher training a five-year program. Teachers of the 1980s have become experts in their role as managers of students and systems. It is reasonable to expect this to continue.

It is probable that the role of our present teacher aides may upgrade to that of teaching paraprofessional. In some areas, a two-year associate degree is already required for these positions. These people may be responsible for

Teachers and their tools change to meet new demands.

supervising student work periods and guided practice sessions after the teacher has taught the new material or lessons. Classroom teachers may assume the responsibility for training greater numbers of paraprofessionals. The teacher's role would be more effectively utilized in planning, designing, organizing and prescribing learning sequences for students.

The impact of computers in the classroom is already significant. Students are becoming computer literate starting in kindergarten. Teachers of the future will use technology for more information and data retrieval. Teachers will do more programming of their own lessons. They may use time with students to teach new skills and objectives and then use the computer lab as a learning resource for student practice and application.

It is improbable that the human factor in education will be significantly diminished in the future. It is possible that more curriculum content will be required. To accommodate this, teachers will undoubtedly utilize more outside human resources. At the secondary level, this is already a well-established practice. Experts in particular fields are brought into the classrooms to teach certain classes.

One example of this is the Chamber of Commerce's Business Education Partnerships, a growing national program that offers a speakers' bureau, student tours, one-to-one visits, teacher workshops, and summer teacher employment opportunities for professional growth. Another example is the growing use of retirees by many school systems. Many retirees have expertise in specialized areas such as math and science, wisdom and experience from many years on the job, unique travel experiences, a willing pair of hands, and a good ear for listening.

Community resource persons may acquire a special license or certification to work in the school system. At the elementary level, such programs as Artists in the Schools and Writers in the Schools are popular for introducing children to working artists and writers who give special insights into their talents and employment opportunities.

Community resource persons help teachers teach.

Within particular buildings or school districts, there may be more departmentalization or specialization. Teachers can teach what they enjoy and do well. If the organizational structure of elementary schools changes in this way, it will involve increased movement of children and/or teachers. Many schools are moving toward the middle-school concept, departmentalizing the upper-elementary grades. Some teachers and psychologists feel this is too stressful for young children, however.

Whatever the role of future teachers becomes, it is certain that facilitating, guiding, and directing will be part of it. The continual adaptations within curriculum areas will certainly affect the teacher's role. If current trends continue, the management and organizational roles will expand. Interacting with students on the personal human relations level continues to be a high priority if our national objective is to nurture loving and caring citizens.

Parent and Community Perspectives

The way parents and community members perceive the teaching profession is an important factor in the operation of a successful school environment. Despite some negative press, the majority of parents are very supportive of their teachers and schools. This positive support is very important to achieve and maintain.

Students spend a large portion of their day under the direct influence of teachers. Parents perceive teachers as the professional vehicle for educating their children. They entrust teachers to pass on the values, such as honesty and responsibility, as well as the content skills they were taught at school. Parents realize that receiving an education is a top priority. They generally hold teachers in high esteem and perceive them as partners in the training of future citizens.

Teachers and administrators recognize the importance of community support for schools and their educational programs. Financial support is crucial, of course. It is very concrete—the necessary funds are either there or they are not. Explicit philosophical support is equally crucial, and it is acquired by various means. The academic community (everyone who works in the school) utilizes a number of activities to inform the physical community. Some of these activities are:

1. *Parent-teacher conferences* provide opportunities for parents and teachers to discuss the academic, social, and emotional growth of students. Conference Day may be the only time teachers have direct contact with some parents.
2. *Curriculum fairs* offer the community an opportunity to come to the school to see what students are experiencing and learning in a particular curriculum area. Student projects are on display.

■ Short Shot

As a parent in the school community, how do you perceive your role?

As a parent in a school community, I see my role as being an overseer of my child's education. I have heard the question asked several times: "If you don't look out for your child, who will?" When I was in school, my parents did not question educators. As a parent in today's society, I feel I have that right—if for no other reason than I am paying the bill.

I feel comfortable talking with teachers and administrators if I feel my child is having a learning or personal problem. I feel having an open line of communication has been a key factor in making my child's school life easier, as teachers know I care and will give all the help and cooperation that is possible.

I also feel that being involved with various school-community volunteer groups has helped pave the way for an open line of communication. If parents would attend PTA, School Board meetings, and conferences, they would learn more about what makes schools function and teachers tick. In turn, the school community has the opportunity to get to know the parent as a person. Parents must make and take the time to find out what they can do to help with every child's education.

Judy Sodeman, Parent

3. *School or district newsletters* are a readily available resource for keeping the community informed about school activities, policies, concerns, and needs.
4. *Various school programs* enable parents and all community members to watch students perform skills and talents (music, plays, sports).
5. *Personal contacts* are made when teachers invite parents and others to visit the school. This is an excellent opportunity to ask for volunteers to help with classroom activities.

The community views teachers in several different ways. Community members perceive the school as a focal point in the neighborhood, and teachers as the primary agents that make it a successful institution. When students are learning and achieving at a reasonable rate, positive feelings are felt in the community. Everyone is proud of the school.

The community at large expects students to learn. People expect teachers to keep up to date on methods and materials so that quality learning can occur. When newspapers or magazines feature articles on topics such as "Are the Schools Doing the Job?" what the message actually means is "Are the Teachers Doing the Job?" Teachers are the power actors in the school. The school community wants to have the best educational system it can afford. It expects the professional staff to be the designers and managers of the knowledge base that students need to become successful, functional citizens. It perceives teachers to be the enthusiastic, positive, nurturing role models who encourage students to achieve at their highest level.

School Organization

Elementary and secondary schools are two major structures in the educational system. Middle schools and junior high schools are important parts of other school systems. The organizational patterns of various school systems may have certain characteristics that are peculiar to a particular area or region. An example of such an organizational pattern could be the procedures for textbook adoption. This is the procedure of one school system:

1. Each grade level or department identifies the instructional goals and objectives for the subject.
2. These goals and objectives are submitted to the curriculum committee for compilation.
3. The curriculum committee chairperson presents these goals to the Parent Advisory Board for approval and further recommendations.
4. Several textbook publishers are invited to make presentations to the full curriculum committee (teachers, administrators, parent representatives).
5. A selection is made based on the established goals and objectives.
6. The selection is presented to the Parent Advisory Board for approval.
7. The curriculum committee chairperson presents the selection to the school board for approval.
8. The new textbook is adopted.

Although this procedure may appear to be tedious, it is a good example of how well organized some schools can be. It also exemplifies parent-teacher-administration cooperation and support. These special characteristics are generally positive and contribute to the unique qualities of a school.

Organization is of vital importance to any working structure. A strong organizational system is the cornerstone of a strong teaching and learning environment. Teachers can deliver effective learning experiences when the organizational structure is conducive to cooperative efforts. Everyone who works in the school plays a part in its efficiency and effectiveness. Some people affect the learning process directly, such as the teachers, teaching assistants, tutors, teacher candidates, and administrators. Others—such as the office staff, custodial staff, and food service personnel—affect the process indirectly. All school employees make contributions to the operation of a school in their own special ways.

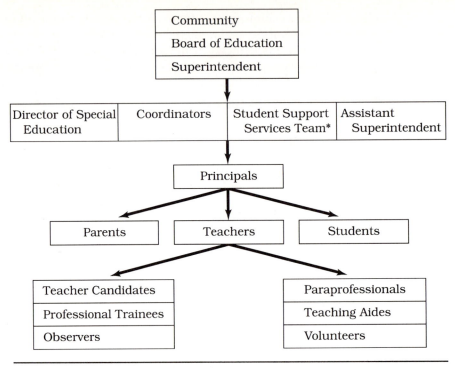

Figure 1.3 The Structure of a Public School

*The student support services team includes such personnel as school psychologists, social workers, counselors, special education teachers, and the nurse. In some areas this group comprises the child study team.

How are effective, efficient schools organized? Who are the people that make up the system and what are their responsibilities? The organizational chart in Figure 1.3 shows one pattern of school structuring. There are various others. We will now examine the specific roles of these people who comprise a school system.

The Community

The community is the geographic area that supports a school system. That support consists of both financial and human resources (students, community members without students in the schools, and parents). A school community can be rather small (a few hundred students in one building) or it can be very large (several thousand students in many buildings). In very large systems, the school community may be divided into more manageable units, each with its own administrative and managerial personnel. In some ways, this management style brings the community closer to the school family while at the same time keeps large areas and student populations active partners in the complete system.

The role of the community is active as well as reactive in terms of school operation. The community includes everyone who lives within the boundaries of the school district. Community education programs, parent advisory groups, the PTA, curriculum committees, fund-raising groups, and other organizations provide opportunities for people to become active members of the school community. The role of the community can become reactive in situations where decisions are made unilaterally without appropriate input from all groups concerned. Schools exist to serve the communities where they are located. Working cooperatively in all matters of school operation generally prevents negative or hostile reactions from occurring. Open lines of communication contribute to good school management.

The Board of Education

The Board of Education is commonly called the *school board* or simply *the board.* It generally consists of six or seven members who are elected for terms of two to four years. The board is directly responsible to the community for its actions and rulings. Local school boards are customarily members of state and national school board associations.

The school board is the governing body of the school district or system. Its role is to make policy decisions of various kinds and to rule on curriculum and instruction recommendations from the superintendent, the professional staff, the community, and other sources. It serves an important function in

---

■ People in Education

Benjamin Bloom

Benjamin Bloom, a noted educational psychologist, has been an important contributor to education for many years. In 1956 his book *The Taxonomy of Educational Objectives* appeared as a major work, identifying six different levels of thinking in the cognitive domain. It served as an impetus for formulating educational objectives for instruction. This work proposes that students can be taught how to think beyond the mere reproduction of factual information (knowledge), which is the lowest step of cognition. Bloom has done extensive work in the areas of mastery learning, the effects of early environment on school achievement, classification of behaviors, task analysis, and others.

the area of labor relations as it negotiates contracts for all employee groups. Keeping abreast of regulations, laws, and recommendations for school operation on the state and national levels is a primary responsibility of school board members. A positive communication style is very important for effective school board operation.

The Superintendent

The superintendent has a dual role in the school system: the educational leader and the general manager. If you were to ask almost any superintendent what his or her responsibilities are, the response would probably be, "Everything!" A school superintendent's role can be compared with the Chief Executive Officer of a major corporation, overseeing the many large and small details that are both educational and managerial.

Some of the superintendent's educational responsibilities include recruiting and hiring all professional staff, guiding and directing the quality of education for the district, initiating and managing needed curriculum and instructional changes, keeping current regarding professional staff needs and concerns, and generally to be the educational leader and innovator in all matters concerned with teaching and instruction. Some of his or her managerial responsibilities would include preparing and presenting the annual budget to the school board, preparing all required local and state reports for the proper authorities, being available for all employee and community groups, positively representing the school district at public and private functions, and being responsible for all school district policies.

Generally speaking, the superintendent is the senior professional manager in the district. He or she is employed by the community and is therefore a public employee. The superintendent reports to the school board on all matters that affect the schools. He or she makes recommendations that reflect the schools' needs and actively seeks support, both financial and philosophical, for those needs. The public relations role of the superintendent to keep both the school board and the community informed is vital.

The Assistant Superintendent

One (or more) assistant superintendent works closely with the superintendent in the total operation of the school system. In some areas an assistant superintendent serves as the general business manager. A large part of this job is managing both administrative and business affairs. The responsibilities of the assistant superintendent might include selected labor-management duties, planning for growth and development, budgetary matters, facilities management, and negotiating with vendors and sales representatives. The school transportation system is frequently the responsibility of the assistant superintendent. Compliance with all state and federal regulations concerning facilities plant management and transportation is also within this job description. He or she is directly accountable to the superintendent and the school board.

Student Support Services Team

The student support services team is a group of specially trained professionals who work to meet particular student needs. In some areas this group is called a *child study team*. The school psychologist, the school social worker, the elementary and secondary counselors, and the school nurse are all members of this team. The special-education teachers may also be included. What is the role of this team? The average school has a number of students with needs that cannot be adequately addressed within the regular classroom. These special needs might be a learning disability, a behavioral problem, a health problem, an emotional disorder, or a child-family problem.

The parents or any professionals who work with the student may request additional services by submitting appropriate documents to the director of support services. The student support services team then works cooperatively to administer any needed tests or surveys, to conduct interviews with teachers, parents, and the student, and possibly to refer the case to any necessary outside sources. A complete physical examination might be one recommendation to clarify a possible physical problem. When all the required data are received, the team meets to thoroughly examine all the information.

At this point, specific recommendations are made to service the student in the school setting. For a learning problem, an Individual Education Plan (IEP) is written so the student can be serviced through the special-education department. A child with a severe emotional disorder would be recommended to the Emotional Behavior Disorders (EDB) teacher. Counseling, physical therapy, speech, or language-delayed services are some other needs that are examined by the child study team.

Coordinators

The role of the coordinators in a school system is partly managerial and partly instructional. Larger districts employ a coordinator for each of the major curriculum areas: math coordinator, language arts coordinator, social studies coordinator, and so on. Some smaller districts use only two: the elementary and the secondary curriculum coordinators.

Curriculum coordinators manage, direct, guide, and influence the course of action their specific area will take. They are responsible for studying the research, evaluating all textbooks and associated materials, and acquiring (or designing) all the necessary materials the teachers need for instruction. The coordinator may also be responsible for staffing and supplying an instructional materials center (IMC). Curriculum coordinators closely observe and track the student test scores on any standardized tests that are administered. Keeping the district's students on an achievement goal is an important responsibility. Providing all the necessary tools and materials for teachers to realize that goal is part of the coordinator's job.

From an instructional standpoint, coordinators are frequently asked to assist new and experienced teachers. Demonstration teaching gives coordina-

■ People in Education
Madeline Hunter

Madeline Hunter (Professor of Education, University of California at Los Angeles) has been a prominent personality in education for many years. Her contributions to education include such areas as how children learn, clinical supervision, methods for increasing the effectiveness of teachers, consulting with other countries to improve their educational systems, working with principals to affect better schools, designing and implementing teaching models, contributing to professional publications, and serving as a guest lecturer for conferences and conventions. Her dedication to effective teaching is paramount.

Hunter developed a cause-and-effect model for establishing the relationship between what teachers do and what students learn. Her Effective Teaching workshops teach the model to administrators and teachers. The basic premise is that effective teaching is based on four elements:

1. *Teach to the objective:* Know specifically what you are going to teach.
2. *Teach to the appropriate level of difficulty:* Plan the lessons for a performance level that students can reasonably be expected to perform—neither too easy nor too hard.
3. *Monitor and adjust:* Carefully observe the students' behaviors and responses during the lesson and make adaptations as needed.
4. *Use, don't abuse, the principles of learning:* Motivation, rate and degree of learning new material, retention, and transfer are the principles that enhance learning; none are eliminated or overemphasized.

The Hunter approach is a positive method for recognizing the many effective things teachers do while they teach. The principal uses a script-tape to record on-task behaviors as a basis for support (praise) or recommendation (try this). The Hunter model is widely used for staff development with experienced and new teachers.

tors opportunities to be in classrooms to interact with students and to assist teachers with particular problem areas. Teachers make special requests for students. One student may have unusual difficulty understanding percents and percentages, for example. The coordinator will attempt to diagnose the particular problem and then search out all the instructional materials she or he has on hand to remedy the problem and help that student to learn.

Coordinators may be responsible for conducting workshops and seminars for all the teachers in the system or for staff members in a particular building. In some areas, curriculum coordinators are called *instructional assistants*. They work closely with the superintendent to plan and manage programs, and with the teachers to implement and evaluate the programs.

Director of Special Education

The director of special education plays an important role in a school system and has many managerial as well as instructional responsibilities. Special-education directors frequently hold a doctorate degree and specialized licenses and certificates for teaching and administration at the elementary and the secondary levels. The passage of Public Law (PL) 94–142, the Education of All Handicapped Children Act of 1975, assured that all handicapped children have a full education available to them in the public schools. This is commonly referred to as *the special education law.*

The special education director reports to the superintendent. He or she is responsible for maintaining the entire special-education program. This program includes such things as Chapter I (previously called Title I), learning disabled, physically handicapped, prekindergarten and early childhood programs, emotional behavior-disorder programs, and limited-English-speaking programs. The director initiates and monitors all special-education programs that are mandated by law, as well as those adopted on a local level.

Preparing special reports, locating and servicing all qualified students, coordinating the appropriate placements in outside sources, monitoring the Individual Education Plans of all special students, supervising, and evaluating the special-education teachers are some of the responsibilities of the special-education director.

Principals

What is the role of the school principal? To list all the responsibilities or jobs the principal performs is an almost impossible task. We will examine some of the more important things he or she does.

The principal's job is one of middle management within the total school system and is the top management position for an individual building. The principal is responsible to the superintendent for all activities in his or her building. He or she is responsible to the professional staff for providing the dynamic leadership, encouragement, and support that enables them to per-

The principal is responsible for the efficient operation of the school.

form their jobs at peak performance levels. "Enable teachers to teach and then let them do it" is a good motto for principals!

An important management role of principals is the supervision and evaluation of teachers. After new teachers have signed contracts, they are typically in a probationary status for two or three years. During this time, teachers are subject to close supervision and evaluation by the administration, usually the building principal. Some principals conduct evaluation observations at an agreed upon day and time; others prefer to drop in unannounced. There are advantages and disadvantages for both the principal and the teacher with each procedure.

Some of the things principals observe are class control (discipline), learning environment (room atmosphere), teacher-student interaction and rapport, presentation of content and concepts, and attitude and personal appearance. A written evaluation form is frequently used and a copy is given to the teacher. A conference is commonly conducted after each formal visit. After completing a successful provisional or probationary period, tenure or a continuing contract is usually granted. Principals are required to evaluate comparably all teachers on continuing contracts. Evaluating instruction and professional performance is a major responsibility of principals.

Principals are responsible to parents and the community for maintaining and improving the quality of education the students receive. Overseeing and evaluating teaching and instructional processes is done by the principal. Strong leadership and guidance directly from the principal is one characteristic of an excellent school. Students readily recognize the principal who expects them to do their job.

Principals are active participants in the student management team (principal, teachers, and parents) that will activate and maintain a strong but fair discipline policy. Principals are usually active members of various organizations that work for school improvement, both in the school itself and the community at large. They attend administrative meetings and they support curriculum committee decisions. Principals make specific recommendations and requests to the superintendent and the school board for school needs. In this respect, they serve as intermediaries and negotiators for their areas of responsibility.

The relationship of the building principal to his or her teachers is very important for everyone at the school. (Figure 1.4 illustrates the role of a building principal.) An effective, confident principal is dedicated and excited about education in general, and his or her role as principal and leader in particular. The principal and the teachers are key persons on the educational team. Although many innovations, new ideas, suggestions, and considerations come from the principal to the teachers, all of these may also come from the teachers (as individuals or as a faculty) to the principal. In schools where site-based management or management-by-objectives procedures are in effect, the principal and the teachers work together as a team to set trends, solve problems (real and potential), determine curriculum goals, establish workable codes of conduct, and accomplish a myriad of other things to improve and maintain an effective teaching and learning environment.

In cooperatively managed schools the principal and all teachers feel free to speak openly and honestly at group meetings and in private conferences. Effective principals are open to suggestions and actively seek information from the teachers. Teachers are frequently closer to a given situation on a daily basis than the principal can possibly be. In most cases cooperative decisions can be made. In some cases, however, the principal must make a decision or act unilaterally. The principal is the manager. Making some difficult or unpopular decisions may not always be easy, but it is part of the job. Principals are human beings too, and they need support from the staff when difficult decisions are made.

In addition to the professional responsibilities, principals and teachers have a social relationship. Having a teacher stop by the office to chat informally is very often a welcome respite from the responsibilities of management and supervision. These informal talks give the principal opportunities to get to know the faculty better as individuals, as community members, and as teachers. Principals enjoy hearing about particular lessons and projects that

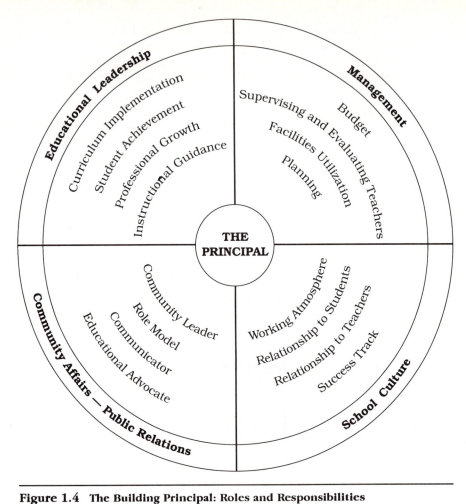

Figure 1.4   The Building Principal: Roles and Responsibilities

are effective and enjoyable for teachers and their students. Hearing about successes is always encouraging and a pleasant experience to end the day. It is unfortunate that some teachers work with the same principal for many years and never meet with him or her to talk informally. Likewise, teachers welcome principals into their classrooms. Principals and teachers are colleagues—not adversaries.

Teachers

Describing the role of teachers is a difficult task! The first role that comes to mind is to teach students. That is what the school board and the community hires teachers to do. A teacher's academic role includes serving on curricu-

■ **Short Shot** _____

What are the rewards and responsibilities of your job as a teacher's assistant?

A teacher's assistant works directly for the teacher. I make copies of worksheets, type, gather worksheets from the curriculum IMCs, design bulletin boards, prepare materials for art projects, and perform other nonteaching duties. The teacher's assistant does whatever the teacher requests to help make instruction more effective and efficient. Sometimes I help children with a reading assignment or project that requires more attention than the teacher can provide at the time.

The rewards come from working in a positive atmosphere where learning and caring go hand in hand. The help you give as an assistant is always appreciated and the friendships you make are valued more than any monetary earnings.

Debbie Felten, Teacher's Assistant

lum and planning committees, faculty councils, and continuing education boards. Serving as an advocate for academic excellence is important. Teachers believe in education at all levels and should actively support it.

The public relations role of teachers is critical. Although parents do interact with the administration at public functions such as open house, curriculum fairs, sports events, and musical performances, the person they encounter most frequently on a professional basis is their child's teacher(s).

When teachers conduct parent-teacher conferences, perform volunteer activities, and participate in PTA events and other activities at school, they are actively sought out by the parents. "How is my child doing?" is usually asked of teachers, even at nonconference times. Parents have many educational concerns regarding their children, but their top priority is the progress *this* year with *this* teacher. The role of the teacher is to represent herself or himself, as well as the school and its programs, in a positive professional manner that is friendly, supportive, and nonthreatening.

Of prime importance for teachers is the role of professional educator. This role is exercised every moment they are interacting with students. It is very critical when interacting with parents during conference times, child study meetings, and other occasions when the student and his or her education are discussed.

School learning and behavior are serious matters and the teacher's role is to convey and affirm this to parents. Parents want factual information from teachers on learning and behavioral matters. They expect a positive, workable, achievable plan for problem areas. Merely being told "Your son is not handing in assignments" has little value to a parent without a remediation plan of action. Part of the teacher's role is to work toward *correcting* problems, not merely to identify them.

It is the teacher's role to help students build self-esteem. Students who feel good about themselves and their relationship with peers will be more positive, ready and willing to learn, and able to perform academic duties. Teachers are responsible for providing the necessary activities for maximum learning to occur for all students. Establishing and maintaining a positive, accepting learning environment contributes to the probability that students will perform at expected levels of competence. A major responsibility of teachers is the evaluation of pupil performance. It is part of the teacher's role to work cooperatively with all other staff members to build and maintain quality programs and to enrich the school environment at all times.

Teachers also have a managerial role to perform (see Figure 1.5). Managing the learning and behavior of students is a major part of that role. Teachers also manage and supervise other adults who work with students. Many schools use teacher aides and volunteers to assist the professional staff with nonteaching duties. Teacher aides and volunteers do such things as correct papers (those with objective responses), prepare bulletin boards or displays, type tests or quizzes, work one-to-one with students, and supervise small groups. Larger districts may have a director of volunteers, whose job is to train these persons; other districts rely on the individual teachers to train, supervise, and evaluate their own assistants. Training these people to use

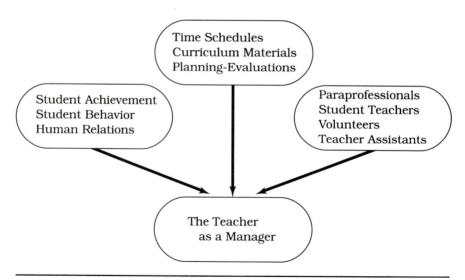

Figure 1.5 Teacher Management Skills

appropriate strategies and methods is very important when they are to work directly with students.

Teacher candidates involved in their clinical experiences are supervised by teachers. The classroom teacher, in cooperation with the university and the student-teaching coordinator, plans, directs, and evaluates all the activities of the student teacher. This role requires tact, honest and positive encouragement, and strong teacher modeling. Teachers are also responsible for the training of any other paraprofessionals who work in the classroom.

Parents and Students

Parents as well as students have important roles in the school organization plan. A school cannot be truly successful or effective unless these two groups consistently perform their roles well.

What is the role of parents in relation to the school family? Parents who do a conscientious job of parenting are a very valuable resource for the school and the community. Preparing children for a successful school experience is critical. This preparation includes such things as providing proper nutrition, rest, clothing, medical care, play experiences, love, and security; developing positive attitudes and responsibilities; and meeting growth and developmental needs. When parents meet various school readiness needs, the potential for academic success is greatly enhanced.

In addition to parenting preschool children in positive ways, parents have other responsibilities. One of them is to support the teacher, the school, and its programs. This is achieved through cooperation, showing interest in the child's academic and social progress, being understanding, and continuing to care for the child throughout the elementary and secondary years.

Caring, successful parents make other contributions to the school system. They are active on committees, boards, and other school organizations. Active, informed parents work for school improvement and academic excellence. Children whose parents are active in school tend to do better academically. If school is important to the parent, it is important to the student.

The primary role of elementary and secondary students is to work toward achieving academic and social goals. Schools exist for students and are the primary sites where academic learning occurs. How the students function as learners determines the success or failure of the school. The community provides the tools and materials teachers need to deliver quality instruction, but the students must do the learning.

The roles of students at the secondary level have some special characteristics. The most important role is academic achievement. Secondary schools traditionally have many extracurricular activities available for students. Sports, debate, chorus, band, academic organizations, and other activities exist to provide particular growth experiences for students. Those

■ **People in Education**

Bernice McCarthy

There are a number of instructional models that classroom teachers use to enhance teaching expertise and the academic achievement of students. David Kolb established a four-quadrant model of learning styles, based on the perceiving and processing of information.

Dr. Bernice McCarthy used this model to describe four types of learners and how the left and right hemispheres of the brain function for the various learning styles. She developed the 4MAT System, which is an eight-step cycle that proceeds sequentially through the four quadrants, using left and right brain techniques for each quadrant. This model is illustrated in *The 4MAT System: Teaching to Learning Styles with Right/Left Mode Techniques* (1980) and subsequent publications. This system can be used successfully for all subject areas and grade levels.

who choose to participate have an important additional role to play. They are to give 100 percent effort and to represent the school in positive ways. Students' roles in public relations reflect on the school, the teachers, the parents, and the community.

Educational Law

The laws pertaining to elementary and secondary education are numerous, complicated, and frequently written with too much legal jargon. Educational laws are enacted by individual states and the federal government. These laws address many issues related to the operation of schools. Issues such as curriculum requirements, the Title programs, special education (PL 94–142), teacher tenure, student policies, teacher-student ratios, student transportation, employment practices, instructional time, accreditation and certification, educational funding, and open enrollments are governed by various state and federal laws. Failure to comply with educational laws results in serious consequences for school districts, employee groups, and students. Other particular educational matters are labeled as recommendations and are usually followed as if they were laws.

The federal government responds to social needs and trends by enacting legislation that affects the education of students in public and private schools. Funding for these programs comes from local, state, and federal resources. The Education for All Handicapped Children Act, the National Defense Education Act, the Elementary and Secondary Education Act, and the Civil Rights Act of 1964 are some of the better known pieces of federal education legislation. There are others. It is recommended that you research these for your own information.

Individual states are concerned and involved with enacting and maintaining quality education for all students. Passing legislation for education requires considerable effort and diligence from parents, teachers, support groups, committees, legislators, school boards, and commissioners.

Legislation that is primarily a matter of funding is important. The state allocates a portion of tax dollars to fund elementary and secondary schools. In addition to this, individual school districts usually have the option of raising additional funds by voting to increase property taxes by a particular amount. For example, an increase of three mils (a mil is one-thousandth of a dollar, or one tenth of a cent) over a two-year period is common. When the school board asks the community for additional funds, those funds are generally earmarked for a specific purpose. Construction of a new school, general operating funds, or major renovations are reasons for seeking more money from the community.

The groups mentioned above are equally concerned about passing laws that affect general classroom education. New laws require school districts to plan, evaluate, and report how they are improving, maintaining, and becoming more accountable for what is taught and learned in all grades, kindergarten through twelve. These are important responsibilities and cannot be taken for granted. Curriculum cycles, testing programs, establishing achievable goals, assurance of mastery, physical plant improvements, and other organizational and management plans are being enacted as part of the newer regulations.

Figure 1.6 gives an overview of the support system for educational legislation.

■ Summary

This chapter has presented some insights into the teaching profession as it exists today. It is a profession that is constantly growing and expanding in responsibilities, preparation, and expectations. Teaching will not become a constant. It if does, then academic achievement will be at a standstill.

Teaching is a profession that demands great dedication, stamina, love, and flexibility. Those who enter the profession can expect many joys as they watch students grow academically and socially. Parents and community members have high expectations for schools and students. The teachers play a critical role in realizing those expectations and quite possibly surpassing them. Teaching is setting goals and objectives and then working toward achieving them.

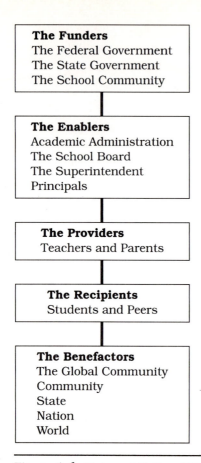

Figure 1.6 State and National Educational Legislation

Teaching is about becoming proficient in methods and strategies that make learning enjoyable, meaningful, and important for students of all ages. It is a profession wherein you will develop a special relationship with students from many backgrounds, cultures, and family systems. Teaching is educating future citizens.

■ The Workshop

At the end of each chapter in this book there will be some activities for you to perform. They will accentuate some of the information, opinions, or topics that are presented in the text. Reading assigned chapters in a textbook is valuable. Using the information as a basis or foundation for further individual investigations adds to its value in many ways.

Activity I

Why do you want to be a teacher? What are the ideas, impressions, events, or feelings that have led you to this consideration? Self-examination is an effective method for sorting out particular, isolated events that affect us. For this activity you will brainstorm (with yourself) all the reasons why you think you want to be a teacher. Write them all down, even if they seem trite or obvious at this particular moment. Next, write down all the factors that influenced your decision to investigate teaching as a possible career choice.

Fold a large piece of paper in half. Label one side Reasons and the other side Influencing Factors. Your instructor may choose to use this activity as the basis for a large group discussion. Keep this activity in a journal until the conclusion of this course, at which time you should reread it. How have your thoughts and ideas changed from when you first listed them?

Activity II

The role of teachers is constantly expanding to meet student, community, and national requirements. During the course of a particular day or week the teacher performs several duties. Some of them include teaching, counseling, parenting, guiding, nurturing, facilitating, prescribing, diagnosing, listening, and many others. For this activity you will need to visit the university library and research the literature on the roles of elementary and secondary teachers. Read at least four articles and prepare a brief summary to share in class. Your instructor may require a written report as well.

■ Questions and Thoughts

1. Research the educational literature and find various definitions of *teaching*. Determine if there are any common factors in the way teaching is defined by the writers. Can you locate some definitions from 10 or 15 years ago? How have the perceptions changed over the span of time?

2. What are the certification and licensing procedures for your state? Are life licenses available? Contact your university certification officer or the appropriate licensing agency (the State Board of Education or the Commission for Teacher Credentialing) for specific information on all certification requirements for elementary and secondary teachers. Are the requirements for the specialists (art, music, and physical education) significantly different than for classroom teachers? Keep this information for future reference.

3. How are professional ethics actually enforced in the average school district? What is the role of the professional association, the school administrators, and the school board?

■ Readings and References

Bloom, B. (1956). *The Taxonomy of Educational Objectives: The Classification of Educational Goals: Handbook 1: Congnitive Domain.* New York: Longman.

Hord, S. M., Rutherford, W. L., Huling-Austin, L., and Hall, G. E. (1987). *Taking Charge of Change.* Alexandria, VA: The Association for Supervision and Curriculum Development.

McCarthy, B. (1980). *The 4Mat System: Teaching to Learning Styles with Right/Left Mode Techniques.* Arlington Heights, IL: EXCEL.

Paul, C. (1987) "To the Trenches." *Clearing House, 62:* 397–399.

Provenzo, E. F., McCloskey, G. N., Kottkamp, R. B., and Cohn, M. M. (1989). "Metaphor and Meaning in the Language of Teachers." *Teachers College Record, 90:* 551–573.

Turner, J. A. (1989). "IBM Plans 5-Year, $25-million Program to Improve Teacher Training." *The Chronicle of Higher Education, 35:* 27.

Wadsworth, B. (1984). *Piaget's Theory of Cognitive and Affective Development.* New York: Longman.

■ ■ ■ **Chapter Two**

Programs
in Education

■ Definitions

Children at Risk: This term is used to indicate those students who have a high dropout rate, are low achievers, and usually have low self-esteem. Under normal conditions, they have a very little chance of succeeding and a very good chance of being lost or dropping through the cracks at school. They can be of any age or grade level, but are usually identifiable in early elementary school or even before they enter the system.

Curriculum: This is the program of studies taught by the school and learned by the students. It may be defined broadly as everything the students learn from all of their school experiences, or more narrowly defined as the specific academic experiences provided by the school. Curriculum development is the planning that goes into providing a specific curriculum for a school.

Early Intervention: It is helpful to intervene in the schooling of a high-risk child as soon as possible to prevent problems before they develop. Various programs identify high-risk students and try to provide help before the problem becomes acute.

Funding: This is the money necessary to operate a special program or to finance an experimental program. Individual schools or school districts may not have money to support these special projects. Possible sources of funding are private corporations and state, national, and local agencies.

Mandated Programs: These are programs that are required by either state or federal law. There is no choice or decision making—the program *will* be in place at the school.

■ Focus Questions

1. How do you feel about new or experimental programs? Would you like to participate in one of these programs?
2. Which of these programs interest you the most? Why?
3. Are there enough programs to adequately meet the diverse academic, social, and cultural needs of students from various backgrounds?

■ Introduction

Projects involving the classroom applications of research are numerous and exciting. Some of these programs may be implemented in your school. At one point the application of research was limited largely to clinical or laboratory school settings. Now these findings are applicable and practical for classroom use. It is very important for teachers to know about pertinent educational research if they are to do the best job possible in their curriculum areas. Participation in a research program can be rewarding for you and your students.

There are many ongoing programs in elementary and secondary education. The implementation of many of these programs in the public schools is directly related to the availability of local, state, or federal funds. A number of private foundations also have funds available for educational programs. The procedure for acquiring these funds is usually to write a grant proposal, submit it to the organization, and wait for an approval or denial. Private foundations frequently approve grant monies for programs that are innovative, highly visible, or directed at special populations such as the academically gifted.

Programs in education include those for teachers, administrators, students, and the schools themselves. This chapter gives an overview of some programs you will probably encounter in subsequent university courses, during clinical experiences (including student teaching), and when you begin professional service. It will not include curriculum programs such as a specific science or reading series.

■ ■ ■

Programs: A Point of View

There are many formal and informal programs in education. Special education is an example of a formal program with its exacting identification procedures and utilization of state and federal funds. An example of informal programming is the teacher who independently provides a differentiated education for his or her high-potential students without allocated funds or materials.

Research indicates that if disadvantaged students are to be successful in school, we must provide early intervention. In other words, we must begin to service them at an early age. National Head Start is a direct result of this philosophy. Early childhood special education, servicing developmentally delayed children (birth to school age), and Chapter I are two others. Based on a philosophy of early intervention (that is, to identify the problem early and attempt to correct it before it is too late), many formal programs are directed at elementary student populations.

■ Short Shot

There is no question that teaching is a serious, demanding profession. It is easy to dwell on the serious aspects and lose track of the humorous, enjoyable, rewarding, and, yes, even the fun part of teaching. Schools are for students, but teaching is for adults who happen to be teachers. Master teachers enjoy their work and openly show it. Someone once said, "There is no fun like work!" Teachers who like their work have fun doing it.

At the secondary level new programs tend to be curricular in nature, such as adding a new computer course for juniors and seniors. Other provisions for secondary students include such things as counseling groups, work study, open enrollment, transitions to the workplace, alternative programs for at-risk students, and extended day programs. A number of secondary programs are directed toward keeping students in the academic environment until graduation. Preventing dropouts and encouraging the minimal 12-year education continues to be a top priority. Our present state of technology requires this as a minimum for gainful employment and a satisfying life.

Programs for public education are expensive. Research, design, materials, teacher training, and other factors are part of the cost to introduce new programs in a particular school district. Mandated statewide programs represent significant funding allocations. State and local boards of education are responsible for setting policies; establishing their fiscal priorities is an important matter. It is unfortunate that new program development (see Figure 2.1) is not a major concern in more school districts. There is a cadre of dedicated, committed teachers who intently study their own teaching, meet the educational needs of their students, and eagerly respond to community expectations. Indeed, they are designing and implementing needs-based programs for their classes, departments, and school districts. Perhaps one day you will be on the faculty with teachers like this!

National Head Start provides programs for low-income and disadvantaged youth.

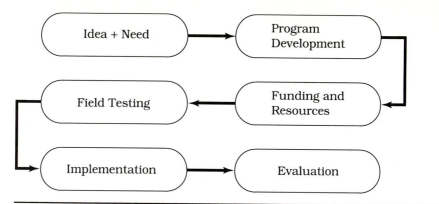

Figure 2.1 **A New Program from Idea to Implementation**

Chapter I

Chapter I is a federally funded program that provides compensatory education for underachieving children of low-income families. Funds are used for purchasing instructional materials, salaries for teachers and teacher assistants, in-service seminars or workshops, and other needs.

Elementary and Secondary Education Act (1965)

This federal legislation served as the impetus for nine title programs to support public education. Title I (now known as Chapter I) is perhaps the most familiar. Some of the others are Title II, library materials and textbooks; Title III, guidance and counseling; Title VII, bilingual education; and Title IX, prohibiting sex discrimination against teachers and students. Title VI, support for educating the handicapped, is now covered under PL 94–142.

National Head Start

The education of low-income disadvantaged children has been a concern for many years. These children typically lack the readiness skills necessary to function successfully when they enter kindergarten and first grade. The Economic Opportunity Act of 1964 provided funds for projects aimed at improving the educational opportunities of these children. Project Head Start was one such program. The basic philosophy is to identify these preschool children and get them into a compensatory program as soon as possible; to provide them with the necessary skills in language development, social development, physical skills, attitudes, health, math concepts, and many others. Providing a very positive success-oriented program for these preschoolers helps to develop the necessary entrance skills to make the adjustment to the public school system more satisfactory for both children and parents.

Open Enrollments

In 1987 the Minnesota Legislature adopted the Voluntary Open Enrollment Program. This allowed students to attend school outside their home district without payment of tuition. During the first year, school districts participated on a voluntary basis, and it came into full participation status during the 1990–91 school term. A student may wish to attend another school to get courses not offered at the home school, or to attend specific classes at a college or university before graduating from high school. Already nationally recognized, other states are designing similar programs. Open enrollment offers students more academic choices as well as location convenience.

Schools for the Creative and Performing Arts

Providing an appropriate education for our creatively talented students is a controversial issue in many states. There have been numerous private arts schools but few public ones. The arts high schools provide a regular secondary curriculum with all the required courses for graduation, in addition to a heavy concentration of music, theater, dance, and art education. Ideally, there should be one in every state. Attendance at a state arts high school is determined by specific entrance standards.

The Gifted

It is estimated that 3 to 5 percent of school-aged children are academically gifted. Identifying them is one thing, providing an appropriate education is quite another matter. Publishers can provide resource books, activities boxes, guides, student workbooks, task cards, and various other materials for teachers to use. One commercially available kit is The Total Creativity Program for Individualizing and Humanizing the Learning Process by Dr. Frank E. Williams. It is designed using his cognitive-affective-interaction model as the foundation.

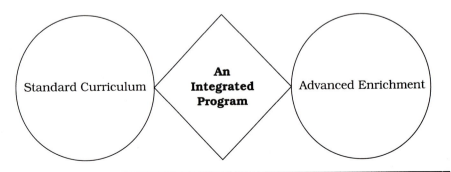

Figure 2.2 An Abbreviated Model for Providing an Education for Gifted and Talented Students

■ **People in Education**

Marian Leibowitz

Marian Leibowitz is an authority in the field of gifted education. She is a popular seminar and workshop leader and has held responsible positions at the national level. She is instrumental in developing strategies for teaching the thinking skills in all academic disciplines at all grade levels.

Some districts have modified programs for the gifted, which consist of accelerated courses, grade skipping (an overused elementary solution to: What can we do with them?), small group after-school classes, some tutoring in a special area provided by a willing teacher, and other curriculum modifications (see Figure 2.2).

Districts do not buy a gifted program the way they purchase a math series. Larger districts may employ a coordinator for the gifted, who primarily trains the professional staff, locates materials, and occasionally performs some demonstration teaching. Districts with a full-time teacher for the gifted are very fortunate. It is unfortunate that many gifted students are serviced primarily by whatever the classroom teacher can find the time to prepare for them. An excellent resource on this topic is *Teaching the Gifted Child* by James J. Gallagher (Allyn and Bacon).

Magnet Schools

Some large school districts have introduced magnet school programs. A magnet school is a specialty school designed to service special student populations as well as to affect social and racial balance. It is possible to have more than one magnet school. For example, one may be known as the math and science school, another as the fine arts school, another as the environmental school, and so on. A magnet school offers high-quality basic skills education as well as concentrated opportunities in its special area. Students from all over the district (or state) have the opportunity to attend these alternative schools.

The High School for the Engineering Professions (HSEP) in Houston is an excellent example of a secondary magnet school. HSEP emphasizes applied math and science for superior students who may choose an engineering major in college. It draws qualified students from diverse social and economic backgrounds. The specialized curriculum is designed by teachers and a group of engineering college deans. Of particular note is the lab that gives students hands-on experiences with machinery of various types, and opportunities to test the theoretical information they learn in class. Graduates of HSEP are highly recruited by engineering colleges and universities.

The Boston University– Chelsea Public Schools Project

Programs in education change and influence public and private education in many ways. There are models for change that are instructional, managerial, financial, evaluative, theoretical, or analytical. Boston University and the Chelsea Public Schools are working together on a national model to improve urban education.

The Chelsea Public Schools had serious problems, including deterioration of the schools, a dropout rate of 50 percent, the lowest academic achievement in the state, 70 percent minority students, and other conditions common to inner-city public schools. The Chelsea School Committee asked Boston University for help and approved a contract giving the university authority to run the school system. The university actually serves as an unpaid consultant to introduce new projects and programs. The university has embarked on a 10-year plan to take over the management of the schools and to initiate major reforms.

Boston University's master plan makes everyone responsible for the education of students and adults via a partnership with the community, businesses, parents, and the university personnel and resources. Funds to support the plan come from state and federal sources, private foundations, and individuals.

New programs for this reformation project are intergenerational to address the non-English-speaking minorities. The literacy project includes language and cultural studies, as well as an experimental literature curriculum to teach responsibility in personal relationships. A creative thinking component of the plan helps teachers use each other's skills and talents for professional development. The community aspect of the plan also addresses the needs of adults. Funds are used to provide daycare services, job training, and literacy and other revitalized programs to raise the expectations and standards of the entire community.

This model represents a long-term commitment between a private university and a public school system to significantly improve and reform urban education. It is suggested that you read the selections listed at the end of this chapter for more information on this cooperative endeavor.

National Teacher Certification

The Carnegie Foundation has underwritten an extensive study of the teaching profession. One of its goals was to define what good teaching is. The National Board for Professional Teaching Standards is charged with defining effective teaching, setting standards to achieve it, and eventually to begin certifying those teachers who meet the standards. These nationally certified teachers would not only be excellent classroom teachers but would also have the necessary skills and abilities to initiate and lead educational reforms and improvements that are needed in their home schools and districts.

This program of national certification would offer qualified teachers the challenge of affecting major changes in the profession and in the entire educational system. Additional plans for these lead teachers include contributing to major changes in undergraduate teacher education programs, designing new master's degrees programs, accepting a larger role in teacher training for new and experienced teachers, and other leadership responsibilities.

The Carnegie Forum's Task Force on Teaching as a Profession (1986) is an important study that examines the teaching profession and makes some critical recommendations for the educational community to consider. Pursuing a national certification would be an honor as well as a significant professional commitment for teachers.

Multicultural Education

Learning about people from different cultures has been one of the major social studies goals for many years. The parameters of that learning were limited to the areas of geography, government, and perhaps trade. If the instructional opportunities expanded beyond these parameters, it was probably due to the intense personal efforts of particular teachers rather than an organized educational program or established educational philosophy.

Multicultural education is no longer a haphazard, incidental instructional matter relegated to an isolated social studies chapter or unit. It is being infused into all curriculum areas in both elementary and secondary schools. This infusion correlates with the ongoing philosophy that the school climate should be a comfortable one for students from all cultural environments. The Native American, Arabic, Southeast Asian, Hispanic, Caribbean, and other groups of students learn about their cultural heritage as well as their adopted American culture by participating in a strong multicultural program.

Multicultural education is both formal and informal. Textbook publishers include this issue in their textbooks, filmstrips, practice books, and other supplementary materials for both students and teachers. Audiovisual materials companies provide a variety of materials for schools to purchase. Curriculum committees are writing and adopting programs that complement their particular community situations. Community education provides programs for adults and children after school and in the evenings.

Funds for multicultural education are provided by regular school district budgeting, by applying for state and federal government grant monies, and by private foundations and other sources. Individual state and local school boards mandate a multicultural education component that addresses the needs of various student populations.

Foreign Language Programs

Foreign languages at the secondary level have been available as an elective or a requirement for many years. Some of the more common languages studied are French, Spanish, and German. Recently the Chinese and Russian languages have become available in some schools. In other schools, Japanese, Italian, and Swedish are available for credit during the regular school period or after school through community education programs. International relations, student exchange programs, travel, and other opportunities highlight the necessity and the advantages of knowing a foreign language. Secondary students are very close to the point in their lives where speaking knowledge of a foreign language is a definite asset.

Teaching foreign languages at the elementary level is a controversial issue. One group of parents and teachers think that young children should have the opportunity to learn a foreign language at the same time they are learning the finer points of English. Another group feels strongly that elementary children have so many curriculum demands that adding foreign language as a requirement would be detrimental. At this point, foreign language is primarily an after-school educational opportunity for younger children.

Educational Cooperative Service Units

In 1976 the state of Minnesota established 10 regional units called Educational Cooperative Service Units (ESCU). Member school districts within each of these regional units work cooperatively to meet and plan for common needs in a cost-effective manner. ECSUs are funded through state grants, membership fees, federal grants, meeting and workshop fees, and other special funding sources. ECSUs provide resources, materials, training, and direction for teachers, administrators, school boards, and students.

The fundamentals of these regional educational cooperatives are superintendents' groups, principals' academies, research studies, early childhood projects, AIDS resources, drug-free school programs, gifted and talented education, personnel development (all employee groups), student-professional mentorships, curriculum development and workshops, and other cooperative efforts.

Other Programs in Education

The Holmes Group: The Holmes Group Consortium is a group of education school deans from large research universities who have proposed a major change in undergraduate teacher education programs. Their recommendations propose the following:

1. A four-year undergraduate degree in the liberal arts and general studies
2. A full year of education courses and study

3. A full year of paid internship in the classroom with continued professional courses and study

Consortium members propose that these additional studies will more fully prepare newly certified teachers for classroom success.

Limited English Speaking: Limited English Speaking (LES) or English as a Second Language (ESL) programs are for those students who cannot speak English or who can only communicate at a minimal level of proficiency. The availability of these programs became very important with the large influx of foreign-speaking students, particularly those from non-Western cultures such as Laos, Cambodia, and Viet Nam. Students in need of these services are taught by the speech and language clinician through the special-education department. They also learn the language by being mainstreamed into the classroom with other children their age.

Early Childhood Special Education: Early Childhood Special Education services children from birth to school age. These children are identified through preschool screening services and referrals from other agencies. Teachers in SE/EC programs must take courses in special education, assessment, early childhood education, and other special courses to obtain this license. (*Note:* SE/EC is not the same as a kindergarten endorsement.)

■ People in Education

Maria Montessori

Maria Montessori is a benchmark in the foundation of early childhood education. The name *Montessori* is immediately associated with preschool, daycare programs, and other educational movements for young children. Her early efforts in education were with mentally retarded children and later with street children in underprivileged areas.

Montessori's theories, methods, and strategies are based on the premise that young children can explore, examine, and learn many things in a relatively free environment, with intervention from adults on an "as-needed" basis. Self-discovery and individualization are stressed in conjunction with group cooperation. She developed activities that permit youngsters to use the senses in order to aid learning. Discovery learning is an important concept in Montessori programs. In some areas, the Montessori educational principles and methods have been extended to include regular public school education through the elementary grades. Most Montessori schools are private academies.

■ Short Shot

Special programs in education are designed and implemented to meet the critical needs of students (i.e., work study, extended day classes, open enrollments, and others). Families with two working parents or single-parent families have some needs that are unique to their particular situations. Before-school and after-school childcare, support systems, a place to get breakfast, and someone to help with homework assignments are samples of those real needs.

Some community education programs are attempting to provide these services for needy families. There is a significant need for positive role models to help students with homework assignments, to praise and reinforce their academic efforts, and simply to read to them in the case of primary-aged students. Are you that special person? If you are, contact the appropriate school or community personnel to volunteer your services!

Daycare and Nursery School: Daycare and nursery school programs are familiar to everyone. With the increased number of mothers working outside the home, there has been a rapid growth of various daycare centers and licensed facilities in private homes. Some centers are located near elementary schools for the convenience of parents and children. School-aged children are on the school bus route and can easily be transported to and from school each day, and the preschool youngsters can be serviced at the same facility as well.

Nursery School: Nursery schools provide many prekindergarten experiences for young children. Typically, young children might attend nursery school two days a week for perhaps two hours. During this time they play games, sing, listen to stories, do fingerplays, enjoy art activities, socialize with other children, and participate in many other planned activities. Nursery schools provide a positive enjoyable opportunity for preschool children. Special licenses are usually required for quality daycare and nursery schools.

Middle School: The middle school, frequently for grades 5 through 7, performs a dual function in the school system. From an organizational-managerial standpoint, it provides more space for the lower-grade students in many overcrowded elementary buildings. It enables the older students to be in a facility that is specially designed for their needs.

The middle school serves as a bridge from the elementary school learning environment to the more socially demanding secondary situation. From the teaching and learning viewpoints, the middle school provides students with courses, programs, and activities that meet their developmental needs in particular ways. This age group of students can interrelate and develop both socially and academically without the interference of significantly younger or older students.

Open School: The open school is an organizational structure that meets the special needs of students who are very independent and self-motivating. Open schools have flexible scheduling, periods for students to pursue personal interests and goals, opportunities to interact with several teachers, and other curricular options within a freer, less rigid environment. The open school remains an option in some larger districts, and students are selected based on a particular set of criteria.

■ Summary

There are a multitude of special programs in our schools today, and this will continue to be so as we work to find new and better ways to teach. New programs are constantly being developed and tried in an effort to find solutions to continually changing problems. You may be involved in some major experiments, or an innovative approach, or something that you devise and try yourself. Whatever the program, you must continually try to remain current in education philosophy and practices.

■ The Workshop

Activity I

Daycare centers and nursery schools are common sites in the average school community. The part they play in the preschool experience of many children is indispensable. It is helpful to observe these facilities to clearly determine the variety of activities and experiences they provide for young children. Make arrangements to visit one and make a notation of activities that could fit into one of these categories:

Language development
Large-muscle development
Small-muscle control
Social skills
Independent activities
Free exploration

Use the following checklist as you observe the children's activities:

**Observer's Guide for Recording Children's Activities
in a Daycare or Nursery School Setting**

	ACTIVITY	OBSERVATIONS	NOTATIONS

1. Language Development
   (sample activities)
   a. listening to stories
   b. telling stories
   c. music, singing
   d. talking
   e. looking at books

2. Large-Muscle Development
   (sample activities)
   a. climbing on play equipment
   b. running, jumping, skipping
   c. riding, balancing
   d. outdoor play

3. Small-Muscle Control
   (sample activities)
   a. fingerplays
   b. rhythmic activities
   c. puzzles, games, coloring
   d. cutting and pasting
   e. art activities

4. Social Skills
   (sample activities)
   a. playing with a friend 1:1
   b. small-group activities
   c. large-group activities
   d. relating to adults
   e. general behavior and
      attitudes

5. Independent Activities
   (sample activities)
   a. reading books
   b. coloring
   c. toy boxes
   d. helping adult leaders
   e. other

6. Free Exploration
   (sample activities)
   a. self-directing activity
   b. making choices
   c. duration
   d. concentration
   e. results

Self-Check: What did you observe? Were the children engaged in meaningful activities? Were the adults positive, reassuring, supportive, and cheerful? Share your observer's guide with a classmate. Be prepared to share your results in class, especially any questions you may have.

Activity II

Children and students who are at risk is a topic that frequently appears in the news media. A number of social and economic factors contribute directly and indirectly to the condition of being at risk. What, if anything, can the educational community contribute to the solution of this problem? Your instructor may lead a discussion on this topic or divide the class into small discussion groups.

■ Questions and Thoughts

1. What is the breakdown of local, state, and national funding for public schools? How are special funds and grants obtained?

2. School restructuring and the influence of the business community are sometimes in disagreement regarding the direction public education should be going. What is the role of the business community and the general public in the process of public education?

3. Should teachers be required to become fluent in another language as a prerequisite for employment in a particular school district or area? Is English the instructional language of our schools? Is such a language requirement discriminatory?

■ Readings and References

"BU Takeover Plan Clears First Hurdle in Chelsea." (1989). *American Teacher, 73:* 3.

Gallagher, J. J. (1985). *Teaching the Gifted Child.* Boston: Allyn and Bacon.

McKenna, B. (1989). "Trouble in Chelsea." *American Teacher, 73:* 10–11.

Norris, B. (1988). "A Debate That Becomes Curiouser and Curiouser (Reform and Control of Public Schools in Chelsea)." *The Times Educational Supplement 3783:* 6.

Norris, W. (1988). "University Takeover of School Runs into Trouble." *The Times Educational Supplement 841:* 11.

Warger, C. (Ed.) (1988). *A Resource Guide to Public School Early Childhood Programs.* Alexandria, VA: The Association for Supervision and Curriculum Development.

Chapter Three

Specialized
Knowledge

■ Definitions

Behavior: This is how a person acts in a given situation. Behavioral psychology is based on the premise that all behavior is learned and can be modified by using appropriate stimuli. The focus is on observable events—what people say and do. Related topics: Behavior modification, stimulus-response, behavioral objectives.

Child Growth and Development: This refers to the study of how children grow and develop. It is usually concerned with the physical growth and change as well as the mental development of children. Of concern to parents and teachers are the sequence and characteristics of the various stages that a child goes through on his or her way to maturity. The teacher must know the characteristics of the age group with which he or she will be working so that the children can be taught accordingly.

Classroom Management: This refers to all of the tasks that go into the operation of a classroom. It includes time management, storage of materials, placement of furniture, student movement, classroom supplies, distributing and collecting materials, and the overall control of the students. In short, it is everything that a teacher must do to be able to teach.

Curriculum Committee: This group, usually composed of teachers, administrators, and parents, makes decisions for a particular curriculum area. Language arts, math, science, social studies, and health are some of the more common curriculum committees.

Educational Psychologist: This person usually is concerned with conducting and interpreting educational research in an effort to help teachers understand how a child learns. He or she also develops teaching strategies that incorporate such findings.

Expository Teaching: This is a type of instruction that depends on the teacher to give the students most of the information they need in the form of lecture, assigned readings, or similar assignments. The teacher is the active participant who gives information, whereas the student is the receptor of the knowledge.

Incidental Teaching: On occasion, teachers may teach a lesson based on a need or interest area that suddenly arises. It is not planned, and the content may not be a stated part of the curriculum. An example might be a fast-breaking news event, such as an earthquake, or a social problem that develops in class.

Pilot Program: This is the procedure of using a given curriculum or process for a stated period of time before it is officially adopted for the school. Typically, one or more teachers will use a program for a year, make evaluations and adjustments, and then give specific recommendations to adopt or reject the program.

Staff Development: School districts provide workshops, lectures, seminars, and advanced training sessions for the professional staff. Frequently, continuing education credits are preapproved for those who participate.

■ Focus Questions

1. Make a list of words that you have heard teachers use or have read in education literature. Can you find definitions for the words or phrases that you do not know?

2. Are you a left-brain or a right-brain learner? Did your teachers meet your learning needs?

3. As a teacher, how will you get everything organized so that you can teach? How will you organize your schedule, yourself, your class, and your furniture?

4. Who controls the class—you or your students? How can you make sure that it is you?

5. What is educational research? How will it help you to be a more effective teacher?

■ Introduction

Every profession has a certain amount of special information that its members should know; the teaching profession is no exception. This body of special information is both incidental (those facts that are needed for particular instances) and essential (the knowledge that is needed on a continual basis). Much of what you learn in the foundations and methods courses forms the background for how you will be teaching in your own classroom. Much of this information becomes automatic and is used without thinking about it. Other things are used consciously and purposefully every day. Conscientious teachers make every effort to acquire as much information as they possibly can about teaching and learning. Not everything is used every day, but when particular situations arise, the information they need will be there.

Specialized knowledge related to the teaching profession includes everything from knowing the procedures for reporting child abuse to understanding all the levels of service for special-education students. It also includes topics such as theory, curriculum, human relations, management, and methodology. Teachers use a myriad of terms that have particular meanings among their colleagues. Some of this jargon is explained in this chapter.

■ ■ ■

Vocabulary

The vocabulary associated with elementary and secondary education is very interesting and useful to know. It is interesting from the standpoint that each curriculum area or department uses particular terms unique to itself. Special education is a prime example of this phenomenon. In addition, there are other terms and phrases commonly used by either elementary or secondary

■ People in Education
Kenneth and Rita Dunn

Kenneth and Rita Dunn are coauthors and collaborators in a number of educational endeavors. *Educator's Self-Teaching Guide to Individualizing Instructional Programs* (1975), *Practical Approaches to Individualizing Instruction* (1972), and *Teaching Students Through Their Individual Learning Styles: A Practical Approach* (1978) are three books that examine classroom implications of student learning styles and the teacher's instructional adaptations to meet them. The Dunns have done extensive work in learning styles and brain behavior, teaching styles, early childhood, and gifted education. These contemporary educators have written numerous articles in professional journals. They designed the Learning Style Inventory that is used to identify student learning strengths.

teachers. When you hear these terms used in conversation with your professional colleagues, you should know what they mean.

Here is a selection of some common educational terms; they may or may not be appropriate to your local situation.

CONTRACT LANGUAGE
A-Schedule: The basic salary schedule for all teachers under contract.

B-Schedule: The extracurricular pay schedule for duties above and beyond the classroom responsibilities. Duties such as coaching, department chairperson, activity advisor, and supervising are covered on the B-schedule salary or hourly rate schedule.

Duty Day: The time teachers are required to be on duty as per contract agreement. Example: 8:00–3:30

Educational Lane: Teachers are placed on an educational lane commensurate with their degrees and/or credits earned. Example: B.A., B.A. plus 15 credits, M.A. plus 45 credits, etc.

Fair Share: A fee assessed to teachers who are not members of the bargaining unit for professional services rendered.

Grievance: A procedure for clarifying real or perceived violations of the master contract. An individual or a group of teachers may file a grievance.

Sabbatical Leave: A leave that is taken for professional advancement. Example: A secondary teacher must perform field service to maintain his or her vocational license.

Seniority List: A list of all tenured teachers in a school system, stating the date of hire, areas of certification, and experience. Position on the seniority list becomes very important during periods of professional staff reductions, lowered enrollments, and district mergers.

Step: An experience increment (number of years of full-time teaching) on the basic salary schedule. Example: A new teacher to the district could be hired on the third step (three years of previous experience at the B.A. level).

Unrequested Leave of Absence: Teachers are placed on unrequested leave due to financial cutbacks, lower student enrollments, discontinuance of position, or other reasons for staff reductions. *See* Seniority list.

SPECIAL EDUCATION TERMS

Adaptive Physical Education: Some physically handicapped students receive additional adaptive physical education services designed to increase and/or maintain physical mobility. Adaptive physical education is frequently on an individual basis with the physical education teacher.

ADD: Attention Deficit Disorder is the inability to concentrate or perform tasks. Research is currently investigating specific brain dysfunctions and hyperactivity connections.

EBD: An Emotional Behavior Disorder student may require removal from the regular classroom for all or part of the school day. Emotionally disturbed students are serviced by teachers with special certifications.

GLD: General Learning Disabled students perform at a lower level in academic areas. Learning-disabled students were formerly identified as educable mentally retarded (EMR).

IEP: An Individual Education Plan that clearly states the objectives for each special-education student. The objectives can be social, emotional, behavioral, academic, or physical.

Out Placements: Some severely handicapped students (Level VII) must be placed in facilities outside of the public school.

PL 94–142: The federal law that requires public schools to provide an appropriate education for all handicapped children. It is frequently referred to as the *special education law*.

Special Education–Early Childhood: A special program for teaching preschool children who are developmentally delayed in one or more areas.

Speech or Language Delayed: Students with oral language or speech performance that is not within the normal range for their ages.

GENERAL TERMINOLOGY

Curriculum Differentiation: Providing special learning activities as needed for special-education or high-potential students.

Curriculum Integrations: Reinforcing one skill by drawing on similar skills in another curriculum area. Example: Teaching the intermediate map directions by correlating that skill with telling time (N = 12 o'clock, NE = fifteen minutes past the hour).

Departmentalized Program: Subject areas taught from a department at the junior high or secondary level. Example: General mathematics, algebra I, geometry, and trigonometry are course offerings in the mathematics department.

Early Promotions: The practice of placing a student in a grade above that of his or her peers; grade skipping.

Grouping: Various instructional-managerial methods of placing students in groups. Examples: *performance group*—all students are performing at a similar level; *ability group*—all students have similar mental capabilities as determined by a given testing instrument such as an IQ test; *cross-age group*—students of various ages work together on particular skills; *pairing*—two students work together, frequently a high achiever is paired with a lower-performing student; *random*—each class has a mixture of high-, average-, low-performing and special-education students.

Intervention: The student support team intervenes (takes an appropriate action, makes specific recommendations) for the student. Such an intervention may be deemed necessary for an acute situation, such as sexual, physical, drug or alcohol abuse.

Open Enrollments: A policy that permits students to attend a school outside the home district; in some cases this expands course offerings for secondary students.

Overachiever: A student who uses excessive, compulsive methods to perform at a superior level in almost all phases of life; a perfectionist. Overachievers frequently impose unrealistic expectations upon themselves at a very early age.

Self-Contained Program: The traditional elementary classroom with one teacher and a group of students. The class spends all day with the same teacher, who teaches all subject areas, usually kindergarten through the sixth grade.

Tracking: Placing students on a specific educational track with predetermined courses. At the secondary level that track may be vocational, college bound, or general.

Underachiever: A student with high abilities who performs significantly below grade-level expectations. This individual may actually be failing in one or all subjects.

Vocational Education: A postsecondary program to prepare students for vocational employment.

In the Classroom

Elementary and secondary teachers are responsible for acquiring a great deal of knowledge (see Figure 3.1). This knowledge falls into several categories: instructional (how to teach), curriculum content (what to teach), human relations (interacting with and managing students), and professional

Instructional	Curricular	Professional	Personal	Human Relations
(How)	(What)	(Skills)	(Private)	(Social)

Figure 3.1 Some Helpful Skills for Successful Teaching

(knowledge and skills related to the profession and one's role in it). Of particular interest at this point are the instructional issues—those related to classroom teaching responsibilities. We will now examine some of these areas.

Left Brain, Right Brain

The terms *left brain* and *right brain* refer to the specific functions of the left and right hemispheres of the brain in relation to learning. Each side of the brain receives and processes information in certain ways. The brain's left hemisphere controls the right side of the body, and the right hemisphere controls the left side of the body. Some specialized functions of the left side are logic; sequencing; convergency; and lateral, factual, and analytical thinking. Some specialized functions of the right side are creativity; divergency; and visual, intuitive, symbolic, lateral, and receptive thinking. (See "Whole Brain Learning," 1983.)

The term *brain dominance* refers to a person's preferred style of learning. A person with left-brain (LB) preference enjoys situations that are very organized, sequential, and carefully planned; he or she knows exactly what

▪ Short Shot

The collection of specialized knowledge in education seems to increase almost daily. At one point the major focus was on New Math. At another time classroom teachers became responsible for teaching mainstreamed special-education students, in addition to individualizing for the gifted and talented. The 1980s ushered in the new requirement that all teachers (yes, even the kindergarten teachers!) become computer literate and prepared to teach computer education to their classes. There are times when teachers wonder what specialized knowledge will be required of them next. The initial four-year college degree is truly a commencement of continuous learning and upgrading of instructional skills.

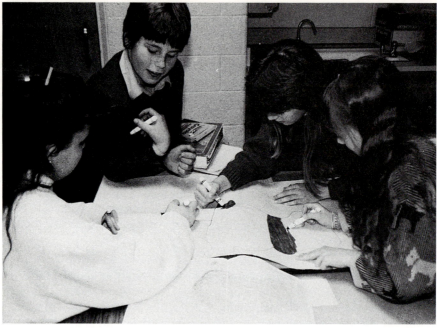

Students with a right-brain preference may be more comfortable in a less formal setting.

the teacher expects and will make every effort to do it. A person with right-brain (RB) preference functions well when he or she has a less formal working situation. Trying several different things, trial and error, creative approaches, and manipulating objects are some of the preferred activities for these students.

In the classroom, teachers provide activities that appeal to students with left- and right-brain preferences. At the secondary level, a lecture class in biology appeals to those with a left-brain preference; whereas the laboratory class appeals to right-brain people. In this instance the teacher provides opportunities for everyone to work in the preferred mode at different times.

Elementary teachers have many opportunities to provide left- and right-brain activities for students. Some examples are:

Math: LB students do a workbook page; RB students play a math game.

Social studies: LB students read the text and answer study questions; RB students write and perform individual impersonations.

Language arts: LB students read folk tales; RB students spontaneously act out a given folk tale.

In these and other ways, teachers plan activities that permit students to learn in the mode that suits them. Teachers do not necessarily label a student as being a left-brain or right-brain person, and then provide only those types of activities for him or her. To do so would severely limit a student's learning capabilities. However, with experience it becomes readily noticeable that certain students gravitate toward particular activities and usually do them very well. It is strongly recommended that students experience activities that are representative of both left- and right-brain hemispheric functioning.

This is a very compact explanation of left- and right-brain functions. It is important to have at least a speaking knowledge of these learning strategies so you can search for and recognize them when you observe in classrooms. As you do further readings in this area, the importance of each hemisphere of the brain will be clarified. It will also become easier to identify particular activities that are associated with each hemisphere. It is the school's responsibility to meet the learning needs of every student. More specifically, it is the teacher's responsibility. Providing activities for left- and right-brain students at both the elementary and the secondary levels is one way of meeting specific learner needs.

Learning Modalities

The modalities of learning are the ways students learn new things. During the average school day, a lot of information is presented to students who receive this information via three basic modalities (see Figure 3.2). They are the visual mode (seeing it), the auditory mode (hearing it), and the tactile-kinesthetic mode (touching, tasting, and smelling it). These three learning modalities are commonly referred to as the *VAT*.

Contemporary schools are very visual. Bulletin boards, display areas, videos, filmstrips, attractive textbooks, supplementary materials, and many

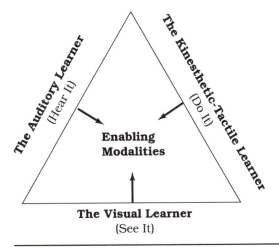

Figure 3.2 Teaching to Access the Three Learning Channels

other things are visually appealing. Even the graphics in computer programs appeal to the visual mode. Consider how much reading is required every day in all of the content areas, especially at the secondary level. It is not difficult to understand why the visual modality is so critical. It is especially important for primary teachers to be sure that young children have good vision to see what they are expected to learn.

The auditory mode enables students to learn through the sense of hearing. It is important that students of all ages develop a strong auditory mode. Both elementary and secondary teachers use expository methods and converse with students in many different situations, and the students converse with each other. The auditory mode is particularly critical for primary children when they are learning many new things. For example, in beginning reading, learning the sound-letter associations is a major skill. Listening skills must be rather acute to differentiate between short *a* and short *e*. At the secondary level, students must be active listeners when attending a lecture and taking notes. Both the auditory and the tactile modes are in operation at this time.

The tactile-kinesthetic modality is used when students touch, feel, smell, manipulate, build, and order objects. Infants and very young children rely on the tactile mode to help them explore and learn about their immediate environment. Holding and touching various objects enables the child to discriminate between them. A soft rubber ball feels different from a building block. Kindergarten and primary children usually have many tactile experiences as integral parts of their curriculum; manipulating objects is strongly encouraged. It is unfortunate that as students move up through the grades they receive fewer and fewer tactile experiences. How many students are reluctant to dissect a cow's eye in the sixth grade or a frog in high school biology? Of the three modalities, the tactile is perhaps the least used throughout the grades.

■ People in Education
Ivan Pavlov

This Russian psychologist ushered in the behaviorist movement with his famous study of classical conditioning. He used a bell (stimulus) to invoke a desired response (salivation) in dogs. The dogs were given meat powder on their tongue, followed by a ringing bell. After a time, the mere sound of the bell could bring the response. The dogs associated the bell with receiving the meat. The research that originated from Pavlov's work significantly affected the theories and practices associated with instructional procedures and learning conditions in the classroom.

The auditory, visual, and tactile learning modalities are important because they help us learn about things in three different ways. It is common to have one modality that is more strongly developed than the other two. One student may always seem to prefer reading about things for herself rather than listening to someone tell about them or actually using them herself. This person obviously enjoys a visual dominance. There is nothing wrong with this, nor is it necessarily a negative work habit. However, as educators we strive to develop all of a student's skills. Given the opportunity, this individual can learn to enjoy auditory and tactile experiences.

Classroom Management

Strong classroom management skills are very important for all teachers. They are significant because good management and clear organization contribute to the learning environment. Likewise, in rooms where the management skills are weak or lax, the learning environment is chaotic or unorganized at best. The teacher may appear unsure of what to do next and the students are equally confused.

When observing in classrooms it is clearly evident which teachers possess strong classroom management skills. The teacher is prepared to teach and all the necessary materials are ready so that lessons begin and proceed in an organized manner. Forethought and careful planning are evident. The students are attentive, responsive, and under control, and the teacher is obviously the leader in the classroom. He or she is in charge.

Classroom management encompasses skills such as planning, organization (for the students and the teacher), human relations, knowledge of the content, self-discipline and confidence. Good teachers are constantly striving to improve their management skills because they dramatically affect teaching success. These management skills are inherent in an individual's personal style, but they are definitely observable.

Management styles are very personal, varying from person to person and certainly between the elementary and secondary grades. The skills required for an elementary science class are quite different from those for a secondary history course. Here are two classroom scenarios to examine.

SCENARIO 1

Mr. Carver teaches a fifth-grade class. Outwardly he appears very low-key and jolly. When the buses arrive in the morning, he greets the students while he is on hall duty. When the bell rings, he enters the room to find the students chatting, putting books away, and hanging coats in the lockers. At a given time, the students go to their desks and appear ready to start the day. Terri takes attendance, gets the lunch count, collects notes, and conducts the morning meeting. At 9:00, the children get out their books and move to various rooms for reading.

You can teach when you are well organized and in control.

Discussion: The preceding scenario takes place in the first 10 to 15 minutes of the school day. How are Mr. Carver's management skills shown? Here are some conclusions we can make:

1. Appearing calm indicates he has self-control.
2. Being cheerful and pleasant shows positive human relations skills.
3. Good management is evidenced by the fact that the students are under control in the room while he is on duty in the hall.
4. He has obviously developed an effective, subtle organizational mode for starting the day (e.g., Terri taking attendance, etc.). The students know the procedures that are expected and they follow them.

Mr. Carver's style takes time and commitment to develop. The students' entrance behaviors would probably not be this good on the first day of school. This teacher's style is relaxed but businesslike, showing that he is in control. One can assume that the school day will proceed in a positive way.

SCENARIO 2
Ms. Redman teaches a third-grade class. Her demeanor appears more reserved as the students enter the room. The desks are arranged in rows, and the work tables and other furniture are largely arranged for expository teaching. Her lessons are primarily teacher directed, the

students raise their hands at appropriate times, and materials are well prepared. The students are respectful and under control.

Discussion: Ms. Redman's management style is an expression of her personality, teaching philosophy, and perhaps her own learning style. Her style works for her, and the students are learning. Here are some observations that can be made about this classroom:

1. The traditional room arrangement is usable and effective for some teachers and some particular groups of students, such as those who function better in a more structured setting (see Figure 3.3).

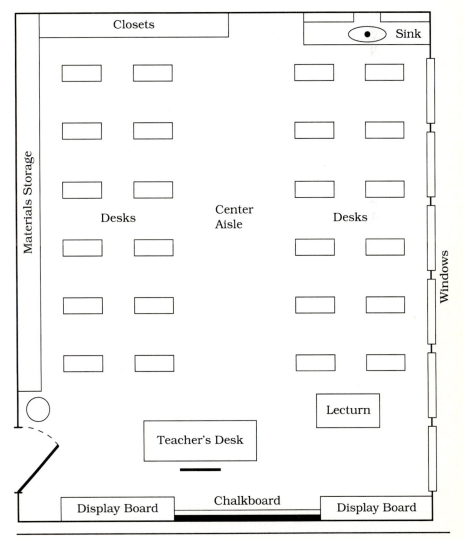

Figure 3.3 A Traditional Classroom Arrangement: Lecture Style

■ Short Shot

Effective time management is an important skill for elementary and secondary teachers. It is a critical part of total classroom management. The instructional day for elementary teachers is divided into periods of 20 to 45 minutes to accommodate all of the curriculum. When the 25-minute math period is over, the teacher must move on to social studies. Likewise at the high school, when the bell rings, classes must be dismissed. Teachers cannot just decide to keep the students 15 more minutes to complete a project. Very precise instructional plans are necessary to accommodate the established time requirements. Time management is indeed an asset.

2. Expository teaching methods are effective for specific classes or lessons. Some teachers use this method very skillfully.
3. Ms. Redman has done her planning, has gathered the materials, and is ready to teach.
4. The students have adapted to her teaching style. They are under control and doing their assignments.
5. She has good human relations skills but does not find it necessary to be flamboyant to earn students' respect.
6. She may have a strong left-brain preference (very structured), which is reflected in her management and organizational style.

Ms. Redman appears to be well organized in several areas. Although some other teachers would feel uncomfortable with her classroom management style, she functions well with it and her students are comfortable and progressing in academic skills.

There are a variety of management styles, ranging from very loose to very controlled. Appearances can be deceiving, however. A quick visual scan of a particular classroom may indicate unorganized confusion to a casual observer, but spending time in that room over a period of days may reveal that it is actually very organized. Students are performing a variety of activities, there is purposeful conversation, the teacher is facilitating and responding to numerous questions and problems, and everyone is busily occupied. Is this a classroom that is dysfunctional? No, it is not. This teacher has simply developed a different management style.

Classroom Control

The term *classroom control* is often used in reference to discipline and student behavior. Regardless of which term is used, it is important to understand clearly that we are referring to two questions: Is the teacher in control and are the students behaving in an acceptable manner?

Effective teachers have good classroom control. Establishing and maintaining control requires a strong plan and a strong commitment to enforce it all year. Some schools have an established discipline plan as part of the policies manual. In these situations it is necessary that all teachers adhere to policy. When there is no school policy, teachers make one for their own rooms. A good discipline plan does the following:

1. It clearly states the rules or expectations.
2. It clearly states the consequences when rules are broken.
3. It establishes procedures for rewarding those who are doing the right thing.
4. It has the support of the administration and teachers using it.

Initially, this may appear very rigid or negative, but it is not. Students need to learn what is and is not acceptable at school. The teacher's prime responsibility is to teach, not to spend the majority of teaching time disciplining. When there are established, written consequences for disruptive behavior, the student knows what to expect and the teacher knows immediately what to do. At the secondary level, the student may be told to leave the room and go to detention for a serious offense. At the elementary level, the teacher may put the student's name on the board and discuss the misbehavior at a more convenient time. There are times when young children become dangerous to themselves or others, and they too must be physically removed from the class.

When expectations are made clear, most students usually make a sincere effort to do their best. These expectations have two components: behavioral and academic. A good discipline plan helps to establish and maintain classroom control. However, having a class that is well behaved is not enough. Students must learn and perform academic tasks. This is the academic component of good classroom control. The primary responsibility of the teacher is to teach all the content areas and provide an atmosphere where students can learn and perform their assignments.

A classroom that is in control, attentive, and respectful is a source of pride for teachers. An effective teacher begins on the very first day of classes to establish positive attitudes and self-esteem for every student. Dynamic teaching contributes to good classroom control. The teacher provides interesting and challenging activities for the students to do, prepares quality materials, plans for any special-needs students, uses a variety of teaching methods, and enables students to make choices. The teacher enjoys teaching and the students know the teacher wants to be there. A teacher's positive attitude is contagious.

Effective teaching and strong human relations skills are congruent in effective classrooms. The following are some *academic* components of good classroom control:

1. The teacher is prepared to teach.
2. Materials are ready.
3. The lesson content is clear and age appropriate.
4. Performance expectations are stated clearly and students are on task.
5. The teacher is positive and supportive.

The following are some *behavioral* aspects of good classroom control:

1. The teacher is clearly in charge.
2. Positive behavior is rewarded and negative behavior is dealt with promptly.
3. Potential discipline situations are recognized before they get out of control; the teacher is alert.
4. Negative behaviors are not escalated (i.e., no arguing with the student, no power plays).
5. Appropriate assignments are given.
6. The teacher is aware of students who need extra reinforcement, supervision, or other controls.

The subject of classroom control and discipline is very complex. Teachers continually search for ideas, methods, strategies, techniques, and programs that will enhance their expertise in the classroom. There are seminars, workshops, lectures, and college courses that provide advanced strategies for teachers at all levels of instruction. A fair amount of common sense is also a big advantage.

School discipline is complex because many factors are involved, such as self-esteem, the home and family situation, health (nutrition, rest, exercise), peer-group problems, academic abilities, the relationship with the teacher, attitudes, and many others that affect a student's behavior at school. You will spend a great deal of time and effort to determine individual student needs and to plan remedial action.

Why Read Research?

As a potential teacher candidate, you are investigating and researching the teaching profession. Your investigations will yield the information you need to answer particular questions or clarify perceptions. Reading about the teaching profession and its various components is interesting and informative. You will also read a lot of educational research.

You may ask: What is educational research and why should I read it? Educational research is the scientific investigation to study and discover facts about a given topic (see Figure 3.4). This research can take several years to conduct and to formulate conclusions. Research is conducted at universities, clinics, private foundations, public elementary and secondary schools, state

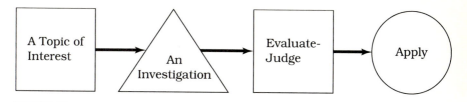

Figure 3.4 **A Sample Process Chart for Educational Research**

facilities, institutes, and even by parents at home. In many instances, two facilities collaborate on a given research project, such as the state university and the nearby public school system. Professional organizations such as Phi Delta Kappa and the Association for Supervision and Curriculum Development (ASCD) finance and conduct research projects for and by their members. These types of research projects can be classified as formal research.

Informal research has particular value for classroom teachers. Some of the most important things teachers learn about instruction are discovered right in their classrooms with their own students. Here is an example of an informal research project.

> *A first-grade teacher was challenged by the building principal: "Do you think our first-graders could learn how to spell without using the textbook approach?" After discussion and consulting with the language arts committee, the teacher agreed to pilot an informal method of teaching spelling, using only a list of 100 commonly used words and a commitment to do her best.*
>
> *In the fall, the class was given a standardized spelling test to determine the entrance skills. The basic premises of this informal research were:*
>
> 1. *If young children are expected to learn how to spell words, they must have many opportunities to write and use words.*
> 2. *Composition will be used for writing (not writing words 10 times or verbal recitations).*
> 3. *Emphasis will be on words that are spelled correctly.*
> 4. *Students are given opportunities to read their own and other stories.*
> 5. *The teacher is able to read the stories.*
>
> *At the end of the year, the spelling test was given again and the class average was established. The same procedure was followed the next year to see if that class could surpass the preceding group. They did. Based on the results of this two-year project, the language arts committee concluded that the first-graders could indeed learn to spell by informal teaching methods without a textbook, workbook, or reproducibles.*

■ People in Education

B. F. Skinner

Behaviorists are concerned with observable behavior; they look for behaviors that indicate that learning has occurred. Skinner proposed a theory of operant conditioning, which stated the relationship between specific behaviors and their consequences. His work investigated the use and effectiveness of positive and negative reinforcers to control behavior. In effect, positive reinforcers are more effective than negative ones. He also made contributions in the areas of programmed instruction and the use of teaching machines—the forerunners of computer-assisted instruction.

This is just one example of how individual teachers and schools can conduct research that directly affects their programs and/or curriculum decisions.

Validity, reliability, statistically significant, mean, median, mode, coefficient of correlation—these and other terms are used in formal research studies and reports. At times the verbiage and terminology can be confusing and even discouraging. At this point in your career it is not necessary to memorize every term. As you begin to read research articles and reports, concentrate on the explanatory sections. Postpone the interpretations of the statistical charts or graphs until you have taken a statistics or test and measurement course.

Teacher candidates and new teachers should read research to become informed and remain current in the professional discoveries and innovations. These readings document the findings in teaching strategies and methodologies, behavior management, teacher preparation programs, curriculum development, school management, and other special interest topics such as gifted and talented education.

It is advised that you begin a schedule for professional reading as soon as possible. Reading the professional literature adds another dimension to your self-discovery and professional portfolio. Some suggested periodicals for your reading program are:

Educational Leadership
Journal of Research and Development in Education
Review of Educational Research
Educational Research

Reading about the teaching profession and its various components is interesting and informative.

Journal of Educational Research
New Directions for Teaching and Learning
Phi Delta Kappan

■ Summary

This chapter has given an overview of some special topics associated with teaching. The topics were chosen based on some common practices, conversational items, and professional terminology used in elementary and secondary schools today. Continued reading in these topic areas is encouraged. As you continue to investigate the profession, visit and observe in schools, and associate with elementary, secondary, and your own university professors, it is beneficial to know what they are talking about and why they do certain things.

Every curriculum area has a great deal of specialized knowledge that teachers must know. Some of this you will learn in the specialized studies courses and during the various clinical experiences. Certain strategies, methods, and activities teachers use may be unfamiliar to you. It is reasonable that you may have questions or want explanations. This chapter serves as an introduction to management and control skills, the vocabulary, and activities you may observe as you prepare to observe in classrooms, which is the major theme of Chapter Four.

■ The Workshop

Activity I

Good classroom control is important if teachers are to teach and learning is to occur. Perhaps you have been a student in a class that was not under control. Can you recall how difficult it was to concentrate and complete assignments? Is that the learning situation you want for your future students?

Having a complete discipline plan is essential. This activity gives you an opportunity to discuss and design a workable plan for either a secondary or an elementary class. Work with two or three other people for this activity. You may need to research the topic of discipline before you begin.

Level (Grade or Class)

Rules

1.

2.

3.

4.

5.

Rewards

1.

2.

3.

4.

5.

Consequences

1.

2.

3.

4.

5.

Administrative Roles

1.

2.

3.

Self-Check: Your group has a tentative discipline plan. What are reasonable rules for a secondary math class? Is "No verbal abuse" a reasonable expectation? What about "All assignments will be turned in on time"? Whichever rules are stated, they must be enforceable in some way. The consequences for failure to remember and follow rules must be consistent. Support by the administration is critical. How can you get it? How can you enlist support from parents? List five ways.

1.

2.

3.

4.

5.

Extension: This is an opportunity to roleplay. One person in your group will be the building principal and the others will be teachers. The teachers' purpose is to get the principal's permission and support to implement your new discipline plan. Take 10 minutes for this activity.

How did you do? Were you able to convince your principal that this is indeed necessary and you need his or her support? What can you do to support each other? Activities such as this are good opportunities to create and defend what you think is important for education.

Activity II

A basic principle of this book is self-discovery. Getting to know yourself better helps you to visualize yourself in the teaching profession. How do you learn? What are the specific ways? Do you learn (and study) most things the same way, or do you vary your style? Which of the three modalities do you prefer?

Knowing how you learn helps to understand and accept the ways other people learn, especially when it is different from your way! Sometimes we learn academic material using one modality and recreational material using another. On the chart below, make a list of some things you prefer to learn using each of the three modalities. Include both academic and recreational activities.

Visual Mode

Academic	*Nonacademic*
1.	1.
2.	2.
3.	3.
4.	4.
5.	5.

Auditory Mode

Academic	*Nonacademic*
1.	1.
2.	2.
3.	3.
4.	4.
5.	5.

Tactile Mode

Academic	*Nonacademic*
1.	1.
2.	2.
3.	3.
4.	4.
5.	5.

Self-Check: This brief exercise can reveal some strategic information in a relatively short amount of time. For example, it is common to learn math principles by reading and memorizing. Do you ever learn math concepts by using manipulative materials? Activities designed for your least preferred mode may be the most difficult for you to plan and/or identify. Were the academic or the nonacademic activities more difficult to list? When adults understand how important the modalities are to various types of learning, we can more readily understand their importance to students who want to be learners!

Activity III

The three modalities help students to learn in special ways. In this activity, you will identify some visual, auditory, and tactile experiences for students in the classroom.

Level: Elementary
Class: Social studies
Unit: Westward Movement

Visual Activities

1.

2.

3.

Auditory Activities

1.

2.

3.

Tactile Activities

1.

2.

3.

Self-Check: Studying about the pioneers and their trek across the country in covered wagons is a favorite unit of elementary students. Even kindergarten children are fascinated with its various aspects. Did you identify the VAT activities that could be used in this unit? Which category was the easiest? The most difficult? At this point you are not expected to plan lessons, but it is helpful to begin thinking of activities students can do. Share your ideas with others in your class. Getting ideas from others is helpful, too. Next, let's do the same for a secondary class!

> *Level:* Secondary
> *Class:* Biology
> *Unit:* Amphibians

Visual Activities

1.

2.

3.

Auditory Activities

1.

2.

3.

Tactile Activities

1.

2.

3.

Self-Check: Can you remember high school biology? Chances are you had many tactile experiences that were required for the course. These lab class lessons were integral to learning the course content. Did you use some of your own experiences for your list? Did your most favorite or least favorite activities come to mind first?

Try something a little more difficult. Do this activity using English Literature as a topic.

Extension: With a partner try to identify each of the student activities above as either a left- or right-brain activity. If you are unsure, consult with your instructor. Once again, it is helpful to examine the kind of planning teachers must do for every lesson they teach.

■ Questions and Thoughts

1. Perhaps you are very interested in educational research. Is there a role for new classroom teachers in this field? How can you make yourself available to participate in a research project?

2. What can teachers do when parents are not fulfilling the home responsibilities as stated in the student's IEP? What is the extent of the school's responsibility in this case?

3. Teachers tend to teach according to their own learning style preference. A person with a strong left-brain dominance may choose teaching strategies that complement his or her learning style.

■ Readings and References

Curwin, R. L., and Mendler, A. N. (1988). *Discipline with Dignity.* Alexandria, VA: Association for Supervision and Curriculum Development.

Dunn, K., and Dunn, R. (1972). *Practical Approaches to Individualized Instruction.* West Nyack, NY: Parker.

Dunn, K., and Dunn, R. (1975). *Educator's Self-Teaching Guide to Individualized Instructional Programs.* West Nyack, NY: Parker.

Dunn, K., and Dunn, R. (1978). *Teaching Students Through Their Individual Learning Styles: A Practical Approach.* Reston, VA: Reston.

Educational Leadership, 48 (October 1990).

Gallagher, J. J. (1985). *Teaching the Gifted Child.* Boston: Allyn and Bacon.

Glathorn, A. A. (1987). *Curriculum Renewal.* Alexandria, VA: Association for Supervision and Curriculum Development.

Hill, D. (1990, April). "Order in the Classsroom." *Teacher Magazine,* 70–77.

Phi Delta Kappan, 71 (March 1990).

Warger, C. (Ed.) (1988). *A Resource Guide to Public School Early Childhood Programs.* Alexandria, VA: The Association for Supervision and Curriculum Development.

"Whole Brain Learning." (1983, June). *The School Administrator.*

Williams, L. V. (1983). *Teaching for the Two-Sided Mind.* New York: Simon and Schuster Inc.

Chapter Four

Observing Teachers and Students in Classrooms

■ Definitions

Affirmation: This is the habit of giving positive, encouraging comments to students when they are doing the right thing, such as following directions or meeting expectations.

Contracts: These are forms of individualized instruction frequently presented in a particular format that includes such items as an objective, materials required, a time limit, open or closed procedures, an evaluation method, and other items prescribed by the teacher. Contracts are frequently used for high-potential students.

Cooperative Learning: This is another term for working in a group. The group members cooperate in order to learn together, although not necessarily at the same rate.

Group Dynamics: This is the study of how people (students) interact and function when involved in a group activity. Educators study how students work together and learn when placed in a group situation. This is especially pertinent in cooperative learning programs.

Learning Environment: This is the physical and mental environment where students are expected to do their work and learn. The tangible, intangible, and aesthetic characteristics of a classroom that make it a pleasant or unpleasant place to be are part of the learning environment. It is a feeling you get when you enter a classroom.

Profile: This is the total picture of a classroom, including the tangible and intangible items. A classroom can be conducive or not conducive to learning, depending on all the factors that are operating in that room. An objective profile can help identify negative factors.

Readiness: This is the state of being able to learn a particular skill or informational set. Example: Most (but not all) first-graders are maturationally ready to learn how to read.

Seatwork: This term, used by elementary teachers, refers to the work students are expected to do at their desks or tables. The word *independent* is frequently used as a modifier. Some students do their seatwork while the teacher works with other groups.

■ Focus Questions

1. What does a classroom teacher really do? What is the best way to find out?

2. Why should you observe classrooms at different grade levels if you already know what grade you want to teach? Why should you observe elementary if you are a secondary major, or secondary if you are an elementary major?

3. How should you dress and behave when you visit a classroom? May you help the teacher if asked?

4. What should you look for in the classroom? What if you see something that you do not think is right?

■ Introduction

Preparing to become a teacher involves participating in many different activities. Taking required courses, selecting majors and minors, and attending seminars and preteaching activities are all part of the preparation. One of the most valuable experiences you can have is to visit and observe in classrooms. Classroom observations give you the opportunity to observe firsthand what teachers and students do during a typical school day, and they can help you decide if you would enjoy participating in those activities.

This chapter gives a rationale and guidelines for your classroom observations on the first- and/or second-level field experiences. It is important to know what to look for in a classroom. Information regarding the teacher, the students, and the classroom environment will help you concentrate on a successful observation experience.

■ ■ ■

The Field Experience

Field experiences are those activities that take you into a classroom or learning environment where you can have actual contact with students. A specific number of hours in field experience activities are frequently required before you are admitted to the teacher education program.

There are three categories of field experiences: (1) initial field experiences, (2) middle-tier experiences, and (3) upper-tier experiences. A different degree of involvement is the distinguishing characteristic of each level in this model. Levels 1 and 2 precede the official practical application of the methods and foundations courses in your college program (i.e., they indirectly prepare you for student teaching.)

The initial field experience is the first level of involvement. It consists primarily of informal or formal (making notations) observations of children or older students in a learning situation. Watching the activities and behaviors of students establishes a foundation for the behaviors and reactions you will be discussing, observing, and analyzing at each step of your professional preparation. The initial field experience does not include planned direct interaction with students.

Some examples of activities for this experience level are watching young children at a daycare center or nursery school, observing a park and recreation director supervise and direct a group of participants, visiting a summer day camp or youth sports training facility, observing in classrooms or in special state facilities, and visiting supervised church or social groups. There are any number of other situations that could qualify.

The initial field experience is planned to provide you with the opportunity to observe students firsthand in a learning experience. Many of you have had initial experiences before you began your program in teacher education. Indeed, your experiences may have been the catalyst that started you toward a career in teaching. You may have worked in a daycare center, been a camp counselor, taught Sunday school, worked with youth groups, or been a cadet teacher in high school. In these cases, your initial experiences did provide a degree of actual involvement with the students. The initial field experience provided by the university will usually consist of structured observations in classrooms.

The second level of field experience is the middle-tier experience, where you start to interact with students. You begin becoming involved in instruction. You may start by observing a specific group or classroom of students, then prepare a lesson for an individual or small group. You may be involved in such things as reading a story, listening to a child read, working with an individual while he or she does an assignment, helping a small group design and construct a bulletin board or display, helping students do research in the library, assisting a teacher in grading classwork or tests, or doing some more formal or structured observations.

Middle-tier experiences enable you to continue observing students to learn more about their characteristics and behavior, as well as provide you with the opportunity to actually teach a lesson you have prepared. At this point, you cannot expect to be given teaching duties as such, or even the possibility of teaching an entire class. You are expected to learn as much as possible about how students learn and react through your observations and actual contacts with students. Discussions in your own classroom with your teacher and your fellow students are also a valuable part of this experience.

The third level of field experience is the culmination of all of your teacher preparation experiences. It is your student-teaching experience. You will be in a classroom, teaching. In most student-teaching situations, you will be in a classroom for 12 to 16 weeks, under the direct supervision of a classroom teacher. You may split the experience between grade levels in the elementary school, or between your major and minor in the secondary school.

Student teaching involves continued observations, as you will observe your students at work and play, your supervising teacher as he or she prepares lessons and works with the class, and perhaps other teachers in the building. You will probably also get to observe parent-teacher conferences.

In addition to student teaching, your third-tier experience will include a seminar with your university coordinator. These seminars usually consist of announcements of interest or concern, discussions of the experiences, and an opportunity to discuss problems and solutions with your instructor and fellow student teachers. You may have lectures, panels, or assignments related to your student teaching.

Third-tier experiences bring you very close to the completion of your professional preparation. Your effort and commitment are very much in evidence at this time. You are expected to act and perform as a professional. Many future employers rely very heavily on your performance and the recommendations you obtain from this third-tier experience.

To summarize, the initial field experience consists of observing, the middle-tier experience is structured observation and some interaction with students, and the third-tier is student teaching, which includes everything.

Why Visit a Classroom?

You are considering the teaching profession as your life's work. In order to get a true picture of what teachers do on the job, it is necessary to have opportunities to observe them doing it. Classroom observations verify some of the ideas and perceptions you already have, and quickly dispel some others. Classroom observations reinforce some positive personal memories you may have about teachers and the teaching they did in your classes. This will be very satisfying for you. Observing contemporary classrooms may dispel some biases or prejudices you have about the teaching process, which is also beneficial.

Observing in a variety of classrooms gives you opportunities to see different groups of students in action, different lessons being taught, varying teaching styles, and other intangibles that will help you understand what teaching really is on a daily basis. It is helpful to observe different grades and classes so that you can see the differences and decide which level is best for you. We would like to emphasize a point: A classroom visitation is a serious undertaking. You are not there to play games or visit with students, but to try to learn classroom realities.

Teacher education programs recognize the value of classroom observations because you, as a student, must be aware of teaching realities before the student-teaching experience. It would be devastating to complete all the necessary coursework, only to discover that teaching is not what you want to do. On the other hand, it is very satisfying to realize that this is definitely what you want to do!

Education programs encourage classroom observations very early in the process because professors, advisors, and teachers are in agreement that this is not only a good idea but a valuable learning experience. Many universities require a specific number of observation hours and volunteering as a prerequisite for admission to the College or School of Education, and use the content of these experiences as a major focus of the admissions interview.

Classroom observations give you a realistic setting in which you can envision yourself in the role of the teacher. During a one-hour observation period you will immediately realize that teachers accomplish many things in that short time. In that hour, a first-grade teacher may teach three lessons: a 30-

minute math lesson, a 20-minute language lesson, and a 10-minute penmanship lesson. That requires careful planning and preparation of materials. Can you place yourself in this role? Why visit a classroom? Visit a classroom to observe the teaching process and your role in it.

What to Look For: A Classroom Profile

When you visit and observe in classrooms, you are a guest of the school. As a guest, it is important to conduct yourself in a professional manner. Your personal attire, your attitude, and your behavior reflect positively or negatively upon yourself and the university. Conducting yourself appropriately is important.

Your role is to be an observer in a classroom (see Figure 4.1). You are not a student teacher, an intern, a critic, or an evaluator. As an observer, your role is to watch and record what you see in the class. You will concentrate on what the teacher does, what the students do, and particular features of the learning environment. (*Note:* If you are a volunteer, then your role and responsibilities will be different.)

Observing in classrooms is an enjoyable experience. It is gratifying to see effective teaching and to watch students in the process of learning. Observing in primary-grade classrooms soon illustrates one important fact: Young children freely gravitate toward any and all adults that are in the room. You are an adult and they will quite naturally come to you for help. It takes time for youngsters to understand your role. Working out an appropriate clarification procedure with the teacher is helpful and necessary.

It is difficult to profile a typical classroom. A primary room is dramatically different from a sixth-grade room, and both of them are unlike a secondary room. One commonality is certain—there will be students and

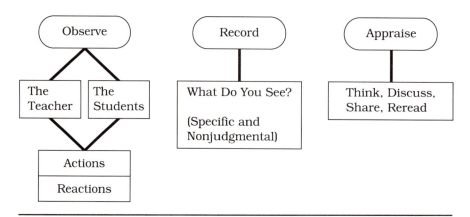

Figure 4.1 Observing—What to Do

■ Short Shot

During the course of your classroom observations it is possible that you will see a lesson presentation that is not going well. There are a variety of reasons why this happens even to the most skillful teachers. Make a special note of how the teacher recovers the lesson and survives this incident, as these recovery techniques are marks of teaching expertise.

teachers. Other classroom features are as diverse as the individual teachers and administrators permit them to be. All schools and classrooms have their own unique cultures and personalities. This will become clear as you conduct observations in a variety of schools and classrooms.

The Students

There are three main reasons for visiting classrooms: to observe students, teachers, and classroom environments. A number of secondary reasons can fit into each of these. One of your tasks during an observation period is to observe students, their behavior, their work habits, and their special and individual characteristics. What you observe in various classrooms at each grade level will be slightly different in some ways and alike in others. There will be greater differences in elementary and secondary classrooms.

Student behavior is a critical factor in the classroom, as it has an important effect on the teacher's ability to teach and the students' ability to learn. Acceptable behavior gives a pleasant tone to a room, whereas consistent maladaptive behavior makes learning very difficult if not impossible. All students can behave. If they do not, then a consistent effort accompanied by a strong discipline plan must be initiated. Each student must learn to be self-disciplined if he or she is to benefit from the school experience.

Student behavior and classroom discipline is a very complex topic to discuss, to examine, and to observe. Behavior has several formative components: physical, emotional, psychological, and neurological. In some cases the student simply has never been taught how to act in various situations and how to control himself or herself. You will surely see some of this behavior in elementary schools, especially in the early grades. Behavior that is acceptable on the playground is not necessarily appropriate in math class.

What behaviors are you likely to see in a primary classroom? Basically, the younger the child, the more diverse behaviors you will see during a given class period. Young children do many things during instructional periods. Some behaviors are appropriate for the child's stage of mental development and will contribute to learning; other behaviors are inappropriate and will detract from the ability to learn and concentrate. In some cases the inappro-

Young children do a variety of things during the instructional period.

priate behavior must be considered a serious handicap. If you are observing a primary-grade class, these are some of the behaviors you may see:

- Whispering and talking out loud
- Looking around for no apparent reason
- Telling others what to do
- Looking to see what others are doing
- Calling out to the teacher
- Asking to go to the bathroom
- Asking to get drinks
- Dropping things (papers, crayons, pencils)
- Raising hands to ask or answer questions, often inappropriate or unrelated to the topic
- Looking back to where you are
- Leaving the desk with or without permission
- Going up to the teacher
- Tattling
- Wiggling, kneeling on chairs, leaning over the desk
- Breaking pencil leads or crayons
- Inability to do the assignment or even get started
- Frustration or crying
- Putting the head down on the desk

- Playing with things inside the desk
- Apathy
- Interrupting the teacher or other students
- Taking turns
- Following directions correctly

These are some very visible behaviors that primary-grade children exhibit. There are others. Some severe behaviors, such as fighting, hitting, kicking, and verbal abuse, may be evident but this is not the norm.

Behavior of young children varies, depending on the type of lesson being presented and the tasks they are expected to do. During a cooperative learning period (working in small groups) you will see how they can function as group members or group leaders. When there are three or four groups functioning in the room, there will probably be some noise. The talking, sharing, moving of furniture or materials may well be necessary and on task, but nevertheless the noise level will be raised.

During a new material lesson presentation, it is reasonable to expect most of the students to be watching and listening to the teacher. You may notice there are no materials on the tables or desks at this time, or the teacher might call the students to leave their desks and sit on the floor. This technique makes it more likely that the students will be attentive; on the other

■ People in Education

Lee Canter

Lee Canter is a pioneer in the field of behavior management. A well-known lecturer, consultant, writer, and teacher, he and his wife Marlene developed the Assertive Discipline programs for teachers, administrators, and parents. Assertive Discipline is a family of seminars, workshops, and materials needed to implement a successful behavior management program for the school and the home.

Basic to the Assertive Discipline concept is the establishment of observable rules, rewards for acceptable behavior, and consistent consequences for unacceptable behavior. This program enables teachers (and others) to manage behavior in all school situations, to deal effectively with severe discipline cases, and to more effectively perform their instructional duties. Assertive Discipline is taught through seminars and workshops throughout the country. The various resource materials can be purchased from Canter and Associates for use after the training sessions.

hand, they will be sitting knee-to-knee in close quarters. Can you perceive some behaviors for this setting? What are they? Each strategy presents some advantages and disadvantages for the teacher as well as the students.

One of the most important activities for young children is the time for seatwork, performing a given task by themselves. This task could be a paper-and-pencil assignment from a workbook or the chalkboard, or constructing something. Performing a task individually is necessary in many instructional settings. The teacher must determine if the child can complete the task successfully. When students are given such a directive, certain behaviors are immediately apparent. Some children will begin the job at once and complete it in a reasonable amount of time, others will begin and then become distracted or disinterested, and still others will lack the organizational skills to even begin. Independent seatwork time is a good opportunity to observe the behaviors of children who do or do not have the necessary readiness skills.

Intermediate-grade students have many of the same behaviors as younger children. Whereas many of the primary behaviors can be categorized as learning behaviors, some of the observable behaviors of older students are social and developmental. Establishing themselves in a social group is very important, and many of the things they do are directed at getting into a certain group or staying in it. Status and roles with peers are significant. Note passing, teasing, name calling, and other such behaviors will probably be seen in many classrooms. An unrealistic preoccupation over clothing, appearance, and contemporary heroes may be evidenced in casual conversations during class.

Older students are more capable of staying on task to complete assignments or listening to instructional presentations. Nevertheless, most classes will probably have a few individuals who do not follow directions or obey class rules. When you are visiting various classrooms, you will notice the disturbing effects these students have on others in the room.

Work habits are those behaviors that enable students to do their required assignments. Establishing and maintaining positive work habits is a critical skill for children to learn. A point of clarification is needed here: Such things as wasting time, talking at inappropriate times, careless or unfinished papers, and many other things students do are nothing more than bad habits, and they prevent growth in learning. The longer these habits or behaviors persist, the more difficult it is to eliminate them and replace them with positive ones. All students have work habits, but they may not all be positive work habits.

Positive work habits help students learn. Student teachers, teachers, and volunteers frequently comment that intermediate students can get so much work done in a given work period. This ability to accomplish objectives is due largely to maturation—they are chronologically older than primary children—and to the acquisition of positive work habits. They have learned some proper procedures to facilitate learning. Keep this in mind when you are observing.

What are work habits? Here are some of the skills you will see.

Productive
- Observing each other or the teacher
- Listening
- Being organized, having materials ready
- Staying on task
- Concentrating
- Taking notes (older students only)
- Asking for assistance when needed
- Ignoring distractions
- Using materials properly
- Doing neat, readable work
- Using time appropriately
- Cooperating in group activities
- Participating as individuals when called on

Unproductive
- Completing assignments that are not legible
- Consistently performing at a level lower than his or her capabilities indicate
- Not completing assignments or even starting them
- Not having the tools and materials available
- Making inappropriate or irrelevant contributions to the class or study group
- Wasting time
- Consistently being late with work
- Negative attention-getting behaviors (disruptive)
- Neglecting to follow established routines or formats
- Investing a good effort only on selected assignments
- Avoiding responsibilities
- Being defiant
- Sleeping

These and other work habits are readily observable with primary and intermediate students in a variety of situations. Positive work habits are necessary for effective learning to take place. Some students have negative work habits that do not help them reach academic goals. It is helpful to be familiar with both positive and negative work habits before you begin looking for them in classrooms.

The average elementary classroom will have some students with significant individual needs, such as a short attention span, a lack of self-confidence, general immaturity, poor retention, inadequate social skills, and weak verbal skills. Special-education students also have specific needs that must be

■ **People in Education**

Robert Mager

Robert Mager, an experimental psychologist, is well known for his research and models in the area of instructional objectives. An instructional objective is a statement of the behavior a student can demonstrate at the end of a lesson. An example of such a statement is: The student will correctly name the capitals of the North Central states on an outline map with 100 percent accuracy.

Instructional objectives are an important initial step in the planning process; they provide guidance for the teacher when planning lessons. They state clearly what students will be able to do at the end of the instructional sequences. In 1962, Mager's book *Preparing Instructional Objectives* gave a comprehensive procedure for writing and using instructional objectives in classrooms. It is still an important resource in university education courses today. Ralph Tyler and Robert Gagne have also contributed in this field of education.

accommodated by the teacher. Particular behavior becomes very visible when these specific needs are not met. Watch for these specific behaviors when you are observing.

The Teacher

The second major concentration for classroom visitations is on the teacher. Teachers come from many different backgrounds, cultures, ethnic groups, and educational institutions. They have varied personalities, philosophies of teaching, ideas, attitudes, and perspectives. If you have a particular idea of what the ideal teacher is like, you may or may not find that person in the rooms you enter. Do not become discouraged or disappointed, but instead look for the good points of the teacher you are observing.

In contemporary schools, principals and other administrators are entering classrooms more than ever before to watch teachers teach. Performing a required number of observations for new and nontenured teachers has been a common practice for many years. Unfortunately, observing the senior staff members occurred rarely in some other schools.

In addition, teachers are observing and coaching each other. It is true that many teachers have never seen any of their colleagues teach. A great number of things can be learned and affirmed from watching another teacher teach. The point is, open-minded, self-confident contemporary teachers are accustomed to having other professionals watch them do their job. Principals and university coordinators or supervisors carefully select these particular

Administrative evaluations help teachers improve their instructional skills.

teachers to participate in visitation programs. You can be confident that these teachers welcome your presence!

The personal appearance of a teacher is very important. A neat, clean, professional appearance gives the nonverbal message that this person respects the profession as well as himself or herself. Appearance for a day of regular classroom teaching is not the same as that for a science field trip to a nature center, but it is appropriate for the specific occasion. A neat appearance is part of projecting a positive adult role model.

Attitude is a critical factor in the success or failure of most life endeavors, and it is an important factor for teaching success. Establishing and maintaining a positive attitude toward the act of teaching and the potential learning of students is a large step in the direction of becoming a successful teacher. Having a positive attitude in itself can be a shallow attribute unless it is accompanied by the positive actions of teaching well. An attitude is a particular state of mind. One's conduct or behavior is a reflection of attitude(s).

▪ Short Shot

If the students aren't learning, then the teacher isn't teaching.

Unknown

A strong positive attitude toward teaching and all of its responsibilities is necessary for success in the profession. It clearly reflects itself in the many things teachers do, ranging from lesson planning to disciplining students. A good attitude does not guarantee that everything will always go smoothly or as well as planned, but it will be one of the factors that clarifies particular situations and provides the impetus to move forward. A good attitude is visible to others and it is curiously contagious.

Many of the things teachers do reflect their attitudes toward the job and the students. These behaviors can be grouped into two categories: teaching and interpersonal (see Figure 4.2). Teaching behaviors are those directly related to job responsibilities. Interpersonal behaviors are those related to the students and other individuals in the school (teachers, parents, volunteers, secretaries, administrators). We will now examine some of the teaching behaviors that show an individual's positive attitude toward the job. The following are some things to consider when you observe in classrooms.

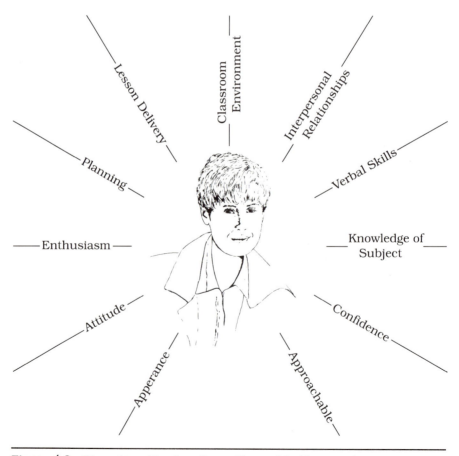

Figure 4.2 Observing a Teacher: Some Observable Characteristics

Planning: The teacher is meticulous about planning lessons that are interesting and stimulating for the students. He or she follows the curriculum guidelines, teaches all content that is required, and makes provisions for spur-of-the-moment lessons. Lesson objectives are clear, and all necessary materials are ready and carefully prepared. It is clear what the teacher is trying to teach and what the students are expected to do. The teacher is clearly in control of the class. There is no question who is managing the class.

Lesson Delivery: The lesson presentation is positive, clear, and concise; flamboyance is unnecessary. The information is accurate and the vocabulary is at a level the students can understand. Directions are short and uncluttered. Lesson objectives are followed and completed, and closure for the lesson is completed.

Assignments: The assignments are at the correct level of difficulty for the abilities of the individual students in the class. Provisions are made for all high-potential and low-performing students. Assignments are directly related to the lesson objectives.

Evaluations: Papers and other assignments are corrected fairly; they are explained as a group or individually. Students must know why something is incorrect if they are to avoid making the same mistake again. Papers are not thrown away by the teacher.

Room Appearance: An attractive classroom shows that the teacher cares enough to make it so. Bulletin boards and display areas are images of the teaching that is taking place and reflect student ownership. The room is neat and clean.

Teachers with a good attitude have very strong interpersonal skills and they are readily visible. A teacher does not have to constantly verbalize "I just love my job!" or "I really enjoy my students!" Certain behaviors make the message very clear. Here are some of them:

Attendance: A person with a good attitude is on the job regularly. Absenteeism is for serious reasons only.

Availability: The teacher is in the room when students are there. Leaving the room is acceptable only for reasons approved by school policies.

Professionalism: Teachers do not degrade or discuss students in the lounge or other places; confidentiality is critical. Ethical behavior is practiced.

Support and Cooperation: Teachers support the administration and each other. Cooperation is evidenced by teaching what is required, following school rules and policies, helping students and other teachers, and sharing ideas.

Interaction with Students: A good attitude shows when teachers speak pleasantly to students. They are firm, understanding, cheerful, flexible, and encouraging. They are available to help those students who need it.

Interaction with Parents: Teachers are courteous and welcome any parents who come to the room. They are willing to answer a quick question or schedule a conference time after school. Visits are welcome.

Body Language: Scowling, hands on hips, harsh voice tones, and other confrontational stances do not reflect positive human relations skills.

Actions: Walking around the room, making encouraging remarks, demonstrating a sense of humor, bending down to the student's eye level (primary grades), a nonverbal message, and other actions are very positive and supportive.

There are many outward signs that clearly show a person's attitude toward the job (teaching) and the clients (students). Any attempt to list all of the signs would be time consuming and unnecessary, if not impossible. Confident teachers exhibit these behaviors so freely and frequently that they are truly second nature and automatic. They are part of a person's teaching personality. Evidence of a good attitude is important to a positive classroom climate.

Class management and organization are two classroom characteristics that are very closely related. A teacher with strong organizational skills will most likely have good class control. Organizational skills such as good planning, staying on task, appropriate individualization, meeting special needs, keeping to a schedule, and other management items help students to feel secure because they know what to expect.

Organization is the framework wherein students can function and they clearly know their limitations and expectations. An organized classroom is one that is properly managed. Control management is not negative. Control management means the students clearly understand what they are expected to do and they make an effort to do it. This type of control does not mean perfect silence, saluting the teacher, or being submissive! Students can be away from their desks or moving around the room for a purpose without being disruptive. Many activities can occur simultaneously when they are

■ People in Education

Robert E. Slavin

Robert Slavin is an educational psychologist at Johns Hopkins University. He has written extensively on cooperative learning, ability grouping, school and classroom organization, mainstreaming, and educational research. He is the author of an educational psychology textbook and is currently a leader in the area of cooperative learning.

planned and supervised by the teacher, by the students, or by the students and the teacher together. Good class management is one positive result of good organizational skills.

The Physical Environment

The third major factor to observe is the physical environment of the class-rooms. The physical environment includes everything in the room—the bul-letin boards, furniture, traffic-flow patterns, lighting, and room temperature. It is important to take notice of the appearance of a classroom. When a per-son enters a classroom, the visual appearance of that room should evoke a positive response. Whether that person is an adult or a student, the general appearance of the room should denote: This is a place where I would like to be.

In any job, good working conditions are important for maximum pro-ductivity. The classroom is no different, as it is the workplace of students and teachers. This is an important point often overlooked or ignored by school boards and taxpayers. The classroom should be bright and cheerful without being gaudy or distracting.

Displays: Attractive bulletin boards and showcases add interest and appeal to the general appearance of a room. What is on the bulletin boards? Display areas have an educational role to perform. They are there to serve one or all of these functions:

1. *A Motivational Instrument:* The teacher displays information, articles, pamphlets, pictures, or artifacts to provoke particular responses, ac-tions, or questions.
2. *An Introductory Technique:* Materials are displayed as part of an intro-duction to a new lesson or unit.
3. *An Instructional Activity:* Specific materials are set up for students to manipulate, use, order, or label during the lesson or unit.
4. *An Evaluation Tool:* Activities or stations are set up for the students to perform required skills to demonstrate what they have learned (mastery of the objective).
5. *A Reporting Device:* Teachers display student papers and projects; this provides the class with an audience to share their work with each other, parents, and visitors.
6. *An Advanced Organizer:* Display materials that arouse curiosity and preview upcoming lessons.

Use of display areas is a reflection of how the teacher feels about class-room responsibilities. If sports posters and faded pictures are what you see, this gives even the casual visitor a very clear message. What is it? If teacher-

Bulletin boards and displays add to the general appearance of the classroom.

prepared activities and sample student projects are attractively displayed, this gives that same casual observer a very different message. What is this one?

As a potential teacher, which type of displays show pride in one's teaching and in students' learning? Changing the displays frequently to keep them current with holidays, special events, and contemporary units takes preparation time before and after school. It is a seemingly never-ending job. However, it is part of the classroom responsibility that teachers welcome and cheerfully perform.

■ **Short Shot**

> The quickest way to meet the objective is the way that eliminates the student's input. Don't lose sight of the student's input.
>
> *Unknown*

Physical Plant—Room and Furniture: What is in a contemporary classroom? The average elementary classroom has student desks or tables and chairs, bookcases, a teacher's desk, chart stands, tables, possibly a study carrel or two, movable carts, and a computer stand. Some rooms may have an overstuffed reading chair or other furniture for special areas. Secondary classrooms should have all the basic furniture that good teaching requires. Special rooms, such as the band room or the science laboratories, have facilities that meet those special requirements. The home economics department has different room requirements than the industrial arts department or the foreign language lab. Not every room at the secondary level requires the same furniture or equipment.

At the secondary level one room may be used by several teachers each day. For the first hour a math class may use the room, then a history lecture class, followed by a study hall, and so on throughout the day. In this case, the typical lecture arrangement of desks in rows or a semi-circle with the teacher's lectern at the front may be the most convenient arrangement for everyone. When several teachers share a room, a cooperative decision regarding room appearance and arrangement is necessary.

In elementary schools it is more common for one teacher to be in the room all day with one group of students (self-contained classroom). Schools that have cross-age grouping or departmentalization require the students to change rooms. Placement of furniture in an elementary classroom is important.

The teacher who uses the expository method will probably use a lecture style of room arrangement, similar to that used in secondary classrooms. The teacher who uses cooperative learning approaches may have the desks or tables grouped in sets of six or eight in various places around the room. Primary teachers use the floor for many activities, so this room could have the desks all on one side of the room. Current research into left- and right-brain learning styles recommends particular room arrangements to accommodate these teaching methods. Teachers use arrangements that fit their teaching styles.

Traffic: Traffic flow is a factor that teachers must consider when arranging their rooms. Students move around the room for many reasons during the course of an average day, so room arrangements must be practical and useable. Students and teachers must be able to perform their duties with a minimum of interference. Consider the following:

1. Are there clear paths to all the necessary destinations that are needed during the day?
2. Are there straight aisles or is it necessary to walk around things and other students that seem to be in the way?

3. Is there enough room for handicapped students to negotiate walkers or wheelchairs around the room?
4. What are the paths most frequently used by the teacher during the typical day?
5. Is there space for students to work on the floor or in small groups?
6. Which pattern of movement will be used to vacate the room quickly, such as in the case of a fire drill or tornado?
7. Are the study carrels in an isolated area?
8. Are the computer stands too close to the windows or strong light sources (eye strain, light reflections)?
9. Is there enough space near the lockers or coat racks?
10. Is there a clear path to the teacher's desk, the sink and drinking fountain, bookcases, pencil sharpener, and other materials?
11. Does a particularly creative room arrangement seem more cumbersome than practical for a particular age group?
12. Does the room arrangement seem to be workable for the teacher and the students?
13. Does the room arrangement enhance learning or contribute to chaos?

■ People in Education

David and Roger Johnson

Roger and David Johnson (Professor of Curriculum and Instruction, Professor of Educational Psychology, University of Minnesota) have done extensive research in the area of cooperative learning. They teach the structure and process of cooperative learning to teachers and administrators throughout the country. The theory and application of cooperative learning are examined in two books, *Circles of Learning: Cooperation in the Classroom* (1984) and *Learning Together and Alone: Cooperation, Competition, and Individualization* (1975), and in numerous articles in the professional literature.

The Johnsons propose that cooperative learning strategies promote academic achievement and improve the quality of student interaction. Some principles of various cooperative learning programs are: a group goal is established, everyone in the group works together to achieve the goal, everyone receives a reward, cooperation is emphasized, ideas and materials are shared, and everyone contributes in his or her own way to achieve group success. Effective cooperative learning situations provide opportunities for students of all abilities to learn and feel successful.

Room arrangements must be practical and useable so students and teachers are able to perform their duties with a minimum of interference or rearranging. Materials and equipment must be located for accessibility; otherwise they may not be used consistently. Traffic flow in a classroom can be a hindrance or a help to teaching and learning.

Other Factors: Teachers must be aware of the physical conditions in the room. Light, heat, and air movement are important things to consider. Light should be adequate but not glaring on the chalkboards or desks. Room temperature should be neither too hot or too cold. Keeping some fresh air in the room keeps both students and teachers alert.

An Observer's Checklist

Classroom visits provide opportunities to practice your observation skills. These valuable opportunities are frequently prearranged for you by the university coordinators, supervisors, and instructors in cooperation with the individual classroom teachers, principals, and school district officials. This opportunity to observe teachers and students is clearly a privilege, and this fact should always be uppermost in your mind.

Professional ethics and manners require that you *do* certain things and *not do* others. It is a good idea to visit the school before your first official observing session. In some areas the instructor or coordinator escorts a group to the various buildings where the observations will take place. Go to the office and introduce yourself to the receptionist or secretary, the teacher, and the principal. This visit accomplishes two important things: It gives these people the chance to know who you are and why you are in the building, and it may eliminate the need to go into the office every time you come. You may also be able to pick up student and teacher handbooks that state school policy regarding dress codes and classroom behavior.

For security reasons, schools are posting notices on all exterior doors to inform visitors that they must report to the office to register and receive an identification badge. You, too, must follow this regulation. However, once the receptionist knows who you are, you may register and get your badge without creating an interruption. A nonverbal signal is frequently agreed upon for regular visitors, but you must follow the procedures established for each building. On the day of your first appointment, come prepared to carry out your given task.

The first day you enter the room, the teacher will introduce you to the class, tell the students why you are there, direct you to some convenient place to sit, and then take care of other organizational and management matters. Once you and the students are aware of these procedures, all subsequent arrivals can be routine. It should be made clear to the students that

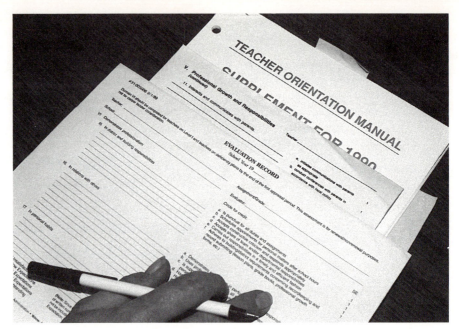

Be familiar with your checklist before you begin to observe.

you are not a student teacher or a volunteer who can help them do their assignments. This is especially important when you go to primary-grade rooms.

Entering the room quietly is important. You do not want to draw attention to yourself and away from the teacher or the lesson. Remember—you are an observer, not an evaluator or social visitor. Go directly to the table, desk, or chair the teacher has provided for you, and begin your observation session.

The following checklist format (Figure 4.3) is designed to help you record specific actions of the teacher and the students, as well as specific physical characteristics of the classrooms. Spaces are provided for any additional notations or observations you wish to record. It is helpful to study the format before you start an observation. As you become familiar with using it, you will quickly record your observations so that you can spend more actual time observing.

The objective is to have this activity be a learning opportunity for you, to observe as many things as you can during the given time period. You are observing classroom activities to help you envision yourself in the role of teacher. Your instructor will provide copies for you. Some additions or deletions may be made as needed.

As you use this checklist there are two things you should do. First, make a check in the column next to the actions or behaviors you observe. Second, write down any consequences that occur. For example, if you observe a

Grade Level:

Subject:

Date–Time:

Observer:

TEACHER ACTIONS	OBSERVED/ NOT OBSERVED	NOTATIONS/ OUTCOMES
Personal Professional appearance Pleasant expressions Open body language Positive nonverbal messages Pleasant voice qualities Pleasant room atmosphere *Comments:*		

Instructional
 	
Content
 	
Lesson objective is clear
Motivational strategies
Introductory activity
Instructional materials:
    audio
    visual
    tactile-kinesthetic
Lesson appears well planned
 	
Strategy
 	
Clear verbal directions
Appropriate vocabulary and
    terminology
Gesturing
Clear explanations
Length of lesson presentation:
    too short
    too long
    acceptable		

(continued)

Figure 4.3 Observer's Checklist

Figure 4.3 Continued

TEACHER ACTIONS	OBSERVED/ NOT OBSERVED	NOTATIONS/ OUTCOMES

Class Management Strategies
 	
The teacher is available:
   moves about the room
   stays seated
Interacts 1:1 with students
Uses positive reinforcers
Is encouraging
Handles inappropriate behavior
Meets time schedules
Identify the teaching style
Lesson procedures are made
   clear
Organizational skills are
   evident
 	
Comments:		

Evaluation
 	
Checks for student
   comprehension
Questioning strategies:
   redirect
   prompting
   probing
Asks pertinent questions
Solicits student questions
Answers questions directly
Lesson closure techniques
Meets individual cultural
   differences
Provides for special-education
   students
Supplementary approach is used
Anticipates student needs
Written assignments reflect lesson
   objectives
 	
Comments:		

STUDENT ACTIONS	OBSERVED/ NOT OBSERVED	NOTATIONS/ OUTCOMES
Behavioral Stays on task Shows respect Works quietly Interruptive Stays seated Works cooperatively in a group Has materials organized Displays positive attitudes Any abusive behaviors Tattling *Comments:*		

Instructional
 	
Asks appropriate questions
Shows understanding of the
     assignment
Shares materials or ideas
Uses materials appropriately
Follows directions; assignments
     are done neatly and correctly
Achieves lesson objectives
Comments:		

PHYSICAL FACTORS Desk or table arrangements Learning centers Materials storage Traffic patterns Lighting and temperature Arrangements for handicapped students Audiovisual center Study carrels *Comments:*		

(continued)

Figure 4.3 Continued

STUDENT ACTIONS	OBSERVED/ NOT OBSERVED	NOTATIONS/ OUTCOMES
DISPLAYS Appropriate for the age, class, or grade Related to academics Current Dated Attractively designed Student effort is shown Displays are: 　motivational 　evaluative 　instructional Cluttered appearance Materials are clearly displayed Displays reflect instructional objectives *Comments:*		

student displaying obvious inappropriate behavior, make a notation. What consequence was there and what did the teacher do? Did he or she ignore the behavior, give a discipline slip, confront the student, remove the student from the situation, or do something else? Make these notes in the last column.

From an instructional standpoint, how did you recognize the lesson objective? At what point specifically was it made clear to you? Some teachers clearly state what the objective is: "Class, today we will learn how to identify details and main ideas in this story" or "Today we will discuss five major factors that led to the American Civil War." Telling students exactly what they are expected to learn or what the lesson is about is a very direct way to make the objective known, but there are other ways. Write down the method your demonstration teacher uses, then proceed in this fashion with other items on the list.

It is helpful to keep your observation sheets in a special folder. As you become a more alert observer and recorder of classroom details, you will notice that you are actually seeing more each time you visit a room. Certain things will catch your attention immediately and others will become routine. These sheets are important records for you to examine. They represent an account of various classroom activities. Some of them are fairly routine and others may be quite exceptional. Some days there may be weak teaching or diversions. Look for patterns, as teachers have good and bad days, too. The teacher's actions and reactions are significant. Which behaviors were representative of teaching expertise? Which ones would you emulate if you were the teacher?

During one of your observations you may see something that appears peculiar; if so, record it on your sheet. This may serve as the basis for a class discussion or an explanation from your instructor. You are not expected to understand fully all the rationale or theoretical background of every teaching behavior. Nevertheless, observing a variety of them can be one first step in your learning process. Your instructor may require additional uses for your observation sheets.

■ Summary

Visiting classrooms is one of the best ways to investigate the teaching profession, as they are the primary location where teaching occurs. Most of the student behaviors you see represent the ways many average students act in school and they are entirely normal. Students have good and bad days, too. Some of the teaching behaviors you observe are outstanding, others are not. Everything you see is valuable from the standpoint of learning something. Classroom visits will help you decide if teaching is really what you want to do. Classroom teaching can become confining at times, and this is one working condition that must be considered. After you have been in a number of classrooms, you may have an answer to this important question.

Accurate observing is a skill that becomes more acute with practice. It is possible (even probable) that you and a friend could observe in the same room and record entirely different things, but this is not a negative reflection on either person. Both persons record what they see; they just see different things. It is nearly impossible to see everything, except perhaps with a video recorder. Seeing everything is not the critical objective of an observation period. Look for specifics and then integrate them into the overall picture. Recording what you see and using that information helps you learn more about the teaching profession. Avail yourself of several opportunities to observe teaching in this manner.

■ The Workshop

Activity I

There are many classroom arrangements that adapt easily to a variety of teaching and learning styles. The traditional lecture arrangement is one of the most familiar in elementary and secondary classrooms. This activity gives you the opportunity to arrange a classroom for the subjects or grade you hope to teach. Decide which type of school you will work in: open school, team teaching, magnet school, departmentalized, or self-contained.

Describe your classroom briefly. The size of the room is 25 feet x 30 feet. The diagram and the picture cut-outs in Figure 4.4 are samples of items that you could find in a typical classroom. Your instructor will provide copies of these and you may add others as needed. You can be creative as well as practical. Here are some things to remember before you begin:

- Teaching style
- Age of the students
- Safety factors
- Traffic patterns
- Curriculum considerations
- Practicality, usefulness
- Handicap accommodations

Feel free to move things around, make changes, and include some things you saw in classrooms you have visited. Did they work? You may design more than one classroom. Try one for an elementary class and one for a secondary class.

Self-Check: Look at your arrangements from a teacher's viewpoint and a student's visual perspective. Can all the students see everything during instructional periods? Where is the teacher? Can he or she see everyone? Are there any obstructions? Are the instructional materials nearby? If there are 25 students in your class, there are probably that many different classroom arrangements. It is helpful to see and discuss these various designs, to learn how other people perceive things, and to hear their explanations. If you are thinking about the elementary grades, you can expand your perceptions by examining a high school diagram. Your instructor may use a class period for each person to share, explain, and defend one of his or her diagrams.

Activity II

Examine your observation sheets. How many of your visits were in primary grades, in the intermediate grades, in secondary classes, special education, or with the specials (physical education, art, or music)? It is important that your observations include more than one type of classroom. There is value in observing different age groups in various instructional settings.

Make arrangements to observe in a classroom setting you have not visited previously. You may have little interest in special education, secondary math, or general science; however, it is helpful to note likenesses and differences in a situation that is unfamiliar to you. How do the teachers teach and how do the students react?

Self-Check: Pair with another person in your class and share the observation sheets from this visit. The purpose of this activity is to see if you had some similar experiences in a situation that was out of your field. Briefly

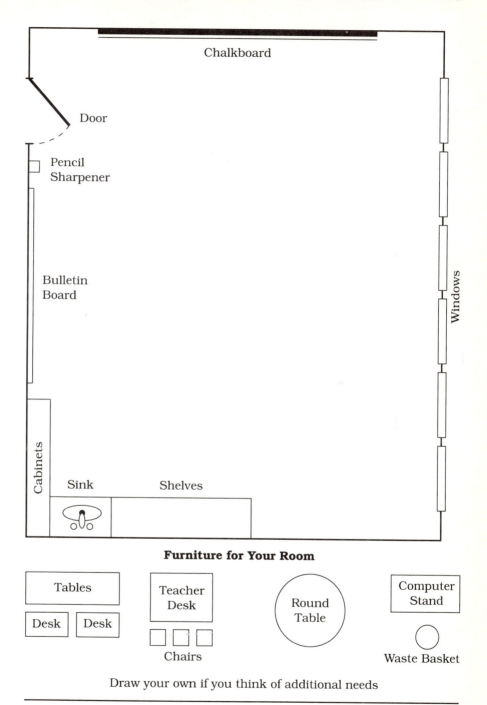

Figure 4.4   Design a Classroom

describe the situation. Point out at least three things that confirmed your initial impressions, and three things that dispelled some others. An additional advantage of this activity is that it may spark an interest in a teaching area you have not seriously considered!

■ Questions and Thoughts

1. What is a typical day for a kindergarten teacher?

2. Why are primary students so restless and fidgety? It seems that too much of the teacher's time revolves around keeping their attention and keeping them on task.
   a. Discuss this in class.
   b. A resource person may speak to the class.
   c. Research some control strategies in the professional literature.
   d. Consult your observation sheets for strategies the teachers used that were successful.

3. What do professional ethics recommend for the following teaching realities? What does the student or teacher handbook say about them?
   a. Abusive language, profanity
   b. Skipping school or cutting classes
   c. Threats
   d. Controversial issues or materials
   e. Defiance
   f. Disruption

4. How might you make your volunteer services available to a teacher you really admire?

■ Readings and References

Cohn, M. M., Kottkamp, R., and Provenzo, E., Jr. (1987). *To Be a Teacher* (Chapter 3, "Looking at Schools, Classrooms, and Teachers"). New York: Random House.

Johnson, R. T., and Johnson, D. W. (1975). *Learning Together and Alone: Cooperation, Competition, and Individualization.* Englewood Cliffs, NJ: Prentice Hall.

Johnson, R. T., and Johnson, D. W. (1984). *Circles of Learning: Cooperation in the Classroom.* Alexandria, VA: Association for Supervision and Curriculum Development (ASCD).

Mager, R. (1975). *Preparing Instructional Objectives* (2nd ed.). Belmont, CA: Fearon.

Moffett, K., St. John, J., and Isken, J. A. (1987, February). "Training and Coaching Beginning Teachers: An Antidote to Reality Shock." *Educational Leadership, 44:* 34–38.

Plodzik, K. T., and George, R. (1989, May). "Interdisciplinary Team Organization." *Middle School Journal, 20:* 14–17.

Ryan, K., and Cooper, J. (1984). *Those Who Can, Teach* (pp. 190–197). Boston: Houghton Mifflin.

Chapter Five

Should I Become a Teacher?

■ Definitions

Adaptive Program: This type of program is specifically designed by the teacher to meet a specific learning or behavioral need. Example: An Individual Education Program (IEP) for a special-education student is an adaptive program.

Affective Learning: This is the area of attitudes, values, and understandings. It is not easy to specifically measure or even to observe affective learning, but it is an important part of a child's schooling. *See* Content Learning.

Assurance of Mastery: Students are required to demonstrate mastery of content objectives before proceeding to the next skill, level, or grade. Students spend as much time and effort as necessary to learn the material or skill, as they are not allowed to move on until they have mastered it. This is also known as Mastery Learning.

Colleagues: The professional and nonprofessional people you work with in your capacity as a teacher are your colleagues.

Content Learning: This is all the facts, concepts, and generalizations to be learned for each area of the curriculum. *See also* Affective Learning.

Developmental: This term refers to a logical, sequential progression of physical and neurological skills and abilities. As children grow, they develop certain skills and abilities in predictable, sequential patterns.

Left-Brain Learning: The left hemisphere of the brain processes information in a linear, sequential, analytical manner. It is the scientific information processing center. Left-brain learners are more organized and analytical, and learn better with structured lessons.

Mainstreaming: This is the practice of placing special-education students with nonhandicapped students in a regular classroom for varying periods of time during the day.

Right-Brain Learning: The right hemisphere of the brain processes information in a spatial, relational manner. It is the intuitive information processing center. Right-brain learners are less organized and prefer imaginative, nonstructured lessons.

Special Education: These are educational programs that are designed for children who have specific problems. Common programs are for the mentally impaired, emotionally impaired, and physically handicapped. There are also special remedial programs such as speech and reading. These programs are usually taught by educational specialists with special certification.

■ Focus Questions

1. Why do you want to be a teacher? Are your reasons valid? Do you really know what you are pursuing?

2. What are the factors that you should consider before making the decision to become a teacher? What are the commitments you must make? How can you find out if you have the personality to be a teacher?

3. What kind of teacher do you want to be? What are your choices?

4. Are you interested in becoming a specialist? What are the options open to you?

■ Introduction

Every teacher has made the conscious decision to choose education over any other profession or career. It is a critical decision because the preparations and commitments to lifelong learning are demanding. Some teachers make this decision (at least subconsciously) early in their life, others reach their decision in high school or college. *When* this decision was reached is not as important as *why* it was made. Why you want to be a teacher—or think you do—should be supported with pertinent information. Emotional responses, fond memories of a particular teacher in your life, or some other isolated but significant event is a weak rationale for such an important decision.

Introduction to Education courses are important avenues to help you to decide whether or not to select teaching as a profession. These courses offer opportunities to examine the act of instruction (lesson presentations), teachers as personalities, course requirements, certifications and licensing, and opportunities to visit and make purposeful observations in actual classroom settings. These and other content offerings provide meaningful background and experiences for you to consider in the decision-making process. All of these offerings focus on the instructional (what the teacher does) and the learning (what the student does) aspects of the profession. Teaching and learning is education. This chapter examines issues that will help you decide if teaching is for you.

■ ■ ■

Is Enjoying Children or My Subject Content Really Enough?

The primary reason or motivation for becoming a teacher is to teach students, or, more specifically, to teach subject content to students. Schools need teachers to share their knowledge, skills, talents, and human resources with learners. If this were not the case, many other individuals could probably do the job.

Is enjoying elementary- or secondary-aged students a strong enough criteria to choose teaching? Enjoying the company of students is certainly an admirable characteristic for persons who want to teach. Respecting them is

■ People in Education
Mary Budd Rowe

Teachers ask a lot of questions during the average school day. Analyzing teacher questioning strategies and student responses is one area of expertise for Mary Budd Rowe. She proposes that students need more wait time—the period before responding to a question or statement—in order to respond more thoughtfully and completely. The wait time allows students to think about their answers and it allows the teacher to formulate succeeding higher-order questions. Mary Budd Rowe, an authority on questioning strategies, teaches science at Columbia University.

important, too. But love and respect are not enough. Love at the emotional level can rapidly disintegrate or diminish when met with apathy, confrontations, stress, and volatile emotions. Love, accompanied by a healthy respect for realistic student needs, both personal and educational, is a critical combination. A good motto for teachers is: Love your students enough to teach them what they need to know.

It is common for teacher candidates to make statements such as, "I just love history. I take every history course that is offered and I want to teach it." It is natural to have favorite subjects and to feel inclinations toward studying them forever. Such feelings are admirable for persons who are considering secondary education. Have you ever heard someone say, "I just love the alphabet and I want to teach sound-letter associations!" Probably not, yet that is a very important step in reading instruction for kindergartners and first-graders.

Individuals who are considering teaching at the secondary level tend to go in that direction because they personally enjoy a particular subject or activity that is associated with secondary schools, such as chemistry or coaching football. Individuals who initially consider the elementary level frequently do so for other reasons, typically because they enjoy being around children of a certain age in social situations. Enjoying children or teenagers and a particular subject are important considerations, but in isolation they are not enough.

The Need to Like Children

Liking children is an important criteria to examine closely. Teachers spend a considerable amount of time in direct one-to-one contact with groups of students; a school day of six or more hours of pupil contact time is not uncommon. The time element is crucial from the standpoint that you, the teacher, are the most important person is each child's educational experience. Being with a classroom of lively, active youngsters for an entire school term certainly requires that you enjoy being around children. If your attitude is one of intolerance or uncertainty, condescension or apathy, it will almost immediately become very clear to the students, and their learning environment will be severely altered. When you enjoy children, it is clearly evident to anyone who enters the classroom. If you dislike children, for whatever reason, strong interest in a particular subject will not be enough to build a successful teaching career.

What do you like or enjoy about children? Which ages and under which circumstances? Take a few moments to record your answers to these two questions on Figure 5.1. Write all your responses, even if they seem trite or obvious. You may have a very long list of reasons or characteristics, or this may be particularly difficult for you to verbalize on paper. The length of your list is not the important factor here, the mental exercise of specificity *is*. Do it now.

How did you do? Now look at your list to see if you can categorize your items under one of these topic headings: family setting, social setting, controlled setting. Under which of these circumstances do you really enjoy the interactions? This quick exercise is intended to give you an opportunity to identify and label the specific reasons why you enjoy children. The school setting is a controlled situation from the teacher's and the students' perspective. The teacher must maintain group order and the students must be in control of their behavior in order to concentrate, to perform required tasks, and to learn. Have you had opportunities to interact with children in controlled situations? Which ones? Which behaviors did you particularly dislike? It is important to put these childhood behaviors in perspective in terms of how they manifest themselves in a classroom setting.

Traditionally, we Americans have always treasured our children and youth and have done everything possible to make childhood and the teen years very special times. Our natural response to the younger generations is certainly an admirable national trait. Enjoying children and youth in a social, recreational, or family setting is one experience that gives you the opportunity to observe how they really are. Avail yourself of these opportunities as often as possible.

Observing behaviors, responses, attitudes, and interactions with peers and adults in noncontrolled situations will give you a fairly accurate idea of how these same children act, behave, and respond in a controlled school setting. Do you like what you see? What do you think about being in a classroom with perhaps 25 other young people all exhibiting basically the same behaviors? Some future courses and seminars will give you pointers on behavior modification, discipline, and group dynamics, but the singular criterion of enjoying children from an observer's point of view needs to be carefully examined and evaluated.

AGE GROUP	CHARACTERISTICS	
Preschool Birth to 5 years	1. 2. 3. 4.	5. 6. 7. 8.
Early Primary (K–2nd grade) 5 to 8 years	1. 2. 3. 4.	5. 6. 7. 8.
Midprimary (3rd–4th grade) 8 to 10 years	1. 2. 3. 4.	5. 6. 7. 8.
Upper Elementary (5th–6th grade) 10 to 13 years	1. 2. 3. 4.	5. 6. 7. 8.
Junior High (7th–9th grade) 13 to 16 years	1. 2. 3. 4.	5. 6. 7. 8.
High School (10th–12th grade) 16 to 18 years	1. 2. 3. 4.	5. 6. 7. 8.

Figure 5.1 Enjoyable Characteristics of Students: A Self-Inventory

Enjoying adolescents and teens is one important factor for considering secondary education. If you are a recent high school graduate, the teen years are fairly recent for you to recall. The high energy level, the excitement, and the activities of the high school experience are still fresh memories. It is necessary to transcend from the teen-student role toward the role and responsibilities of adult and teacher. Think about the behaviors and characteristics of the high school students you know. Which ones do you like and dislike? It is recommended that you observe in secondary classrooms to verify firsthand what teaching this age group is really like. Refer to Chapter Four for specific guidelines.

Teaching at the secondary level is quite different from teaching at the elementary level. The chronological ages of the students and the larger range of performance levels are very important. At the secondary level, students are experiencing both physical and psychological growth and developmental changes. Teachers, parents, and administrators must address the manifestations of these changes on a daily basis.

Suppose you are a social studies teacher and your course is required for all tenth-graders. Some of the students are interested and conscientious, some are marginal and in the class because they are required to be there, and others are clearly apathetic or belligerent. You are very interested in United States history and want to do a good job of teaching it to your class. The motivations to study and perform in a course that is required are clearly different from those for an elective course. Is your interest in United States history strong enough to engage all the students in purposeful learning? In addition to a strong commitment to your subject area (this is a very important factor for successful teaching), you must be prepared to deal with factors such as volatile emotions, apathy, belligerency or disruptive behavior, outside interests, tardiness, mediocre performance, and other stresses related to those students who do not really want to be in your class for whatever reasons.

Is enjoying children or teens enough? When viewed in isolation from other factors related to teaching, it probably is not. In combination with other characteristics that teachers must have, yes it is very important. Along with enjoying teens, it is important to be very strong in the areas of commitment, energy, flexibility, adaptability, character, self-control, and endurance. A strong commitment to a particular subject or curricular area, such as the language arts, is desirable and necessary. If you are not committed to it, it will be difficult for you to convey its importance to students. Being highly enthusiastic about your curriculum must be accompanied by an equally strong enthusiasm for the students who will learn it from you.

Teaching or Playing Games: A Differentiation

By definition, *teaching* is the sharing of one's knowledge with others. In a school setting this knowledge is largely the course content and the other skill areas required in the curriculum. It is common to hear uninformed persons

*Will you fill one of
these classrooms?*

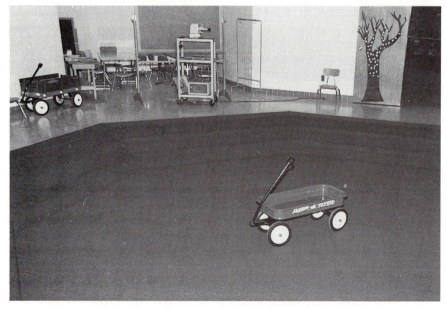

say things such as, "Teaching is easy—all they do is play games," or "They just babysit," or "It doesn't look like teachers do much whenever I'm around the school." Remarks such as these are disconcerting to those who are in the profession, and certainly misleading to those who are seriously considering entering the profession. Disparaging remarks surely damage the reputations of schools, teachers, and students, but dwelling on them serves no useful purpose.

Games are activities people engage in for sport, amusement, or an enjoyable pastime. This type of activity can hardly be compared with the high-skill level that teaching requires. Do teachers play games? Yes, they do. A well-designed learning game can be an excellent tool to teach or reinforce a specific skill in almost any subject. Planning to use a game for teaching is an acceptable activity when used purposefully under the guidance of the teacher. Using a game to fill time is not acceptable.

Primary teachers use games for several reasons. Games allow young children to learn a specific skill in a play setting that is nonthreatening. Play settings are familiar and comfortable for them. They can easily relate to peers in the group and concentrate on the skill they are trying to learn. Finger plays, nursery rhymes, board games, large-muscle movement games, and others are important activities in primary-grade classrooms. Keep in mind the game strategy is not the ultimate goal; rather, it is a means to successfully achieve the goal. Using this criterion, upper-elementary and secondary teachers use games with their classes.

It has been said that all teaching is skill teaching. That is a good principle to keep in mind when trying to differentiate teaching from other things adults do with children or adolescents. Working with youngsters in a recreational setting, such as youth camps, city parks, or recreation programs, is a valuable experience, as is performing childcare services at a daycare center. Caution must be exercised not to rely totally on these experiences as a criterion for generalizing, "I really enjoyed this; therefore, I think I'll become a teacher." If you have special skills and talents in these fields, perhaps you should investigate the childcare services field more closely. The school community needs teachers who can successfully teach all the skills students need to become functional, productive citizens. Teachers must be willing and prepared to teach the curriculum, as this is one of their most important responsibilities.

Factors in Deciding on Teaching as a Profession

Examine some of the possible factors of teaching for a broader perspective. Each factor you observe or experience plays a key role in helping you achieve a realistic picture of what teaching is like now.

Your School-Related Experiences

Direct personal experience is the best way to fully appreciate or understand almost everything. Saying "Don't touch, it's hot" has little meaning to a toddler until he accidentally touches something hot. At this point, meaning is attached to the word *hot* as well as the tone of mother's voice when she says it again. Experience is a good teacher. This example is perhaps a dramatic one to stress the point, but it does emphasize the fact that prior experiences are meaningful.

What experiences have you had that influenced you to investigate the teaching profession? Have you spent time in classrooms, other than as a student? What are your motivations? Do you have a hidden agenda of some kind? Prior experiences can be direct or indirect and both have considerable influence over you.

Direct experiences with children or adolescents include such experiences as being a cadet teacher or summer camp counselor, working on playgrounds or recreational areas, teaching youth groups or Sunday School, working at a daycare center or nursery school, or even volunteering at an elementary or secondary school. Each of these experiences is valuable only to the extent that it gives you some insights that relate directly to teacher-student roles in an academic setting. Why did you participate in them and what specifically did you observe or learn? How did you feel or react when

Volunteer experience with children and youth influences your perceptions of teaching.

nothing seemed to go the way you planned it? Were you able to recover the situation and get things on track again? Enjoying successful experiences and regrouping to energize some not-so-successful activities are routine procedures for teachers.

Think specifically of the direct experiences you have had with children. Identify (1) what you actually observed and experienced, (2) what you did, and (3) what you learned from it. This type of exercise is important for you at this point. Are you cognizant of particular occurrences and are you willing to learn from them? Use the following chart to help you.

Experiences with Children and/or Youth

My Experience	What I Did	What I Learned
1.		
2.		
3.		
4.		
5.		
6.		
7.		
8.		
9.		
10.		

Now examine your "What I Learned" column. Put a check next to those items you think have relevance to classroom teaching. Your instructor may decide to conduct a discussion on this topic.

Perhaps the most valuable direct experience is visiting classrooms. (See Chapter Four). Nothing that can affect your impressions of teaching in quite the same manner as actually being in an elementary or secondary classroom! Observing a variety of teachers and groups of students will immediately give you impressions about teaching. Because you are not a certified teacher, you cannot go into a room and actually experience it. Carefully observing other teachers teach is the best way to experience teaching vicariously until the time arrives for your own student-teaching clinical experience.

■ **Short Shot** _____

What can I expect in my first year of teaching?

The first year of teaching, you will experience many joys, frustrations, successes, and professional growth opportunities. Studying all the curriculum guides and teaching all the required skills will be your biggest responsibility. Preparing your instructional materials will be very time consuming; this is accomplished during your preparation periods and at home on weekends. Accept the fact that a portion of your private time must be designated for school work throughout your teaching career. Effective teaching requires a lot of energy, so at the end of the day you may feel exhausted! Expect to fall victim to a myriad of colds, sore throats, viruses, strep throat, and perhaps even chicken pox and the blahs. Don't become discouraged; it gets better! Your first class will be a very special group in your life. Your relationship with them will carry you through all the trials and tribulations of your first year.

Another important factor that helps you to decide about teaching is your indirect experiences. Growing up in a family that respects education is a factor that influences many individuals to become teachers. Being in a family of teachers is another powerful influence. There are many families that have several members enter the same profession. The home environment, goals, values, and personal characteristics all seem to come together in ways that result in producing a series of doctors, lawyers, mechanics, or merchants. This is true of some teaching families, too. If one or both of your parents are teachers or administrators, or if you have a brother or sister who is a teacher, this indirect influence is very powerful. The family influence can also be quite subliminal. You may find it difficult or even impossible to verbalize just exactly why you are looking into the teaching profession. Are these valid influencing factors? Yes they are, if they do not fall into the category of coercion. Several members of a family may be teachers and perform at a high level of competence. They may be very happy with their career choice. But is it the right choice for you? That is the critical factor to isolate. *You* must do the job, so remember to put family influences in perspective.

Interest Inventories and Personality Surveys

Getting to know yourself better is an important step in the process of entering any profession. The information that you obtain from an inventory or survey helps you to do this.

An *interest inventory* is a standardized instrument that gives you informational data regarding vocational interests, likes, and dislikes. Interest inventories are geared toward specific activities that can help you make a better occupational choice. It is important to know that *interests* are not synonymous with *abilities*. A person may be very skilled in mathematics but at the same time not be particularly interested in the field or even enjoy it. An interest inventory helps you to identify your preferences.

Completing an interest inventory can be a profitable experience for you. Go to the university testing center and inquire about the various instruments that are available. The counselors are specifically trained to administer and interpret test results. The interpretation-evaluation of the results is very important. If you decide to participate in this exercise, remember to respond to each item honestly. Trying to fake or give responses you perceive as the most socially acceptable will defeat your purpose. Taking an interest inventory requires perhaps an hour of your time. It is an educational and guidance tool that will clarify your interests and help your advisor or counselor get to know you better.

A *personality survey* is an instrument that identifies personality traits, characteristics, and behaviors. It is frequently projective in nature and takes the format of a self-report inventory. A personality survey helps you and your counselor identify your unique characteristics, some of which may be very enlightening. For example, if you tend to be a loner, moody, and have difficulty communicating with people, these are important factors to know about yourself. Functioning successfully in a classroom of verbal, active students would be very difficult for a person with these personality characteristics. Can you tell why? Various personality surveys may be available at your university testing center. Taking a survey and using the results are only valid to the degree they assist you in getting to know yourself better, and how they serve you in making a career choice.

Some of the better known interest inventories and personality surveys are the following:

Heston Personal Adjustment Inventory
Bernreuter Personality Inventory
Bell Adjustment Inventory
Strong Vocational Interest Blank
Kuder Occupational Interest Survey
California Psychological Inventory

■ **Short Shot** _____

Many personality and interest questionnaires are designated "inventories," since they appraise an individual's status in several personal characteristics, or his level of interest in a variety of types of activities.

William A. Mehrens and Irvin J. Lehmann

Your Commitment

To be successful in any profession, it is necessary to acquire and maintain a deep commitment to that profession. A strong commitment is especially critical for teachers because what they do on the job, or fail to do, directly affects the lives of students. A strong commitment causes teachers to strive constantly for excellence in their own performance. It causes them to set high standards of performance for students. Minimal performance is not acceptable.

Commitment is an inner sense of tension or anxiety that causes you to give a total effort on a consistent basis. It leads you (perhaps unconsciously) to remain positive, supportive, and inspired when circumstances may not be ideal. Commitment leads you to make a constant effort to improve your school, the curriculum, and the teaching profession itself. It is the basic inner drive that gets you out of indecision to seek every possible way to help students learn.

What is your commitment? Can you define it? It would be unreasonable to expect the level of your commitment to be the same as that of a master or cooperating teacher. There is an anecdote about teaching that goes like this:

Question: Why did you become a teacher?
Response: For three basic reasons: June, July, and August.

If this is an important factor in your reasons for considering the teaching profession, it is very weak, unprofessional, and, yes, even inconsiderate of your future students and colleagues. If the issue of vacation is the only reason important to you, you should question the thinking behind this motive right now.

Be advised that effective teaching is *not* an easy job, even though it may appear to be so to casual observers. Commitment to the profession includes one major factor: a firm decision to improve one's teaching skills. If possible, contact a teacher whom you consider to be an outstanding master teacher. When you are discussing the possibility of becoming a teacher, chances are you will hear such things as, "I just took an excellent class on left- and right-brain learning" or "I wanted some new ideas for parent-teacher conferences and took a conferencing class." The most outstanding teachers are always eager to learn new strategies, techniques, and outcomes of the latest research. A life license is no assurance of mastery for teachers. Your level of commitment is a motivating force for you to always seek those new ideas and better ways to teach. Commitment fosters self-improvement.

The Specialists:
Physical Education, Art, and Music

You are considering becoming a teacher, but what kind of teacher do you want to be? At the elementary level, the majority of teachers who teach in self-contained classrooms are certified to teach all subjects at one or more grade levels in the elementary school program. At the secondary level, each teacher specializes in one or two subject areas and teaches only those subjects in the departmentalized secondary school program. Some teachers are in special education and their certifications are specialized for teaching the learning disabled, the emotionally disturbed, and other students with specific educational needs. In addition to these, there are teachers who specialize in physical education, art, and music. Let's examine these three areas of elementary and secondary education.

Teaching Physical Education: If you enjoy participating in team sports, working out, and other physical activities, teaching physical education may appeal to you. Working with elementary students in this capacity is very different from teaching in a classroom. Visiting a gymnasium during a physical education class makes two things clear: It can get very noisy and the students become very competitive and excited. Elementary physical education begins in kindergarten with very basic large-muscle activities. Many of these activities are taught in conjunction with music. Some major units include basic movements (walking, marching, running, skipping, starting and stopping), exercises (jumping jacks, leg lifts, arm movements, sit-ups), rhythms (creative movements with music, dances, singing games), rope jumping, and beginning tumbling stunts. The kindergarten teacher presents one or more of these every day, in addition to the periods with the physical education teacher.

Physical education skills in the first, second, and third grades build on those established in kindergarten. Each year the children gain more control of their bodies and are capable of performing more difficult activities. In the fifth grade some of the major units might include apparatus gymnastics (vaulting, parallel bars, uneven bars, balance beam, floor exercise), basketball, floor hockey, exercises, modern dance, rope jumping, soccer, softball, track and field, and volleyball. Participation in team sports is emphasized more in the upper-elementary grades.

Teaching elementary physical education has advantages and disadvantages. In some school districts, physical education teachers work in more than one building, so travel is necessary during the day. Some demonstration teaching is done at each building, in addition to providing lesson plans for the classroom teachers to follow until the next scheduled class.

Coordinating the program is a major responsibility. When teaching in a specialized field, you quickly learn to appreciate the importance of promptness and schedules. When a second-grade class appears at the door, you must be there and be prepared to start the class. At the appropriate time, you must have the students lined up and ready for the classroom teacher. Another class will appear shortly. The physical education teacher frequently schedules all the physical education classes for the building, being certain each class receives the required number of instructional minutes per week. In some districts, the physically handicapped students are serviced through the physical education department (adaptive physical education).

The physical education teacher must constantly adapt to changing groups of students. Therefore, there is limited bonding. Some after-school activities may be included as part of his or her contractual responsibilities. Consider this scenario: In an elementary school of 700 students, there are four or five classes at each grade. You will teach each class twice a week. When the unit is volleyball, that involves 28 classes for the introductory, the guided practice, and the advanced skills areas. That is a lot of volleyball!

Is your commitment strong enough to maintain a high level of excitement over a period of two or three weeks? This is very important for the students. Considering all the units that are required for elementary students, you must be highly committed to all of them if you expect to do a good job. Being very skilled at one or two, or teaching only what you like, is not an acceptable reason for choosing to teach physical education.

At the secondary level, physical education and health education are frequently a combined department and taught by the same person(s). Physical education is usually required of all students, even those with limited physical abilities. Some individuals decide to teach physical education in conjunction with coaching a particular sport. Remember, coaching takes place after school and teaching physical education is done during the school day. Keep the two in balance.

The physical education and health departments offer courses that give students a wider range of activities for both boys and girls. Besides the tradi-

The secondary physical education teacher teaches higher-level skills.

tional courses, some new high-interest ones are available. The national emphasis on personal life-styles and health decisions provide the impetus for some courses students select. Certification classes in CPR (cardiopulmonary resuscitation) and first-aid training are popular choices. Team sports, individual sports, beginning and advanced conditioning, and adaptive or developmental courses are also available. The school nurse frequently works closely with the physical education teacher to design special classes or activities for students with specific health problems such as asthma or diabetes.

Teaching Art: Art education in the elementary school is an important part of a student's academic experience. Learning to experience and appreciate the various forms of art adds a special dimension to everyone's life. Going to art class is one of the favorite activities for students of all ages and ability levels. It is an area in which everyone can experience success. This is a strong advantage for the art teacher. The motivations and expectations are high.

If you have particular artistic talents, you may be considering art education. Elementary art gives children many experiences and it is much more than coloring, drawing, and finger painting. Some major emphasis units include design, painting, drawing, printmaking, sculpture and construction, and fabrics. Each of these emphasizes several skill areas.

A fifth-grade class may have opportunities to make blockprints, vegetable prints, linoleum prints, as well as cardboard, sponge, and string prints in a printmaking unit. In a drawing unit, third-graders will use pencil, ink, chalks, oil crayons, charcoal, and other media for their projects.

Is art education for you? Teaching art involves lessons using several different media. You must be willing to use them all, to clean up after each class, and to get ready for the next one. Keeping to a definite schedule is also important; therefore, planning must be done carefully. Serving as a consultant to other teachers on the staff may be part of your job description. Do you like this one curriculum area well enough to teach it all day?

Teaching art at the secondary level is a very rewarding experience. The students are chronologically older and their abilities or talents can be very pronounced. Some art courses may be required, others are elective or taken at the recommendation of the instructor. This is a distinct advantage because the students want to be there. Projects are planned that may take longer than one or two class periods to complete, allowing the teacher to guide and direct all the necessary steps for a successful experience and product.

Secondary teachers are very close to the point in a student's life when he or she is making initial career decisions. Teaching a particular student who has outstanding artistic talent is very challenging and rewarding, as is encouraging and counseling that person into the field. Personal contact is more likely to be maintained as you play the mentor role.

Teaching Music: Music education is an important part of a child's school experience. It is the international language, as everyone seems to find pleasure in listening to it in some form. Music is very enjoyable for young children, for they seem to have a natural feeling for its rhythms and experience it openly. Elementary music includes both vocal and instrumental performance. The typical elementary music teacher is responsible for large-group instruction as well as individual or small-group instruction (i.e., band, sectionals, or private lessons). Preparing musical programs is another responsibility of the music teacher. Cooperation with the secondary music department is necessary to ensure a smooth progression of content and performance expectations.

What do music teachers teach? Some major units are theory recognition, rhythm concepts, melody concepts, form, dynamics, tone color, music history, texture, and music appreciation. Each of these has individual skills that must be emphasized or mastered before new skills are introduced. Vocal music and instrumental performance (band) are probably the most visible. Like the physical education and the art teacher, the music teacher must cope with schedules, rehearsals, and other management responsibilities, as well as interschool travel. Coordinating the classroom music lessons and keeping the program on a success track is part of the music teacher's job.

Music education at the secondary level builds on the foundation established at the elementary level. Secondary music includes both vocal and instrumental classes. A secondary music teacher must be willing to accept responsibilities that extend beyond the regular school day and school year. High school bands and vocal groups are frequently invited to perform at various local and state celebrations. These performances are an important part of our heritage, and preparing for them is a time and talent commitment the teacher must accept. Weekend, summer, and evening performances are routine. Participating in exchange concerts with other schools is an additional possibility. Music appreciation, history, introduction to theory, choir, jazz or rock ensembles, band, and private lessons are some of the courses that are offered at the secondary level.

Music teachers have the advantage of using the audition technique for admittance into courses or activities that are optional, such as concert band or concert choir. This guarantees that the students have at least minimal talents, as well as the motivation to be in class regularly and perform well. Teachers frequently have the option of removing individuals who do not meet the minimal standards and expectations.

Special relationships form easily with secondary choir and band directors. The practice sessions, performances, tours, and activities are very special times in a student's high school career. These bondings are very meaningful and can endure far beyond graduation.

Discussion: Art, music, and physical education are specialty fields that require particular talents and a strong commitment to one area. Flexibility and patience are two personal characteristics that are important for the special area teachers. Listed below are factors that relate to these characteristics. How would you react to these statements?

Statements and Concerns in Special Area Teaching

Actions, Reactions, or Comments

1. The students may not be as "talented" as you would like them to be in your special field.
2. Accepting varying degrees of performance can be difficult for beginning teachers who enter with high expectations.
3. You obviously are very dedicated to your one area; getting some students to enjoy it as much as you do can be frustrating.
4. Some colleagues feel that special area teachers have an easy job.
5. Some students register for art or music classes with the attitude of "It's an easy credit."
6. The special area teacher must relate successfully with all other persons on the staff to facilitate cooperative scheduling.
7. Care must be taken so that the *performance* aspect of these three areas does not overshadow the curriculum aspects.
8. Special area teachers must be aware of the boredom factor; teaching one subject can become tedious after a period of time, but it is still new and fresh for the students.

Art, music, or physical education may be the area of teaching that interests you. Some aspects are obviously more appealing than others. Observing and visiting with individuals who teach your specialty will give you realistic facts regarding their daily routines and responsibilities, and how they relate to the general operation of a successful elementary or secondary school. Observing and visiting will help you to decide if teaching a special area is for you.

Special Education

Public Law 94–142 is the federal law requiring appropriate education for all handicapped children. It is commonly referred to as the *special education law*. This legislation requires school districts to provide educational services for all students with special needs, whether they be physical, mental, or social. The goal is for handicapped students to receive an education that allows them to reach their highest performance level while being with nonhandicapped students whenever it is appropriate. Special-education classes and mainstreaming are the outcomes of this legislation.

There are several teaching fields in special education, but all teachers must possess many special talents and characteristics if they are to be effective in the classroom. The label *special education* should not be viewed as an indicator that teachers of the handicapped are more special than other teachers. The same is true of art, music, and physical education teachers. Over time they have simply been known as "the specials." All teachers are special to the students and their parents! Perhaps teaching in one of the special education areas is for you.

Physically Handicapped

Physically handicapped students are those individuals with physical conditions that impair, to a greater or lesser degree, their ability to perform or participate in the regular classroom. Students with cerebral palsy, a hearing or vision impairment, or a birth defect may qualify for service in special education. Some students have multiple handicaps and have serious needs in more than one area. What would the special-education teacher do with a physically handicapped student? Some goals might include:

1. To emphasize what the student can do and minimize what the limitations indicate he or she cannot do
2. To obtain any materials he or she may need to increase functioning in the regular classroom (i.e., large print or Braille printed materials, special writing instruments)

■ **Short Shot**

Children receiving remedial education are distinct from normal readers in that they did not learn as a result of educational procedures that were effective with most children.

Emerald V. Dechant

3. To provide direct instruction when necessary
4. To demonstrate any needed instructional techniques or strategies the classroom teachers may request
5. To write and monitor the student's Individual Education Plan (IEP)
6. To work closely with all other teachers to achieve maximum success for the student

Mainstream education for the physically handicapped has achieved many important objectives. One of the most important, from a human relations standpoint, is that handicapped students are not feared, ridiculed, or isolated. A student with limited use of the legs may prefer to crawl instead of being pushed around in a wheelchair. In the eyes of other children, especially younger children, that is simply "the way he goes places." It is a matter of fact and it is accepted as perfectly normal for that particular child: I walk, he crawls.

Mainstream education has also made significant contributions to educational philosophies. At one time, the predominant attitude toward handicapped students (as well as many other students) was unfortunately slanted toward the negatives: "She can't do that like (or with) the other students." We have, hopefully, developed a more positive attitude. Yes, a particular student may not be capable of performing a skill at the same level as others in the class, but she is capable of performing that skill at her level—a level that gives her a feeling of success, accomplishment, and participation. Teaching handicapped students to recognize their condition, to participate in the educational process to the fullest extent, and to encourage positive self-concepts are important factors in working with the physically handicapped.

Teachers of physically handicapped students work closely with the nurse, the physical therapist, the physical education teacher, parents, and other outside sources (the medical doctor, vocational resources). They serve as the resource person who manages and coordinates a student's entire educational process, including classroom goals, adaptive physical education, and any necessary medical or personal needs. Coordinating educational goals with achievable, reasonable home and family expectations is one of the greatest aspects of this job.

General Learning Disability (GLD)

Students with a general learning disability are usually defined as those with an IQ of below 80 on measures of intelligence. These students were formerly labeled as the *educable mentally retarded* (EMRs). The achievement levels, perceptual skills, emotional development, general information, and language skills of these students are not at an appropriate level for their chronological age. GLD students frequently exhibit inappropriate behavior for their age, and this becomes an important part of their inability to cope with traditional classroom expectations.

■ People in Education

Seymour Papert

Do you recognize this name? If you have ever used LOGO, then you have an acquaintance with Seymour Papert! He is a Professor of Mathematics at the Massachusetts Institute of Technology and an expert educational theorist. His book, *Mindstorms: Children, Computers, and Powerful Ideas* (1980), tells how he designed this powerful computer language for use by children. It is based on two fundamental premises: Computers can be designed so that children can communicate with them using natural processes, and learning to communicate with a computer may change the way(s) that other learning takes place.

Papert's idea is that the children can program the computer, as opposed to using the computer to teach the children. The work of Jean Piaget is an important foundation for the building of LOGO and artificial intelligence. The possibilities for the LOGO family of computer languages in the schools is an exciting prospect. The Papert book is an important source for information on the topic of computer education.

Teaching GLD students involves several levels of service for each student. At the time the student is evaluated, the appropriate level of service is determined. The necessary amount of service may be set for one or two hours a day, reading and mathematics instruction only, language and behavior modification, or full-time direct service for more severely disabled individuals.

Mainstreaming GLD students into the regular classroom to the degree they can experience success is very important, and requires cooperation between the special-education teacher and the regular classroom teacher. Specialists believe the appropriate personal and behavioral skills are learned more readily when GLD students are with other students who are modeling for them. Providing opportunities for these students to practice appropriate behavior is important. Learning-disabled children can learn a great deal from other children when given the chance to do so.

The GLD teacher is a resource person for parents and classroom teachers. She or he is responsible for teaching the students, frequently on a one-to-one basis. Writing achievable goals for the classroom teacher and parents and helping them achieve those goals is another part of the job. Goals (or objectives) for a GLD student might seem very basic at first, when compared to the achievement capabilities of some other students. Teachers readily realize that setting very small, short-term goals is necessary. A student from an environmentally deprived situation may need to learn many personal-social skills before the academic skills are approached. Some of these could be to use the bathroom alone, to eat with a fork or spoon, to walk in the school halls, to dress himself or herself properly, to play with another child without aggressive behavior, and many other skills. Teaching coping skills to primary-aged students is very important at the beginning of their school experience, and they need to be repeated as long as the students are in school.

Teaching academic skills to GLD students is very challenging and demands great patience, understanding, and a positive attitude. The learning increments or steps are small at times and require many repetitions. These students want to learn—it just takes them a long time to do it. GLD teachers must learn to be satisfied with very small gains and rewards for very small successes.

Teachers sometimes use the same textbooks and materials the other classroom students use, and at other times special books and materials are needed. GLD teachers seek ways for the students to experience success. This search for success can be taxing at times, but it must be done. Special-education students need more positive reinforcers. That is why their learning steps are presented in smaller pieces. A goal that takes a week to achieve may be inappropriate for one individual, especially a kindergarten or first-grade child at the beginning of the year.

If you visit a special-education classroom, you will probably notice several charts and graphs with student names and stickers on them. These serve two important purposes: They tell the teacher at a glance which particular skill each student is currently working on and they are visual motivators and reinforcers for the students themselves. Each time the child correctly performs a given skill, he or she can attach a sticker, draw a smiley face, or give himself or herself a star. This may appear silly or trite to the observer, but it is a powerful reinforcement (reward) technique for the classroom. Visiting will also confirm that GLD students are generally pleasant, happy children to teach. Each skill they learn is a major event. They feel so good about it, and so will you!

At the secondary level, the delivery of special-education services includes more options that meet the needs of older students. The special-education teacher continues to teach the appropriate academic and life skills that are needed to live successfully in the community. Some classes are taken with other students. Individual tutoring is an option. Older students often qualify for special classes at the area vocational technical facility. Seminars and supervised occupational experiences are available on a work-release basis. Prevocational counseling occurs at the high school level to screen those students who can successfully function in dual programs.

Speech and/or Language Delayed

Speech and language clinicians teach students with communication disorders. These disorders include fluency, articulation, voice, and language. At the primary level, some common articulation problems are the *r* sounds, *th*, *ch*, *sh*, and *w*. Language-delayed students are those students whose language skills are not appropriate, within a normal range, for their age. Oral language development is an important factor for successful early elementary experiences.

The speech clinician teaches students and performs various program development as well as personnel and coordinating duties. Identifying and planning the appropriate remediation for students on the caseload is a primary responsibility. Another task is to coordinate closely with all other teachers and the parents to affect a successful plan for the student. Sometimes outside sources are needed to meet the student's needs. New legislation has required the servicing of preschoolers to age 3 years. Many of these children require language development services, and the speech teacher works with them as needed. Early intervention frequently diminishes problems before formal school learning begins.

Reading Specialists

The ability to read well is a vital skill. Students who cannot read are severely handicapped in almost all school and job-related activities. It has been said that every teacher is a reading teacher. Obviously, the primary teacher must be very skilled at teaching the beginning reading skills of sound-letter associations, oral fluency, comprehension, and other basic skills.

Reading instruction does not discontinue after the third grade or after the reading period. Teaching and reinforcing the reading skills should occur in all subjects. Students must read materials for everything they study— math, social studies, language, science, and other areas. Every teacher is responsible for teaching the necessary reading skills for each subject. Reading for science content is not the same as reading for social studies content. Being certain the students know how to read is every teacher's responsibility.

Students who have not mastered the necessary reading skills for successful learning (both school learning and life learning) may require the services of a reading specialist. School systems employ reading specialists to meet the special needs of these students. A reading specialist is a teacher who has taken highly specialized postgraduate courses in reading and met the necessary certification requirements of the state. He or she usually holds a master's degree in the field. A reading specialist is qualified to administer and evaluate survey, diagnostic, readiness, and other specialized reading tests to specifically determine reading problems, deficiencies, or needs.

A student may be unable to read within the normal range of his or her age or grade placement for various reasons. An undetected vision or hearing impairment will significantly affect a child's ability to learn to read. Aphasia and dyslexia are two important conditions that affect reading abilities. Sometimes there is an emotional block that prevents a child from learning to read, especially at the beginning stages of reading instruction. Whatever the cause, the reading specialist's job is to determine the problem and then develop a program to correct it.

The reading specialist typically works in a reading center and the students come to her or him for instruction during the reading period. Many special materials and approaches to reading instruction are available that address each student's particular problem. In some cases, working on a one-to-one basis is necessary. A reading specialist frequently services more than one building. He or she serves as a resource person for the classroom teachers, and may work with the principal to evaluate, strengthen, and revitalize the entire reading program.

Emotional Behavior Disorders (EBD)

Teaching students with emotional or behavior disorders requires unique qualities of inner strength and stamina. A deep concern and understanding for each student's particular situation is critical. Emotionally disturbed students can be very difficult to handle and control during periods of inappropriate behavior. When a student is out of control, it may take two or more adults to restrain the student and administer any necessary modification procedures. An EBD student has serious, prolonged maladaptive behavior that interferes with his or her ability to learn. At times this behavior interrupts the learning of others in the class. Removal from the classroom is necessary to learn self-control and to perform required academic skills. Testing instruments, observations, interviews, and behavior rating scales are used to accurately identify those students who can be serviced in this area. A child-study team usually assists the teacher in the identification process.

Teaching the emotionally disturbed may be one of the areas you are investigating as a possible career choice. Why does this specialized field appeal to you? Have you spent any time in an EBD classroom or interviewed teachers currently in the field? It is easy to fall into the trap of feeling sorry for EBD students. Yes, the students with emotional-behavioral problems are victims of unfortunate circumstances. It is easy to feel sorry for them, as it is for all special-education students. How long do you think these sad feelings will support you in the classroom? In reality, not very long. If this is the primary reason for your interest, it is not strong enough to carry you successfully through the necessary coursework, clinical experiences, or your first year of professional service.

Emotional sentimentality is unproductive for the student and potentially unhealthy for you. It will eventually affect your instructional performance. Commitment, dedication, specific training in strategies and methodologies, and consistency are much stronger reinforcers for you and the students.

■ Summary

Is teaching for you? This chapter has examined some criteria to help you gather the necessary data to make an informed decision. Being the teacher yourself is very different from your perceptions of the person who was in the room when you were an elementary or secondary student. It is important to begin seeing yourself in the teacher role for the particular grade, department, or specialized area that interests you at this point. You must begin to disassociate yourself from the student role, its juvenile impressions and reactions. You are now the adult, and you must begin to envision yourself as the adult role model.

Enjoying the company of children and teens is an important factor. You will be with them several hours every day for nine to ten months. Students are your clients and you must be able to interact with them successfully. Teaching the curriculum content is an important responsibility, so you must be very knowledgeable in all subjects you teach. Elementary teachers are frequently referred to as *generalists* because they are required to teach all the subjects in the elementary curriculum. Secondary teachers are perceived as *specialists* because they teach one or two subjects in a departmentalized program. This debate over labels has been going on for a long time, and it should not unduly affect your decision to choose elementary over secondary or vice versa. Every teacher who works toward excellence is a specialist in what he or she teaches!

There are some critical factors that play important roles in your decision as to whether or not teaching is the right profession for you. Such things as your love of learning, commitment, interests, personality traits, family influences, motivations, cultural values, and other intangibles all contribute in positive or negative ways to your decision. Assigning a weight value to a long list of critical factors may be an interesting exercise in statistics or list making, but it probably will not realistically influence you one way or the other. This does not negate the value of carefully considering the numerous factors that comprise a teaching career, however. If an exercise such as this appeals to you, examine Activity II in The Workshop. It may be valuable for you.

There are many things about teaching special education that contribute to its distinctive role in our educational system. Surely it is an honorable calling to teach students with very specific, complex learning and emotional needs. Realizing that they usually have to work twice as hard to accomplish smaller goals, it is very satisfying for teachers whenever the students achieve an established goal. Working closely with parents to set standards and goals for a successful life outside of the school setting is extremely gratifying. Teaching special education is very special for the right persons. Maybe you will be one of them.

■ The Workshop

Activity I

To be a successful teacher it is necessary to be an unselfish, giving person. If teachers were continually required to *give* without much *receiving,* there would not be many teachers staying in education! It is important to know what you as an individual want to share with students. It is equally important to know what you expect to get from them. The things you receive are critical for assisting students in developing self-esteem, contentment, and motivation. In this exercise you are to list all the things you can share with students, as well as what you expect to receive as an educator. You are not looking at material gains, but at mental and emotional gains. Use the chart below to list your ideas.

What I Want to Share with Students

1.	6.
2.	7.
3.	8.
4.	9.
5.	10.

What I Hope to Receive from Students

1.	6.
2.	7.
3.	8.
4.	9.
5.	10.

Self-Check: After you have completed your list (if you have more than 10 ideas, include them all) answer these questions carefully.

1. Which level of teaching are you considering: elementary, junior high, secondary?
2. Look at your Share list. Which responses are academic, social, and human relations items? Label them with an *A* (academic), *S* (social), or *HR* (human relations). This will give you a quick indicator of your personal inclinations.
3. Examine your Receiving list next. Use the same labels for each of your items as you did for number 2 above. Do they indicate altruistic motivations or realistic expectations? At this point you may wish to rework this list.
4. Are there any direct correlations between your two lists? Which ones? Was this deliberate or chance? Share your two lists in a small-group discussion or with your instructor.

Activity II

Many factors influence a person's decision to become a teacher. There are also many important characteristics that effective teachers have in abundance. This activity gives you the opportunity to examine both of these. First, complete the lists. This may be done individually, in a group, or in class. Now, assign a value to each item based on how you perceive the importance of the item (value: 1 = very important, 2 = important, 3 = marginal). Complete the activity by rating your personal strength on each item (1 = I am weak, 2 = I am average, 3 = I am strong).

Am I a Future Teacher?

Influencing Factors	*Value*	*Personal Strength*
1.		
2.		
3.		
4.		
5.		
6.		
7.		
8.		
9.		
10.		

Characteristics of a Good Teacher	Value	Personal Strength
1.		
2.		
3.		
4.		
5.		
6.		
7.		
8.		
9.		
10.		

Self-Check: This activity is not an exercise in statistical validity. It is merely an exercise in specifically stating the factors that are presently influencing you to consider the teaching profession. It is an opportunity for you to think seriously about the characteristics that are important for teachers to possess, and to decide how critical they are in terms of teacher effectiveness.

1. Examine the point values you assigned to each item in your two lists. How many 1s and 2s did you write?
2. Examine your teacher characteristics list. Do you now possess any of those characteristics to which you assigned a value of 1? To what degree? Is this a strong personal characteristic? If you think these characteristics are very important, they should really become a very important part of your personality profile.
3. Read three articles in the professional journals that examine the topic of teacher characteristics. Which characteristics do research studies indicate are the most significant? Do you agree? Why or why not? Use your data as the basis for a discussion with your group.

■ Questions and Thoughts

1. Why would you be an effective teacher? State three significant reasons and write a rationale to support each one.

2. "Those who can, do. Those who can't, teach." List five reasons why anecdotes such as this one are so damaging to the teaching profession.

3. What is good about mainstream education?
   For the teacher:
   a.
   b.
   c.
   For the special-education student:
   a.
   b.
   c.
   For the other students:
   a.
   b.
   c.

■ Readings and References

Dechant, E. V. (1960). *Improving the Teaching of Reading.* Englewood Cliffs, NJ: Prentice-Hall.

Johnson, K. (1989, May/June). "Handling the Tough Ones: Teacher Trauma." *Thrust, 18*: 201–111.

Manning, B. H., and Payne, P. D. (1988). "Analysis of Private Self-Talk of Preservice Teachers." *Educational Research Quarterly, 12:* 46–50.

Mehrens, W. A., and Lehmann, I. J. (1980). *Standarized Tests in Education.* New York: Holt, Rinehart and Winston, p. 304.

Papert, S. (1982). *Mindstorm: Children, Computers, and Powerful Ideas.* New York: Basic Books.

Pate, R. H., Derdeyn, M. J., and Goodnough, G. E. (1989, May). "Perceptions Held by Academically Talented High School Students of Teaching as a Career." *The School Counselor, 36*: 352–358.

"Teachers Under Stress." (1989). *The Times Educational Supplement, 3805*: April 16, June 2.

Tiedt, P. and Tiedt, I. (1990). *Multicultural Teaching.* Boston: Allyn and Bacon.

Weiner, L. (1989, October/November). "Why High Achieving Students Choose to Teach: Policy Makers Take Note." *High School Journal 73*: 1–6.

■ ■ ■ **Chapter Six**

Becoming
a Teacher

■ Definitions

Academic Advisor: This member of the university faculty meets with students to help them interpret and understand the university bulletin, curriculum requirements, and scheduling. An advisor helps you plan your program, select majors and minors, and counsels when necessary.

Catalog (or Bulletin): This official university handbook usually lists requirements for all university degrees, curriculums, and certifications. It contains information about admission standards, fees, tuition, grading, scholarships, student rights and responsibilities, faculty, and administration.

Experiential Credit: This term pertains to your past experiences. Many schools are giving credit for various experiences in a student's chosen area. This is becoming more common as nontraditional students return to the campus with valuable life experiences.

General Education: Many universities require a common core of liberal arts coursework for all students regardless of major or degree. It may consist of work in the humanities, English, math, science, arts, and physical education. It is based on the assumption that all students must have a basic knowledge of these areas if they are to be a university graduate. Other names: core curriculum, university program, or Gen. Ed.

Supervising Teacher: In student teaching, this is the classroom teacher who will take you into his or her class and supervise your work. This individual works closely with you and your university teacher as he or she assigns you work, critiques the work, observes your teaching, and makes recommendations regarding your fitness as a teacher.

Testing Center: There are many types of testing centers, but in general the term refers to a place where you can go to be tested. It usually operates in conjunction with a counseling center and provides academic information, standardized test results, and interpretation of test results.

■ Focus Questions

1. What curriculum must you follow to become a teacher? How can you be sure that you follow the right one?

2. How do you get admitted to a teacher education program? Are there any special requirements that you must meet before admission?

3. What is the university catalog and how do you get a copy? Why is it so important?

4. When do you get to student teach? What are some considerations that you must know about? Do you have to arrange your own student-teaching experiences?

5. How do you decide on majors and minors? Who can provide some help? What are some concerns to be explored?

■ Introduction

Chapter Five presented information to help you make the critical decision of whether or not teaching is for you. There are some avenues to explore that give you data about yourself and the teaching profession, and the compatible elements of each. Can you fit into the profession and does the profession fit into your personality, life-style, and career goals? If your response to these questions is a strong yes, then you can proceed to the next step: examining and identifying the various procedures and processes for preparing to become a teacher.

■ ■ ■

Curriculum Requirements

There are many important steps, some intangible and others very concrete that you must take to become a teacher. Figure 6.1 illustrates the steps in deciding for or against a teaching career. Enrolling in an introduction to teaching course is one step. It indicates that you have progressed from just thinking about teaching as a possible career choice to actually starting introductory coursework. Education courses give you insights into the profession that show you the special characteristics that differentiate a teacher from any other person who is knowledgeable about a particular topic and attempts to teach it to others.

Becoming a doctor, a lawyer, an accountant, or any other professional person requires the individual to successfully complete a specified curriculum. The same is required for persons who intend to become teachers. Curriculum requirements are established to provide preservice teachers with the knowledge and experiential bases they need for success in the classroom. These requirements are based on educational needs as perceived by the various professionals already in the field. Boards of education, boards of teaching, curriculum associations, teacher organizations, and other professional groups make specific recommendations to the appropriate officials

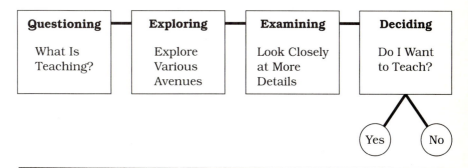

Figure 6.1 Becoming a Teacher: A Process

based on their perception of the knowledge, skills, and foundations new teachers must have to be successful in the classroom.

Some basic curriculum requirements remain constant, while others are new. These new and perhaps novel requirements are instituted in response to local, regional, and national trends or demands. Teachers must be properly educated to teach what society and the local communities deem is necessary. At one time the new curriculum requirement was a course in audiovisual materials. Today the new requirement might be a course in computer literacy, human relations, group dynamics, or site-based management.

Curriculum requirements vary somewhat among universities and states. All teacher education institutions must meet the minimum requirements of the state where they are located, if their graduates are to be certified to teach. Curriculum requirements are those courses, activities, and experiences you must have to graduate. Do not plan to negotiate with your advisor to substitute one course for another simply because you do not want to take it. Courses are required for important reasons and you must complete them successfully. Teacher education programs allow for a certain number of elective courses. To avoid any misunderstandings, it is sensible to consult with your advisor regarding these electives.

There may be some curriculum requirements that all students must meet regardless of their chosen academic program. These are frequently referred to as *basic courses* or *general education*. These basic requirements may include such courses as English composition, introduction to computer science, state history, basic mathematics, physical education, communications, and an introductory course in the natural sciences. These general education courses may comprise 40 to 45 credit hours in your program.

What is the purpose of these basic general education courses? The 1990–1991 Central Michigan University Bulletin proposes this rationale: "The purpose of General Education is to expose all students to a range of study inhvolving basic educational skills necessary for successful lives and careers" (p. 72). This clearly states the importance of a comprehensive educational experience for all graduates. A sound basic education program is helpful in preparing teacher candidates for their professional courses.

■ Short Shot

In every class, you should be working hard to prepare for the final exam. Contrary to what you may think, the real final does not come at the end of the semester, but in a year or two when you have convinced an unsuspecting principal that you are a teacher and have been hired to teach. When you walk into your own classroom for the first time, with no one to fall back on—that is when the real final exam comes. You will know rather quickly whether or not you have learned anything in your previous coursework. And the exam will continue for as long as you teach.

University Requirements

To become an accredited teacher, you must fulfill all requirements of and graduate from a university or college. There usually are three required steps: admission to the university, admission to the teacher education program, and student teaching. Most of you reading this text have already completed the first step, but an overview of the process is given for your review. High school and nontraditional students can read and start preparing for admission. Once you are admitted to the university, start planning to get into the teacher education program. All future teachers look forward to student teaching, as it is the culmination of all of your work and a signal that your undergraduate career is almost over. You can then look forward to that day when you can apply for a job as a teacher.

Admission to the University

Admission to the university of your choice is a process that begins (informally) as early as the junior year in high school. The beginning of the senior year is the time to apply formally for admission to the top two or three colleges or universities you have selected. We currently have a maturing population that is making career changes for various reasons, or returning to college after a number of years have elapsed. These individuals usually have used other criteria and procedures to select and gain admission to the university of their choice.

The searching out and investigating of various educational institutions is important, as it provides initial information regarding the programs they offer, as well as other factors that affect your decision to apply for admission at one place over another. Selecting a good university for your educational goals is important, so begin the process early.

A strong academic background in English, mathematics, science, and the social sciences is highly recommended at major universities. Teachers especially need to be strong in these areas. You cannot teach what you do not know. Foreign language, computer science, and the fine arts are factors the admissions committees may also consider. It is your responsibility to fill out the application form(s) and submit them early. It may be necessary for nontraditional students to take the ACT (American College Test). These test results are considered as one indicator of a successful performance at the university level, in conjunction with other data in your portfolio. Additional procedures are necessary if you apply for admission as a transfer student.

Admission to the university is dependent on several important factors. The courses you have taken in high school, or at another institution of higher learning in the case of transfer students, are important. To a large extent, they determine your ability to approach the challenges of college work. The grade point average (GPA) is one indicator of performance in relation to others in the class. Admissions counselors examine grades carefully; they recruit students who exhibit a strong foundation in college preparatory courses.

In addition to the grade point average, they examine the candidate's personal character references, participation in extracurricular activities, life experiences, employment records, leadership roles, and special talents or aptitudes. Students with a comprehensive background are an asset to the university and its program, as well as the professions they will enter after graduation.

Soon after your admission is confirmed, it is advisable to become familiar with the current catalogue. It contains important information regarding the College of Education you are about to enter. The catalogue states the sequential steps you must follow in terms of coursework, deadlines, competency tests, student-teaching requirements, advising, and other useful information. Reading the catalogue carefully results in many questions being answered without unnecessary calls to the education office or an advisor. Some advisors will ask if you have read your catalog and, if not, will send you home to read it before advising you.

We recommend that students contact an academic advisor as soon as possible. Your advisor serves as a coach or mentor to help plan your program and lead you most directly to graduation and to obtaining your degree and teaching certificate. Communicating honestly and candidly is necessary if this guidance process is to be successful. Misunderstandings can result in unnecessary disruptions, such as taking classes that are not acceptable as electives, taking classes that are inappropriate choices for the major or minor, missing deadlines for student teaching placement, late or incorrect information for tests or screening procedures, and other unforeseen mistakes.

Academic advisors sincerely want to make your college experience as error-free as possible. It is so much easier on the student and the advisor if a program is cooperatively planned early in the process, rather than trying to

■ People in Education

Carol Cummings

Cummings's book *Teaching Makes a Difference* is used in many methods courses throughout the country. This easy-to-read paperback thoroughly examines instructional skill, the many decisions that teachers make regarding what to do to help their students learn and progress. This book stresses the fact that a person cannot just enter a room and "teach." A very complete set of skills is necessary to teach—to establish instructional objectives and a definitive plan to accomplish them. This text clearly defines what teachers must do to teach effectively. *Managing to Teach* is another very useful book by Cummings. Watch for this interesting speaker at conferences and conventions.

straighten out a serious mistake that was caused by a student who thought that he or she didn't need an advisor. Every year we see seniors who cannot student teach or graduate on time because they listened to a friend who had a roommate in education, and not to a qualified university advisor.

Admission to the Teacher Education Program

Applying for admission to the teacher education program is another important step. Submitting the application with all the necessary recommendations and verifications should be done as soon as possible. Submitting your application early in your freshman year or very soon after transferring to the university is highly recommended.

A standard application for admission to the teacher education program requests a variety of information about you. Residence information, transfer data, tentative selection of major and minor(s), character references, citizenship status, elementary or secondary interests, and a written composition describing your interest in teaching are some of the things that may be included on the application. Care must be taken to respond completely and honestly to all items. Incomplete applications can keep you out of the program or, at the very least, delay your admission. Dishonesty or false answers can be grounds for dismissal from the program.

This application is reviewed by an admissions committee, a department representative, or other selected personnel. The information you submit assists in determining your specific qualifications and special interests in teaching before the entrance interview or other admissions procedures can happen. The appropriate application forms are available at the teacher education department offices.

University programs and faculty members want to make the admissions process and subsequent progress through the program as organized and foolproof as possible. As an example, the Department of Teacher Education and Professional Development at Central Michigan University has developed and initiated the Admission to Teacher Education Program to facilitate this. The main tenets of this program are:

1. An early experience in teacher education that will allow potential teacher candidates to engage in a screening process
2. A mentoring system that provides teacher education candidates with a professional mentor who will assist the student in advisement, program review and planning, and portfolio development of professional experiences and work samples
3. A continuing candidacy process with three cycles that the student completes in sequence
4. The concept of multiple criteria for admission to and continuance in the program

This program provides teacher candidates with a sequential and closely supervised management system that tracks the academic program. The admission process is organized into three cycles of candidacy: the entry candidacy, the continuing candidacy, and the exit candidacy. As can be seen in Figure 6.2, some of the major points of these cycles of candidacy are:

Cycle I
1. Demonstrate the following competencies: written English (a minimum of five pages on a given topic), oral communication, and mathematics competency (written test).
2. Present evidence of at least 90 contact hours of experience working with, directing, or supervising children and youth, 45 of which must be in a regular classroom.
3. Present a letter of recommendation.
4. Make an appointment with the advisor.

Cycle II
1. Majors and minors are properly authorized.
2. Methods courses are completed.
3. Complete 75 percent of major and minor classes and meet requirements of the departments.
4. Have a minimum 2.50 GPA.
5. Make another appointment with the advisor.
6. Complete the teacher's oath (a state requirement).
7. Submit the application for student teaching.

Cycle III
1. Successfully complete student teaching.
2. Meet with the advisor.
3. Meet the minimum 2.50 GPA.
4. Complete major and minor(s) department requirements.

Of particular note is the number of hours required working directly with children and youth. These hours of direct experience are an important prerequisite at the beginning of the academic process. They provide opportunities to determine whether or not the individual can cope with small and large groups of children or adolescents. They provide some indicators of success or failure in the student-teaching experience. This and other similar admissions programs help candidates successfully complete all of the requirements for graduation and certification.

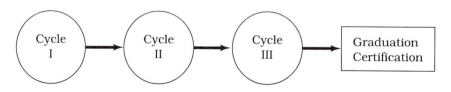

Figure 6.2 Cycles of Candidacy

Admission to the teacher education program may require some specific courses, experiences, or activities that are peculiar to a certain region or area. Requirements, such as the grade point average in general coursework and professional courses, may be different. Completion of an introduction to education course may be a prerequisite. Some written competencies (standardized tests) may be required in addition to the ACT that is taken before admission is granted. Competencies in math, oral language, and written language may also be required. All universities have their own unique requirements that are established to help attract and maintain the quality of teacher candidates they intend to graduate and recommend for certification. This is also a good time to start a portfolio to showcase your preparatory work (see Figure 6.3).

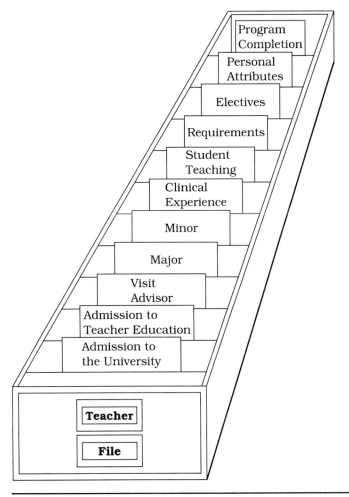

Figure 6.3 Creating a Professional Portfolio: Decisions, Procedures, and Competencies

Student Teaching

Becoming a teacher involves many important decisions, commitments, and academic courses. Each of these play an important role in your educational experience. The attitudes and dedication you bring into each experience will, to a large extent, determine your degree of success. The program established by your university has two important goals: to adequately prepare you for a successful student-teaching experience and ultimately to prepare you for full-time classroom teaching as a licensed professional.

Preservice teachers must fulfill a period of supervised teaching before they can apply for a teaching certificate or license. This period of supervision is called *student teaching* or the *clinical experience*. Achieving a high grade point average is important; however, your GPA takes on validity only to the degree that it prepares you to teach students in a classroom. Grades are important, but what did you learn? What you learned becomes very evident in a relatively short time when you begin your student teaching.

Approaching the student-teaching experience with a positive attitude is critical. A cavalier attitude is both unprofessional and unacceptable. Supervising teachers are carefully selected by building principals and the university coordinator for their exemplary teaching skill and dedication to the training of new professionals. They can recognize a mediocre effort right from the start. You cannot "just get by" and expect to receive a strong recommendation or evaluation from the supervising teacher.

Do not plan to complete student teaching with less than a total effort. This is the time for you to use the content material, methods, strategies, and theories you have learned, under the supervision and direction of an experienced teacher. This is the time for you to demonstrate that you do indeed have the necessary background and basic skills to effectively teach the curriculum to students. You must demonstrate these skills to your supervising teacher on a daily basis with every lesson you teach. As a preprofessional member of the school staff, your responsibility is to teach the curriculum that is adopted by the district. You will be teaching the skills and units that are on schedule for the time when you join the staff. Some flexibility will be necessary, but you must be willing to adapt to the curriculum cycles of skills teaching.

The student-teaching period is very rewarding and enjoyable. There is a particular sense of pride when a lesson you have taught is successful and effective. Your planning and effort have made it so! Planning and designing good lessons is work, but you will enjoy the feeling of pride that comes from a job well done. It also provides professional satisfaction for the supervisor who is guiding and directing your work.

Working together as a team is mutually rewarding. Your supervisor wants you to succeed, to become a very good teacher. Suggestions, critiques, and observations are given to assist you in that process of becoming a teacher. Open, honest communication with this person is critical. Ask questions, clarify, observe, and discuss. Share in the critical review of your work. You are

Bring a complete and accurate set of application forms when you apply for student teaching.

there to learn. Critiques are an evaluation of your work made to help you see the strengths and weaknesses of your lesson; they are not a personal criticism of you. If you cannot take constructive criticism, you will not learn much from your student-teaching experience. Indeed, you may develop a dislike for teaching.

Your supervising teacher is the person who will most directly oversee your classroom performance. She or he examines your lesson plan, watches you teach, and confers with you afterwards.

Other persons on the staff directly and indirectly contribute to your student-teaching experiences. Building principals frequently come into the classrooms to observe student teachers. They do this for several reasons. It is good public relations for the school and the university, it enhances the working relationship between the coordinator and the school administration, it reinforces and affirms the supervisory skills of the teacher, and it provides *observed data* (not just hearsay) for possible job recommendations in the future. In smaller districts, the superintendent and the curriculum coordinator may visit the class for similar reasons.

The university student-teaching coordinator is an important person in your journey to become a teacher. He or she has done a considerable amount of work in the field long before you enter your classroom on that first day. Examining schools, interviewing principals and prospective supervising teachers, scheduling, advising, and other responsibilities are handled in advance. He or she takes care to place you and every other student teacher with just the right teacher in the right classroom setting. Remember this when you enter the room. Details and reasons may not appear evident to you at first, but trust they are indeed professionally decided.

Your coordinator will come to watch you teach and confer with you on a regular basis (as established by university policies). He or she also consults with your supervising teacher regarding your progress and daily perfor-mance. Some universities require a seminar class in conjunction with the student-teaching experience. Your coordinator conducts this class for all of his or her student teachers. This individual is there to help, so take advantage of his or her expertise and resources.

The length of the student-teaching experience varies. Some states re-quire a six- to eight-week primary experience and an equal intermediate ex-perience for elementary candidates. This is important to note. Some individ-

■ People in Education
Joseph Renzulli

The subject of special education for academically and creatively talented students is a concern of teachers, parents, and legislators. A basic premise is that high-achieving students are our future leaders; thus, our educational system must provide a challenging, appropriate learning en-vironment for them.

Dr. Joseph Renzulli (Professor of Educational Psychology, University of Connecticut) and his associates are doing extensive teaching and re-search to bring workable gifted and talented education to these students. The Scales for Rating the Behavioral Characteristics of Superior Students is an instrument used to estimate a student's strengths in the areas of learning, motivation, creativity, leadership, art, music, drama, communi-cations, and planning. The Enrichment Triad Model emphasizes a three pronged approach:

Type I   General exploratory activities
Type II   Group training activities
Type III   Individual and small-group investigations of real problems

Although some programs for the gifted are conducted outside of the regular classroom, Renzulli's Revolving Door Model allows students to move into and out of special programs at various points during the year for a specific reason and for a specific period of time. Renzulli and his associates publish extensively on the topic of gifted and talented education.

uals may want to teach only the upper grades and so plan to student teach in fifth or sixth grade. This plan may not be acceptable, as you will probably be certified to teach all levels in the elementary school. Secondary candidates must complete their student-teaching assignment teaching in their major or minor concentration. Special-education candidates usually serve eight weeks in a regular classroom and eight weeks in a special-education situation. Length of service may vary for those who seek certification for kindergarten through grade twelve in such areas as music, art, or physical education.

Several key elements contribute to the success or failure of the student-teaching experience. Your preparation and attitudes, the supervising teacher, the coordinator, the classroom environment, and many other elements are important and must be seriously considered.

What about the students? What is their role in this process? Whether you are teaching third-grade grammar or honors calculus, the role of the students is critical. They are the recipients of your teaching efforts. If you plan and prepare yourself well, they will learn and clearly benefit from their relationship with you. On the other hand, if you come to class ill-prepared, their learning experience will be severely altered. As a student teacher, you have the responsibility to teach particular skills to the class, not just to practice your skills of instructing.

During your six- or eight-week tenure, the students must progress. At the end of this period, the classroom teacher cannot go back and reteach all the curriculum; she or he must move on to other material. You may have another opportunity to student teach, but the students will not have another opportunity to repeat the academic experiences they had with you. The point is, your relationship (both personal and professional) with the students is very important. Teach and relate to them the best way you possibly can, while you can.

Majors and Minors

Choosing a major and/or minor is not always an easy task. There are so many things to consider: What majors and minors are certifiable? Where is the demand? What do I really like? If I pick a demand major or minor, can I make decent grades in it? What if I really like a particular major/minor combination such as psychology and sociology—can I get a job, or can I even get placed for student teaching? There is a lot to think about. You do want to teach in areas you enjoy, but you also want to get a job when you graduate!

Majors and Minors in Demand

Traditionally there have been some majors and minors that are more in demand than others for both the elementary and the secondary level. When society decided that students should become physically fit beginning in the

Many majors and minors are selected based upon your interests.

primary grades of their school experience, a need for certified physical education teachers arose. Our present societal needs indicate that teachers with computer science, bilingual education, and counseling are required. The demand for teachers with particular certification, or a certain major and minor combination, or specific majors or minors can appear rather suddenly. It is to your advantage to be aware of the most obvious current needs.

Choosing a major or minor that is certifiable but remotely in demand is probably unwise. In areas such as Texas, California, and the general Southwest, having a major, minor, or fluency in Spanish is a definite advantage. These states and others need teachers who can communicate with large numbers of students who cannot speak English, or who have only minimal oral and comprehension skills in English. The primary language that is spoken in the home is an important factor in a student's ability to be successful in school. English as a Second Language courses, commonly referred to as ESL, are valuable to have.

Choosing Majors and Minors

Selecting a major and minor is an important step in preparing to become a teacher. As with most major decisions in life, concentrated thought and self-discovery are necessary. What do you really enjoy studying and how success-

■ Short Shot

The role of athletics in our educational system is important. Both boys and girls begin training at an early age for the various school athletic teams. Coaching them well is important, too. Coaching is basically an after-school responsibility for teachers. It is time consuming, stressful, and demanding in many ways. In addition to the classroom certificates and licenses, coaches must maintain their coaching status with the state department of education. Continued courses, seminars, and workshops are required to maintain these licenses and certificates.

ful are you with it? A person may really enjoy taking art classes, for example, creating art for self-satisfaction and recreation. But what is the quality of the work? Is it exceptional? And can this individual withstand the rigors of art education and become skilled enough to teach it to others? A teacher must not only enjoy the content area but also be capable of teaching it.

Enjoying a particular area of study is important. You probably know yourself well enough to name a few areas that are your obvious strengths. Write them down. Think about them. Review your files for any tests or inventories that indicate your areas of strengths and weaknesses. Investigate the possibility of taking some tests at the university testing center that could indicate other potential strengths.

Consulting with your academic advisor or mentor is critical to assuring that you are considering all possible factors when deciding what your major and minor should be. Haphazardly choosing a certifiable major or minor can lead to dissatisfaction with your course of study, causing a change in majors and/or minors, which in turn prolongs your date of graduation. Discussion with friends and fellow students can also be valuable, as they may give you a different view of a major or minor. But remember, in the final analysis, *you* must be comfortable with your choice. Seek assistance from the professionals in this decision-making process. Go to the departments under consideration and ask about their majors and minors. They are in the best position to give you the information you need to make a valid choice.

Selecting a major or minor can be confusing even when you are sure which content area you want. Perhaps you have determined to major in music. Your decision is final. Or is it? Which baccalaureate degree do you really want? A university Department of Music may offer these degree programs for music majors: Bachelor of Music, Bachelor of Arts, Bachelor of Science, Bachelor of Music Education, and Bachelor of Science in Education. What is the difference? Those seeking the Bachelor of Music Education degree must major *and* minor in music. These individuals must take the required general education courses, professional education courses, courses outside the major, music common cores, instrumental and vocal concentration, and others. The confusion is evident.

This example shows the need to meet with an advisor and carefully consult the university catalogue. It becomes clear that you must be specific as to which major and minor you really want, as well as the specific baccalaureate degree you intend to receive.

■ Summary

Becoming a teacher is a careful, somewhat predetermined process that leads to the completion of a degree and obtaining certification. Although tradition, the university, the state, and the boards of teaching exert considerable influence over the process of becoming a teacher, the journey is intended to be a rewarding and satisfying one for you. The curriculum requirements, certification requirements, standards of performance, tests, and other steps toward graduation are deemed necessary and valid to ensure that teacher graduates can indeed perform all the responsibilities of classroom teaching. Care and consideration for every aspect of your preparation is as important to all of the advisors and instructors as it is to you.

■ The Workshop

Activity I

Reading the catalogue is necessary if you are to know what to do to graduate from the university. The catalogue is usually large and sometimes cumbersome to handle on a regular basis. Having a list of things to do, in order of importance (deadlines and dates), and courses you need to take during specific quarters or semesters is a handy tool to keep you on a directed path. Get your catalogue and make a large chart for yourself with these headings:

Important Dates
Major Courses
Candidacy Requirements
General Education Courses
Minor Courses
Office Phone Numbers, Locations
Other Important Things

Place this chart in a key location above your desk and you can check off each responsibility as it is completed. It will also let you know at a glance what is coming up in the near future. Make an appointment with your advisor to be sure you have a complete list. He or she may find some omissions.

Activity II

There are a number of books on the topic of student teaching. The Education Index and ERIC feature sources for articles that cover many factors of student teaching, from evaluation, to criteria, to lengthening the requirements. Spend some time reading about these clinical experiences. These articles and books are valuable resources that examine many different aspects of student teaching from the point of view of supervisors, universities, state departments of education, and student teachers.

■ Questions and Thoughts

1. What are the advantages and disadvantages of attending a traditional teachers' college or the state university?

2. "Is it possible to do my student-teaching in a private or parochial school? I don't want to lose my campus job and a particular teacher is willing to supervise me." Will this work?

3. Distinguish between the State Board of Education and the Board of Teaching.

4. A teaching position in your minor area of concentration is available in a particular school district. You really want to teach full-time in your major. Should you accept this position or wait for another? Discuss the pros and cons of each choice.

■ Readings and References

Cleary, M. J., and Gobble, O. (1990, February). "The Changing Nature of Public Schools: Implications for Teacher Preparation." *Journal of School Health, 60:* 53–55.

Cummings, C. (1980). *Teaching Makes a Difference.* Edmonds, WA: Teaching.

Cummings, C. (1983). *Managing to Teach.* Edmonds, WA: Teaching.

Freeman, D. J., Martin, R. J., Brosseau, B.A., and West. B. B. (1989, May/June). "Do Higher Program Admission Standards Alter Profiles of Entering Teacher Candidates?" *Journal of Teacher Education, 40:* 33–41.

The Journal of Teacher Education, 40: 49–56 (May/June 1989).

Lindholm, K. (1989, April). "Student Teachers: More Than Luck Is Required." *Clearing House, 62:* 332.

Peterson, S. K., and Hudson, P. J. (1989, Winter/Spring). "Coaching: A Strategy to Enhance Preservice Teacher Behaviors." *Teacher Education and Special Education, 12:* 55–60.

Seefeldt, C. (1989, May). "Who Meets the Standards for Early Childhood Teachers?" *The Education Digest, 54:* 21–24.

Wells, D., and Parette, H. P. (1989, Spring) "Admissions, Retentions, and Graduation Standards Used by Selected Colleges of Education." *College Student Journal, 23:* 41–46.

■ ■ ■ **Chapter Seven**

Marketing Your Teaching Skills

■ Definitions

Accreditation: This term refers to the granting of approved status to an academic institution by an accrediting body after examination of its courses, standards, and so on. The North Central Accreditation Association (NCAA) accredits elementary, secondary, and higher education institutions. The National Council of Accreditation for Teacher Education (NCATE) accredits the teacher education programs for colleges and universities.

Departmentalized Classroom: In a departmentalized program, such as that found in almost all secondary schools, students move from classroom to classroom for each different subject.

Endorsement: This is another major, minor, or special qualification that is added to your regular certification. You might go back to school and complete another major or minor so that you can teach in an area other than your undergraduate program, or you might do additional work to become a reading specialist.

Portfolio: This consists of all the materials you have gathered over your university career that you may show to a potential employer or to a graduate school. You may collect documents and papers from your personnel file at the university placement office, grade reports, personal and professional recommendations, awards and citations, and other personal papers that are a part of the credentials you bring to a potential employer.

Provisional Certificate: An elementary or secondary provisional certificate is issued upon completion of your undergraduate program, provided you have met all certification requirements. The provisional certificate entitles you to teach for a specific period of time (usually three to five years) while you complete the requirements for a Continuing Certificate (or in some states, a Life License).

Self-Contained Classroom: This is a classroom where one group of students remains for most of the school day with the same teacher. They may go to a special teacher for art, music, or physical education, or an individual may go to another room for special instruction, such as speech or remedial reading, but the main instruction is in the same room.

■ Focus Questions

1. What is the difference between your needs when applying for a teaching position and an employer's needs when hiring a teacher?

2. What should you consider when deciding on your major and/or minor? Is this choice really important? How do choices affect employability?

3. What do employers look for when they interview prospective teachers? Will your job experiences and extracurricular activities enhance or diminish your chance of getting hired?

4. Which level should you teach: elementary or secondary? What is the difference? Why can't a person teach any and all grades or subjects?

▪ Introduction

Everyone hopes to secure the perfect job—one that matches the individual's personality, talents, skills, abilities, and creative interests. This is a reasonable expectation in life. Being accepted at the university of your choice, admittance to the teacher education program, successful completion of student teaching, and graduating with a bachelor's degree are necessary steps toward securing satisfying employment in the teaching profession.

Teacher candidates should realistically examine the job market in relation to their academic preparation. Academic choices prepare (or may not prepare) you for the teaching positions that will be available three or four years in the future. Reports indicate that secondary science and math continue to be critical areas for teacher recruitment. It is not too early to begin making those important decisions that will make you a viable, employable teacher. Becoming employable in the profession of your choice is very important. This chapter discusses the academic and personal preparations that enable you to become marketable and employable in the field of education.

▪ ▪ ▪

Employer Needs

Elementary and secondary schools need good teachers. The number of available teaching positions is not unlimited, but qualified teachers are needed as long as students enroll in schools. It is common knowledge that the number of teacher graduates far exceeds the number of available full-time teaching positions. Graduating with a degree does not guarantee an easy search or a signed teaching contract. It is not uncommon in many suburban, metropolitan, and rural areas for several hundred applicants to apply for each available position. Which applicants will be selected for the initial group interview? Which ones will be chosen, for the final interview process? And which person will ultimately be offered a contract? (See Table 7.1.) In many communities, employers enjoy the position of having a very large pool of applicants from which to select their new teachers. They are not forced to hire minimally qualified personnel. They are in a position to hire only the best.

Schools need teachers who are capable and willing to teach students. In addition to the formal instructional responsibilities, employers need teachers

Table 7.1 A Professional Employee Selection Process

PROCEDURE	PERSON(S) INVOLVED
Step 1: Credentials Search (the portfolio examination)	Personnel director or building principal(s)
Step 2: Group Interviews (5 or 6 applicants)	Building principal and department chairperson
Step 3: Individual Interview (top 2 or 3 applicants)	Superintendent or personnel director
Step 4: Contract Offer (the new teacher)	Superintendent or school board

who are good employees from the standpoint of attitudes, cooperation, self-improvement and continued education, support, energy, honesty, positive role modeling, and cooperation. In many ways, schools are looking for out-standing "superhumans" to teach their students. The social, emotional, and educational needs of students are great, and the educational system requires excellent personnel to meet those needs. There is a lot of work to be done in

Schools need teachers who are capable and willing to teach students.

▪ Short Shot

Competition for that first teaching position will be keen. To give yourself an extra edge over the competition, you must take charge of those elements of the interview over which you have control.

The first element is your general appearance. You do not need to wear a designer wardrobe or have a $50 hair styling, but you do need to be clean and neatly dressed. Remember: You are a professional applying for a professional-level faculty position, and you have only one chance to make a good first impression. If the final selection comes down to two equally qualified candidates, personal appearance might be the deciding factor.

You also have control over your behavior. Be alert, attentive, and assertive throughout the interview and do not chew gum. Watch out for false fronts. Most interviewers are experts in seeing through insincere behavior and mannerisms. Present a confident appearance, but avoid any hint of arrogance. Try to maintain close eye contact with your interviewer and concentrate on listening to what is being said. Before answering any question, put your thoughts in order. Know what you are going to say before you say it. A moment of silence will not hurt you; speaking before you think may. Answer questions truthfully and as completely as you can.

At some point during your interview, you will be given the chance to ask questions. Do not fail to take advantage of this opportunity. By asking job-related questions, you tell the interviewer that you are interested in the position. The manner in which you phrase your questions, as well as the content, gives the interviewer an insight into how you plan and organize your thoughts and how well you think on your feet.

By mastering the techniques of interviewing, you enhance your chances of being selected for your first teaching position. From then on, your success depends on how well you apply yourself and the skills you have learned in your college career.

---

a school, and teachers are an important part of the team that accomplishes a variety of educational and social goals. Employers need strong teacher members for that team.

Majors and Minors

Majors and minors provide opportunities to concentrate your courses in particular fields of study. A predetermined number of semester hours are necessary to fulfill the requirements for a certifiable major or minor. Usually a major consists of at least 30 semester hours and a minor of at least 20 semester hours of coursework. A major in psychology and a minor in physical education may enable you to graduate, but these choices may not be certifiable for a teaching license, student teaching, other clinical experiences, and ultimately securing a teaching position. The discussion and investigation of choosing certifiable majors and minors was presented in Chapter Six. The requirements for majors and minors vary in different states and universities.

The newspaper and broadcast media regularly report the need for secondary math and science teachers. Teachers in these two fields are also recruited by business and industry, and individuals do leave education for various reasons, such as advancement, higher salaries, professional recognition, opportunities for research and creative endeavors, and mobility. Table 7.2 will assist you in your search for a teaching position.

Other positions are in demand, such as special education (elementary and secondary) and bilingual education. Both of these tend to fluctuate in terms of geographical location, specific student populations, funding priorities, and funding capabilities.

There will be teaching positions available for both elementary and secondary teachers with a variety of majors and minors. These positions become available due to retirements, attrition, and population growth. The question "What teaching positions are currently in demand?" can be misleading. The phrase *in demand* does not imply that school districts are willing to employ a math major with a 2.5 grade-point ratio, when another applicant has a 3.9 in addition to other significant qualifications. It does not indicate that school districts are zealously recruiting every teacher education graduate. The responsibility is on the teacher to seek out the available positions for which she or he is certified to teach, and then submit an application for employment application.

Special Qualities, Training, and Experiences

Superintendents, personnel administrators, and building principals examine many components when screening teacher applicants. Grade-point ratio is certainly an important one. However, a number of other criteria are also significant. The mission of these individuals is to select and hire the person most likely to fit into their educational system. The responsibility of the candidates is to possess and/or develop the qualities, experiences, and assets necessary to obtain the desired teaching position. What are some of the qualities, personal experiences, and specific training that make one person more marketable and employable than many others?

Successful teachers possess many special qualities. It may be difficult to make a list, or even to assign each of them a specific label. However, potential employers do look for special qualities and place a point value on such

■ People in Education

Jerome Bruner

> Bruner is a cognitive learning theorist who is known for his model of discovery learning. The student learns by active involvement in the solving of a problem. This is used extensively in the teaching of science. He also proposed three ways of knowing: the enactive, cognitive, and symbolic modes.

traits during the initial screening process. Dedication, scholarship, flexibility, character, loyalty, commitment, written communications skills (as evidenced in your letter of application as well as the employment application forms), references, employment record, experiences with children or youth, volunteerism, attitude, professionalism, and many other features are evident long before the employment interview. Qualities such as respect for students, positive human relations skills, teaching skill, knowledge of subject matter content, honor, dedication, and other personal qualities are valued and necessary for good teachers to possess. The records you submit to potential employers clearly show many of these qualities.

■ Short Shot

With the large numbers of applications you receive for each available position, how do you determine those who will be called in for an interview?

The single most important element of the employee selection process is the personal interview. Unfortunately, because of time and cost limitations, it is generally not possible to interview all job applicants. Therefore, candidates for a position must be ranked or prioritized to determine who will make the "cut" for an interview. For new graduates, the GPA in the major area of study is frequently considered the top priority. A close second is the applicant's extracurricular activities or work experiences, either for pay or nonpay. Experiences or activities related to the field of study are valued higher than unrelated efforts. Those applicants with the highest GPAs and the most directly related experiences are consistently selected to interview.

A Professional Recruiter

Table 7.2 Where the Jobs Are

It is hard to believe, but despite dire predictions of teacher shortages, apparently no one has collected state-by-state or district-by-district statistics on supply and demand.

The availability of teaching positions across the country varies considerably by location and by teaching field. There is widespread demand for teachers in the sciences, mathematics, computer science, and special and bilingual education. Minority teachers are desperately needed, especially as enrollment of minority children continues to grow.

The table below shows teacher supply and demand, by regions of the country and by field, based on a survey of teacher placement officers. Keep in mind that there can be wide disparities among the states within a region, as well as among districts within each state.

FIELD	Alaska	Hawaii	REGION									NATIONAL 1990
			1	2	3	4	5	6	7	8	9	
Agriculture	2.00	4.00	3.50	3.00	2.75	2.77	2.00	2.77	3.54	4.00	—	3.03
Art	2.00	1.00	1.25	2.28	2.00	2.52	2.05	2.48	2.18	2.00	1.86	1.96
Bilingual Education	4.00	4.00	4.13	4.79	4.75	4.36	4.76	4.00	4.50	4.53	4.00	4.35
Business	3.00	4.00	2.75	2.46	2.60	2.62	2.44	4.05	2.51	3.30	4.00	3.07
Computer Science	4.00	4.00	3.66	3.45	4.00	3.83	3.66	4.16	3.73	3.56	4.17	3.84
Elementary–Primary	5.00	2.00	3.14	3.26	2.57	2.16	3.40	3.48	1.80	2.26	2.08	2.83
Elem.–Intermediate	5.00	2.00	3.14	3.20	2.77	2.22	3.25	3.38	1.84	2.13	2.00	2.81
English	5.00	5.00	3.37	3.00	3.10	2.80	2.90	3.07	2.51	2.84	2.45	3.28
ESL	4.00	4.00	3.16	4.44	4.80	4.23	4.00	3.73	3.89	4.18	3.66	4.00
Home Economics	4.00	4.00	1.66	2.30	2.00	2.23	2.55	3.05	2.04	2.75	3.00	2.69
Industrial Arts	4.00	5.00	3.00	3.00	2.16	2.41	3.33	3.09	3.00	3.20	3.33	3.23
Language–Spanish	4.00	3.00	3.57	3.66	4.25	3.55	3.53	4.04	3.59	3.37	4.86	3.76
Language–Other	4.00	3.00	3.00	3.28	3.75	3.40	3.62	3.64	3.71	3.16	3.00	3.41
Library Science	5.00	5.00	3.20	4.14	3.00	3.78	3.70	3.35	3.89	3.33	3.00	3.76
Mathematics	4.00	5.00	3.37	4.35	3.37	3.61	4.10	4.21	3.71	3.71	3.54	3.91

Musical–Instrumental	5.00	2.00	3.88	3.25	3.43	3.57	3.16	3.15	2.79	2.52	2.75	3.23
Music–Vocal	5.00	2.00	4.12	3.06	3.00	3.57	2.55	2.86	2.75	2.65	2.75	3.12
Physical Education	2.00	1.00	1.43	2.27	1.43	1.41	1.94	2.05	1.56	1.70	2.14	1.72
Science–Biology	4.00	2.00	2.75	3.60	2.66	3.12	3.60	3.78	3.29	3.13	3.00	3.17
Science–Chemistry	4.00	4.00	3.37	3.66	3.66	3.70	3.80	3.72	3.74	2.97	3.20	3.62
Science–Earth	2.00	3.00	3.12	3.60	2.62	3.24	3.68	3.81	3.20	3.25	3.14	3.15
Science–General	4.00	3.00	3.11	3.46	2.50	3.18	3.44	3.71	3.32	3.17	3.00	3.26
Science–Physics	4.00	4.00	3.71	4.10	3.70	3.95	4.05	4.37	3.77	3.89	3.66	3.93
Science–Other Areas	3.00	4.00	3.25	3.44	2.50	3.23	3.66	3.86	3.39	3.60	3.00	3.36
Social Sciences	2.00	1.00	1.43	3.26	1.44	1.54	2.17	2.08	1.73	2.03	2.10	1.89
School Social Worker	4.00	3.00	2.83	3.33	3.50	2.82	2.50	3.08	2.90	2.00	3.00	2.99
Spec. Ed.–LD	5.00	5.00	4.66	4.33	4.66	4.43	4.46	4.54	4.23	4.05	4.00	4.49
Spec. Ed.–Ment. Hand.	5.00	5.00	4.75	4.35	4.66	4.19	4.63	4.52	4.10	4.10	4.00	4.48
Spec. Ed.–Multi. Hand.	5.00	4.00	4.75	4.50	4.83	4.25	4.54	4.47	3.88	4.05	4.00	4.39
Spec. Ed.–Reading	5.00	3.00	4.00	3.13	3.66	3.19	3.93	3.77	3.27	3.32	2.80	3.55

5 = considerable shortage   4 = some shortage   3 = balanced   2 = some surplus   1 = considerable surplus

Region 1: Idaho, Oregon, Washington **2:** Arizona, California, Nevada, Utah **3:** Colorado, Montana, New Mexico, Wyoming **4:** Iowa, Kansas, Minnesota, Missouri, Nebraska, North Dakota, South Dakota **5:** Arkansas, Louisiana, Oklahoma, Texas **6:** Alabama, Florida, Georgia, Kentucky, Mississippi, North Carolina, South Carolina, Tennessee, Virginia, West Virginia **7:** Illinois, Indiana, Michigan, Ohio, Wisconsin **8:** Delaware, District of Columbia, Maryland, New Jersey, New York, Pennsylvania **9:** Connecticut, Maine, Massachusetts, New Hampshire, Rhode Island, Vermont

Source: Association for School, College, and University Staffing, Inc.

Knowledge of the subject matter you intend to teach is indicated by the grades you receive. You cannot expect to teach others what you do not know. This is equally important for your majors, minors, electives, and general education courses. Do you really care enough to get the highest grade you possibly can, or are you content to settle for an average grade?

Dedication to the profession is evidenced in many ways. One of them is the record of your student-teaching performance and evaluation. This is critical. Did your supervisors indicate that you gave a 100 percent effort, or did you exhibit a cavalier attitude? Such qualities as professionalism, attendance, stamina, flexibility, teacher-student rapport, knowledge of subject matter content, cooperation, teaching skills and behaviors, and dedication are recorded in this report. The quality of your student-teaching experience serves as a very important marketability asset. Employers weigh this very carefully.

The personal experiences you have are an important part of your teaching portfolio. These experiences do not have to be grandiose in order to be pertinent. Spending a summer backpacking through Europe can be very exciting for you. How can this qualify as an employment asset? If you take a large number of quality slides that comprise a good tape-slide presentation, if you have a number of representative artifacts, mementos, pamphlets, and maps that could enrich your social studies curriculum, then this personal experience becomes an asset.

Other personal experiences contribute toward making you a well-rounded teacher candidate. Traditionally, persons who are considering the teaching profession gravitate toward activities that provide direct interaction with children and teens. These activities are volunteer as well as paid positions and may include any number of possibilities, such as working at a day-care center or nursery school, as a playground supervisor with the parks and recreation department, as a summer camp counselor, as a Boy Scouts or Campfire Girls leader, as a church youth group leader or Sunday school teacher, with a civic theater group, in a summer school, with sports teams, as a YMCA or YWCA leader, as a piano or guitar teacher, and almost any other involvement with children.

These experiences are beneficial for the community at large—interested persons are willing to accept the challenge and the responsibility. They provide opportunities for you to actually work with children and youth in the age range of the students you someday hope to teach. These experiences also enable you to make preliminary decisions such as:

1. Is this the age group I really like?
2. Does this age child relate well to me and vice versa?
3. Can I successfully interact with these individuals for long periods of time, six or seven hours a day?
4. How are my large-group management skills?
5. Am I more comfortable on a one-to-one basis?

6. Is the social aspect of this experience more important and satisfying to me than the responsibilities (goal completion, skills development, planning) aspect?

Another benefit of these experiences is that if one type of activity or group is not successful, you can always try another. Each activity enables you to build a background of management, supervision, and interaction skills. Each provides a number of potentially valuable preeducation opportunities.

The training you receive at the university is critical in preparing you for a teaching career. The courses that are required, your choice of majors and minors, and your choice of elective courses all play a significant role in the type of teacher you will become.

Required courses are determined by the state's Department of Education and implemented by the university or college. Your choice of certifiable majors and minors are approved by your advisor and/or department head. What about the elective courses you choose? As an elementary teacher candidate, did you take Youth in the Juvenile Justice System (of general interest but probably minimally related to elementary classroom teaching), or did you select Advanced Reading Methods (very pertinent)? As a secondary teacher candidate, did you take an elective course on how to play golf (a good personal recreation course, but not applicable to your teaching), or a course in multicultural awareness to help you work with the diversity of students in your future classes? These are examples of your training that you control.

Course selections that relate most directly to the subject matter content and/or the students you will be teaching reflect positively on your professionalism. Training experiences such as teaching piano lessons relate directly to the skills you will need to teach elementary or secondary music. Such things as planning, evaluating, time commitment, self-improvement, sharing knowledge and skills, coordinating programs, and other skills are indicative of your ability to teach someone else what you know. Other training experiences you have are also beneficial.

Extracurricular Activities

Participation in extracurricular activities is another important part of the college experience. These activities benefit the community, the university, and the participants in a variety of ways. Participation in extracurricular activities indicates various qualities you have:

- Special interests and talents
- Willingness to participate and contribute
- Special skills
- Ability as a team player

Extracurricular activities are also important.

- Human relations and social skills
- Attitude
- Motivation and energy
- Time management ability

Your participation in some select extracurricular activities is another indication that you are a well-rounded individual. Extracurricular activities are vehicles for receiving special honors and awards in addition to your scholarship endeavors. These activities may relate directly to your chosen career field. For example, working on the campus newspaper, radio station, or yearbook staff gives very valuable practical experience if you intend to teach communications skills or journalism at the secondary level. Extracurricular activities add another dimension to your teaching portfolio.

Discovering Elementary and Secondary Education

Because you are interested in education as a career field, this book and other personal investigations are designed to help you make decisions about your future. Which level of education attracts you the most? Perhaps you are not

■ **Short Shot**

> I have been teaching the elementary grades for more than 20 years. As a
> student in elementary and high school, I really enjoyed studying geogra-
> phy and history. I had strong reading, spelling, and writing skills as well. I
> decided to major in social sciences and minor in English. Both of these
> have proven to be good choices for me. It seems as though I teach lan-
> guage arts all day; reading, spelling, language, writing and speaking occur
> in every curriculum area, first through sixth grades. I am very pleased with
> my choices for the major and minor.
>
> *A First-Grade Teacher*

really sure if elementary or secondary is the better choice. In addition to
making subject matter choices, you need to determine if you want to teach
elementary or secondary students. Let's examine what is special and perhaps
unique about each level.

Elementary Education

The elementary school experience for most people brings memories that are
happy and pleasant. These strong, positive memories are very important, especially if you are considering becoming an elementary teacher. The many
joyful stages of development that young children experience are exciting and
very rewarding for adults to observe, guide, and share. Stage development is
one of the crucial factors that lead certain individuals toward elementary education.

Some states provide elementary teachers with a choice of certifications:
(1) early childhood, nursery school through grade 2; (2) elementary, grades 3
through 8; and (3) elementary, grades 1 through 6.

The college preparation of elementary education majors is special. At
one midwestern university, elementary education majors must complete a
minimum of 137 hours to graduate and qualify for a teaching license. The
majors and minors selected by elementary candidates are special in the sense
that they must be relevant to what is actually taught in the elementary grades,
as well as to the mental development of the students. Some possible major
fields could include bilingual education, math, language arts, science, social
studies, music, art, physical education, library science, reading, psychology,
physical science, family life and sex education, earth science, and many others. Minors are also available in most of these areas. A major field will usually
require 30 to 36 semester hours, and a minor field 18 to 24 semester hours.

The professional education of elementary teachers includes the student-
teaching experience as well as a combination of other education courses.
These courses may include an introduction to teaching, the education of

young children, elementary math, reading, science and social studies education/methods, learning and evaluation, social foundations of American education, remedial reading, and elementary seminars. Combined with student teaching, these could require as many as 30 or more hours of coursework. Elementary teachers must also exhibit specific competencies, such as written and oral language or math proficiency, which are determined through various teacher testing programs. Other specialized studies and curricular requirements are part of teacher education programs.

The teaching conditions for elementary teachers are unique. A large percentage of elementary schools follow the self-contained classroom management and organization plan. This means that if you decide to teach fourth grade, you will be in the classroom virtually all day with about 26 boys and girls all approximately the same age. Accepting, enjoying, and tolerating the various behaviors of typical fourth-graders becomes very important! At some point, many elementary teachers feel very confined. This is due to the fact that they are in the classroom almost the entire duty day—and so are the children! Can you picture yourself in this situation?

Elementary teachers do have some mobility. They are usually certified to teach grades 1 through 6, and have the option of adding the kindergarten endorsement to their credentials. This enables them to change grade levels when the opportunity arises. A teacher may teach first grade for a number of years, then move to an upper grade for a totally different instructional opportunity. The possibility of changing grade levels is an important option to remember.

Elementary teachers have many responsibilities, both in and outside of the classroom. In class, they are responsible for teaching all of the curriculum areas, not just the areas of one's major and minor. They are indeed specialists in many fields. They are management experts, managing and organizing a variety of personality types, student abilities, and classroom schedules. Outside of the normal duty day, elementary teachers are responsible for attending a variety of school functions, such as the monthly PTA meeting, fund-raising events, school programs (the Christmas program, music performances, curriculum fairs), parent-teacher conferences, the carnival, student plays, and other events.

The personal rewards of elementary teachers are very special. Being closely associated with a group of students all year, watching them make great educational and personal strides under your direction, is very satisfying. Almost nothing can compare to this sense of pride and achievement! At the end of the year, teachers are tired but the feeling and the evidence that "I really made a difference in that student's life" is truly incredible.

Teaching effort and student growth are irrevocably intertwined. There are lasting rewards associated with your relationship with colleagues. The teacher next door, the master teacher who welcomed you the first day, and many others affect you in a number of ways. You will feel special when you take a graduate course or a workshop that gives you workable, tangible ideas

■ **People in Education**
Ned Flanders

In 1960, Ned Flanders developed a basic teaching model called a *social-interaction model.* This model focuses on the verbal interactions (statements) between the teacher and the students, as well as periods of silence. Flanders categorizes the statements into 10 areas. In a later study, the classifications were expanded to include nonverbal activities as well.

The interaction model attempts to establish the relationship between teacher influence and student dependence and achievement. The composite scores of teacher talk and student talk indicate a teacher-centered or a student-centered learning atmosphere. Basic concepts of this teaching model are used in interaction analysis seminars and workshops for staff development.

that you can use in your classroom with your students. The college preparations, the unique teaching conditions, and other personal rewards are some of the things that are special about elementary education.

Secondary Education

The secondary experience is in the recent past for many college students. The memories of extracurricular activities, the various courses you took, the opportunity to be instructed by a large number of teachers, meeting new friends from other schools, and other events are special reasons to consider becoming a secondary-level teacher. Other things, such as wanting to work with older students, wanting to teach only one or two subjects, teaching a different group of students each period, and having opportunities to coach or advise extracurricular activities, are part of a secondary teacher's experience.

The college preparation of a secondary teacher is special, and in many ways quite different than that of elementary teachers. Secondary teachers can teach only in the areas for which they are certified—usually the areas of the major and minor. If a teacher has a major in social studies and a minor in math, he or she cannot legally or ethically teach French or home economics. Also, that individual cannot move into the elementary school and teach, although social studies and math are part of the elementary curriculum, unless he or she goes back to school and becomes recertified. Certification for elementary and secondary teaching is entirely different.

The classes typically offered at the average secondary school are the areas from which certifiable majors and minors can be selected. Some possible major areas of study could include speech and theater, political science, foreign languages, math, earth science, art, and music (including vocal performance, instrumental, and music theory). Some areas for a minor are health education, distributive education, business, chemistry, journalism, and many others. Remember—these are only partial lists.

The professional education of secondary teachers may include such courses as an introduction to teaching, psychological foundations, social foundations, improving reading skills of secondary students, a media course, seminar in education, clinical experiences, and student teaching. Competency requirements in math and language are necessary in many states.

The effects of technology in the workplace and in our private lives are impacting our educational systems. The result is that courses in computer science are becoming a standard for graduation from many universities. There is increasing demand for secondary students to be computer literate. Their teachers must be capable of using and teaching the new technological media.

Secondary student-teaching requirements are variable. One university may require 16 weeks of full-time teaching, 8 weeks in the major and 8 weeks in the minor areas of study. Another university may require 10 weeks (National Council of Accreditation for Teacher Education requirement) wherein both the major and the minor are taught simultaneously. Because NCATE standards are changing, universities are also changing to meet the new standards. Whichever university you attend, you can expect to student teach in both the major and minor areas.

The teaching conditions of a typical secondary teacher are quite different from those of an elementary teacher. Instructing older students enables you to converse with a higher level of interaction. Directions, lecture material, demonstrations, subject matter content, and other factors related to instruction are more sophisticated and mature. This instructional-level issue is important. It is very difficult to determine the instructional level of many elementary learners (what do they already know, where does teaching begin?) and then teach at an appropriate level.

Secondary education offers teachers mobility during the average school day. For example, the business education teacher may teach Typing I in the typing room, Shorthand II in a regular classroom, Introduction to Computers in the computer lab, then supervise a study hall, and then coordinate students in the work-study program in the afternoon. Flexibility is necessary, but having the opportunity to change locations and environments during the day can be good for your mental health. Another type of mobility is the opportunity to teach in major and minor areas with students of different ages. Government, history, and geography at the ninth, tenth, and twelfth grades are all unique.

Secondary teachers have instructional as well as supplemental responsibilities. Supplementary responsibilities enable teachers to interact with students in different situations, oftentimes out of the classroom. These include

Secondary teachers specialize in one or two areas.

supervising study halls, being a member of the student support team, coaching, advising, monitoring the cafeteria, sponsoring an at-risk student on a work-study program, tutoring, chaperoning social events, and other activities. Secondary teachers can expect to perform a number of these supplementary duties in any given school term.

The relationship with students can be very special. The spirit, positive attitudes, energy, vitality, and other characteristics of secondary students are very refreshing to the adults who work with them. The academic progress they make is very motivational for teachers. These students are very close to moving into the workplace or into higher education. They are making course decisions and career-track decisions. Teachers and counselors assist them and guide them into areas where they can perform successfully and gain personal satisfaction. When good decisions are made and things proceed smoothly, everyone feels good!

There is a great deal of satisfaction when you watch your students proceed successfully through the system. It is very gratifying when students come back after graduation, often years later, and tell you about their lives. The rewards of secondary education do not stop after a particular student leaves your class.

A typical secondary school is divided into various departments, such as the math department (grades 9 through 12), social studies, language arts, and

■ **Short Shot** _____

If you do not obtain a full-time teaching contract soon after your graduation, it is advisable to apply for substitute teaching in a number of school districts. Submit a letter of application with all of your credentials to the personnel director. School districts frequently conduct seminars or workshops for all potential substitute teachers to familiarize them with expectations, procedures, requirements, and policies. Your attendance at these meetings indicates your sincerity and willingness to work. This is very important for daily substitute teachers as well as long-term (a month or more) substitutes.

so on. Whichever subject(s) you teach, you will be a member of that department. Department members usually work together on scheduling, staff development, extracurricular duties, workshops, meetings, and other professional responsibilities. When the school district sponsors a science fair, for example, the members of the science department have a large job to plan, direct, organize, and evaluate the event. Department members become very close on a personal as well as a professional basis.

There are many special things associated with teaching at the secondary level. This discussion has been a representative sampling of the reasons why you may choose to teach at the secondary level.

■ Summary

Becoming a marketable, employable new teacher is a big task. Can I get a job? This is certainly an important consideration to every potential teacher education candidate. It would be a tragedy to complete a four-year degree program with a teaching license and then discover your credentials do not qualify you for a teaching position. It is necessary to have the best education, experiences, training, knowledge, realistic goals, and other credentials to help you acquire the teaching position you want.

It is not too early to begin preparing yourself for employment as a teacher. Selecting a reputable teacher education institution is an important initial step. Investigating the estimated population reports, student enrollments, and professional staff projections for your particular state or desired geographical area is encouraged. It is also helpful to make visits to a variety of elementary and secondary schools to observe firsthand how they operate, what students do, and what teachers do during an average day. This will add considerably to your knowledge of what is special about elementary and secondary education.

■ The Workshop

Activity I

Special qualities are necessary for effective teachers. What special qualities do you have now, and which ones do you need to develop? If you are to develop them, you need to know what they are! In a small group, make a list of special qualities you think a teacher needs. It is not egotistical to admit "I am strong in this area," nor is it negative to admit "I really need to work on that area." After you have completed the list, at the side of each item list some things you can do to improve in that area. This type of activity will prepare you for teacher evaluation procedures that occur during student teaching and when you are a contracted teacher.

Activity II

It is agreed that some majors and minors are more in demand than others. By this time you probably have some ideas regarding majors and minors that you would like to investigate further. This activity may require some additional research. You are to do the following:

1. Choose a major and minor that you think you may pursue. Make your selection based on genuine interest, not on apparent demand.
2. Investigate this major and minor combination.
3. Write a one- or two-page position paper to defend this choice of a major and minor combination.
4. Submit your paper to the instructor.

■ Questions and Thoughts

1. Is it advisable to become certified for both elementary and secondary education? What are the advantages and disadvantages for holding licenses in both levels for special education, music, or physical education? Would it require longer than the normal four years of university study? Discuss the ramifications of this situation.
2. What is a typical teacher interview? Are there any specific strategies for obtaining an initial interview? Discuss ethics, etiquette, portfolio preparation, and your questioning strategies.
3. What is *usually* the determining factor that decides if a person chooses elementary or secondary education?
4. Not every new teacher will obtain a full-time teaching position the first year after graduation. In these cases, it is advisable to get on a number of substitute teaching lists with various school districts. Substitute teaching provides opportunities to teach a variety of grade levels. It enables prin-

cipals and administrators to watch you teach; they do this to screen potential new hires. Positions do become available during the year. Good substitute teachers are always in demand.

▪ Readings and References

Campbell, E. (1990, January). "Middle School Kids." *Middle School Journal, 21:* 39.

Doe, B. (1990). "Why Incentive Payments Do Not Ease Shortages." *The Time Educational Supplement, 3839* (January 26): 15.

Nicklos, L. B., and Brown, L. S. (1989, December). "Recruiting Minority Teachers." *Education Digest, 55:* 28–31.

Phi Delta Kappan, 70 (June 1989): 771–776.

Short, P. M., and Short, R. J. (1988). "Perceived Classroom Environment and Student Behavior in Secondary Schools." *Educational Research Quarterly, 12,* no. 3: 35–39.

Young, M. W. (1989–90, Winter). "Characteristics of High Potential and At Risk Teachers." *Action in Teacher Education, 11:* 35–40.

Chapter Eight

Looking
Ahead

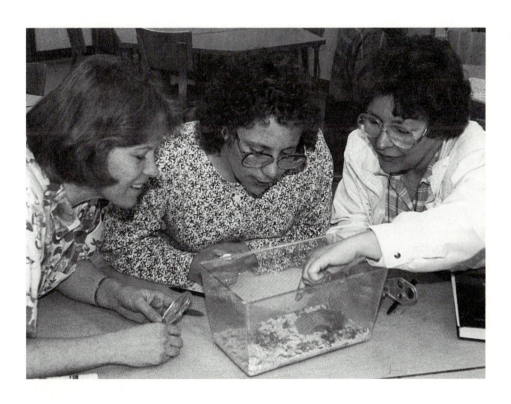

■ Definitions

Accountability: This refers to all the professional responsibilities and duties teachers are required to perform. You are accountable for what you do or fail to do as a teacher.

Cause: This is a legal term that refers to the grounds for action (dismissal of a teacher) that must be settled in court. Cause for termination of the teaching contract could be for immorality, incompetence, or insubordination.

Consolidation: Finances, student populations, demographics, teacher shortages, and other important factors cause school districts to join together, or consolidate, in order to continue to provide educational services.

Continuing Education Units: Commonly called CEUs, these are the credits required of teachers by school districts to maintain their proficiency and tenure. Some states also require CEUs to maintain certification. They may be obtained by additional university coursework, workshops, in-service programs, or other preapproved activities.

Due Process: This is the method of determining one's guilt or innocence in a court of law. It usually refers to the steps that must be followed if a teacher is to be terminated.

■ Focus Questions

1. What is *certification*? Why is it important? How do you get it?
2. Can you lose your certificate? How and under what circumstance? What are your rights?
3. What are professional organizations? Which ones should you join?
4. What are your rights and responsibilities? How are your rights protected? Who are you responsible to?
5. If you want to go out of state to teach, what should you do?

■ Introduction

Up to now, you have been concerned with what a teacher does and how to become one. We will look ahead for a change of pace. Three or four years from now may seem like a long time, but if you look back at the past four years and how quickly they have passed, you can see the need for planning ahead. You want to be ready when the time comes for you to enter the job market.

Think ahead to the time when you have fulfilled all of the university requirements and are ready to enter teaching as a qualified professional. We are sure that you have many questions and concerns. In this chapter, we will try to answer some of the more common concerns that teacher candidates ask as they look to the future.

▪ ▪ ▪

Becoming Certified

To become certified, you must first meet your state requirements (discussed in Chapter Six). Your university degree program should be designed so that you can meet the curriculum requirements. Other requirements, such as meeting a minimum grade-point average (GPA), letters of recommendation, affirming a teacher's oath, and passing a qualifying or exit examination, may be required in your state. These requirements are listed in your college bulletin. Do not hesitate to contact an advisor to be sure that you know all of the requirements.

It is very helpful to make a list and check each item as you complete it. This avoids nasty surprises when you make a final audit before graduation. Imagine finding out that you missed some detail that causes you to remain in school for another semester. An advisor's nightmare is a senior who has never read the bulletin or contacted an advisor, but has relied on information from friends who are in the teacher education program. Go to an advisor, make a checklist, and complete the requirements as they come due.

After you meet the requirements for certification, you must apply in some manner to your state certification agency for your teaching certificate. You do not automatically receive certification when you graduate. Most colleges and universities will extend varying amounts of help. Some will automatically process your application and submit it when you complete all of your requirements, whereas others may require the completion of the necessary forms as a part of your application for graduation packet. Some states require *the university* to submit verification of your completion of requirements, whereas other states require that *you personally* submit the request for certification as well as a transcript and/or other verification information.

There are 50 states and therefore 50 different ways of handling this process. Learn the procedure for your school by reading the catalog or asking an advisor. Do be aware that many states have application fees that must be paid before they will process your application. Your school may do most of the work for you, but it is your responsibility to have all of the required information and necessary fees submitted so the office personnel can do their work. In the final analysis, it is your responsibility to see that your application for certification is processed and sent to the appropriate certification office. Figure 8.1 shows you the factors encountered in becoming a professional teacher and in maintaining your certification.

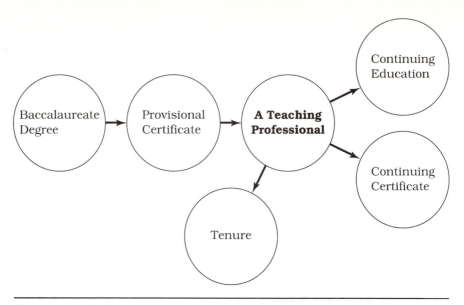

Figure 8.1 **The Teaching Professional**

Maintaining Certification

Very few states issue permanent certificates. The general practice is to issue a provisional certification that must be upgraded to a continuing certification by completion of specific requirements. Some states initially issue a continuing certificate, which are usually in effect as long as the holder is actively teaching and meets stated requirements. An example from a specific state may help you see how this works.

In Michigan, you would receive a provisional certificate that is good for 5 years. During this time, you are expected to complete 3 years of successful teaching and 18 semester hours of coursework appropriate to your teaching assignment. If you do not complete the 3 years of successful teaching or the 18 hours, you can request an extension of your provisional certification. Upon completion of the requirements, you can apply for a continuing certificate. This certificate remains in effect as long as you continue to teach and obtain 6 Continuing Education Units (CEUs) every 5 years. These credits may be obtained by taking appropriate college courses, by attending approved workshops or in-service programs, or by completing other preapproved activities.

Many states now require that you do appropriate work to maintain your proficiency in order to maintain your certification, and many more states are joining this trend. The number of CEUs required, the way they are determined, the types of activities that are acceptable, and the time frame may vary from state to state, but the purpose is the same: to require teachers to refresh their skills and upgrade their knowledge. You will be responsible for applying for your continuing certification and for fulfilling all of the requirements to do so. No one will contact you and ask you to get your paperwork in or to take courses to maintain your certification.

One other topic should be mentioned at this time—substitute teaching. You may do a little or a lot of substitute teaching before you get a regular full-time teaching position. How will this count toward your 3 years of successful teaching? First of all, substitute teaching is not the same as regular teaching, but most states allow you to apply it toward your continuing certificate. However, the total days must add up to a predetermined number of days, usually well over 100, for you to receive credit for the entire year. You are responsible for the documentation of your experience.

Professional Organizations

Every profession has an organization created by the members to serve their own needs and interests; teaching is no exception. The teaching profession is unique in that it has so many different organizations available. For convenience, we will divide professional organizations into two groups, which we call *teacher organizations* and *subject organizations*.

Teacher Organizations

These organizations are concerned with the teaching profession and the people in it. The two major national organizations are the American Federation of Teachers (AFT) and the National Education Association (NEA). You will probably be a member of one of these organizations. The AFT is a teachers' union devoted to the welfare and well-being of teachers. Albert Shanker has been the leader for many years and the AFT has developed under his leadership into a strong unit that represents teachers in contract negotiations, grievances, and job security. If you teach in a school system where the

---

■ People in Education

Albert Shanker

Albert Shanker is a very vocal supporter of teachers and the teaching profession. He has been the president of the American Federation of Teachers for 25 years. As president, he has vigorously represented teacher needs through the process of collective bargaining. Salaries, benefits, retirement, and other issues are primary concerns of the AFT.

AFT is the bargaining unit or local union affiliation, you will be expected or even required to join.

The NEA has a much larger membership than the AFT and has been in existence longer. The original purpose of the NEA was to be an organization for teachers, promoting such things as ethics, proper training, and good teaching. It has become more militant in the past several decades, especially through the state and local affiliates.

Every state has a professional teachers' organization that is affiliated with the NEA, and almost all school districts (except those that are affiliated with the AFT) have a local unit of the state organization. For example, a teacher might be a member of the Clare Education Association (CEA), the Michigan Education Association (MEA), and the National Education Association (NEA).

Your local and state organizations are usually concerned with teacher welfare. They negotiate contracts, lobby for better support of schools, and engage in other similar activities in an effort to make teaching a more attractive profession and to make schools better. You will probably be expected to join all three organizations when you start teaching. This is known as a *unified membership.*

Subject Organizations

Almost every subject matter area has an organization devoted to the improvement of teaching the subject. Some examples of these subject organizations are:

National Science Teachers Association (NSTA)
National Council for the Social Studies (NCSS)
National Council of Teachers of Mathematics (NCTM)
International Reading Council (IRC)

There are also state chapters of each of these organizations. You may be more interested in your state chapter than in the national, as the meetings are closer to home and may be more oriented to your specific needs. Both state and national organizations hold annual conventions or conferences that provide workshops, material displays, and speakers.

If you go to a convention or conference, you can attend workshops covering a wide variety of topics, ranging from new teaching methods, to current research, to new products. Material displays will have all the latest textbooks and teaching materials for you to see and, in many cases, to purchase. You can talk to the sales representatives who want to explain the materials and how to use them; you may even meet some of the authors. Speakers talk on new technology, current trends, or new methodology, and they are the pep leaders of the conference. After attending a conference, you will come back to work full of new ideas and an eagerness to use them in your own classroom.

There is a professional organization for almost every curriculum area.

National organizations usually publish a magazine that you will receive as a part of your membership. They may also send you teaching tips, current research notes, and other related materials.

Joining Professional Organizations

It is beneficial to join professional organizations, but be selective. Very few people can afford the dues for all of the organizations and no one has the time to participate fully in more than a few. First of all, you will be expected or even required to join one of the teachers organizations. Which one will be determined by the school in which you teach. When you join, be active. You then have a say in your profession and possibly in your teaching conditions.

Deciding which subject organization to join is not always an easy task. You may talk to other teachers to find out which organizations are more active in your area. You may want to join a large, active group because it can offer good conferences and lots of ideas. On the other hand, you may want to join a small, but growing group so that you can be a part of the growth. Most likely, though, you will select the organization that represents your favorite subject areas or your major or minor. No matter what your reason for joining, plan to be active. Go to the conferences, meet other teachers, become a presenter or even an officer. You pay your dues to become a part of the organization, so take advantage of the opportunity to really be a part of it. The more you contribute, the more you get in return.

One last note: You do not have to wait until you graduate and get a teaching job to join a professional organization. Almost all have student memberships at a reduced rate, which entitles you to receive publications and attend conferences. It is a good way to become acquainted with the organization of your choice.

Tenure

Tenure is a term used to denote continuing employment. Once you gain tenure, you cannot be terminated (fired) without cause and due process. This does not mean you cannot be fired for incompetence, failure to do your job, or other compelling reasons, but it does give you protection from frivolous or capricious termination. For example, your employer cannot terminate you because you can be replaced by someone else for less money.

Not all states have a tenure program. Some have continuing contracts, which allow you to continue teaching from year to year. These contracts are very similar to tenure, but without all of the protections of tenure. Teacher unions and organizations take a strong stand against this practice. Teachers in private and parochial schools usually do not have tenure protection.

Tenure is not an automatic right. You must earn it by being a competent teacher. When you sign a contract with a school system, you are a probationary teacher. You will be observed and evaluated according to school or contractual procedures. If you are not doing a satisfactory job, you can be terminated at the end of the year. If you are doing satisfactory work, then you will continue to work there and will again be observed and evaluated periodically. Usually at the end of the second year (this varies from state to state) the tenure decision is made. At this time, one of three actions will be taken by your employer.

1. You will be terminated if you are not performing well and show no signs of improving.
2. Your probation will be extended if you are weak, but improving. Your employer is giving you one last chance.
3. You are granted tenure. You have proven yourself and your employer thinks you will be a long-term asset to the school.

There are two very important things to remember. First, during your probationary period you will be observed and evaluated. Listen to your critiques and ask for help if needed. Work on your weaknesses. You are a new teacher and still have much to learn. Pick out those whom you consider to be the best teachers and talk to them and observe their teaching. They want you to succeed and will give you all the help they can, but you must make the effort to ask and to learn.

Second, once you gain tenure you cannot relax. You must continue to learn and be the best teacher you can be. In granting tenure, your employer took a chance on you, betting that you would prove to be a valuable asset in the years to come. It is up to you to prove that your employer's faith in you is justified.

Professional Rights and Responsibilities

This is a difficult topic to address in a concise manner because there are so many aspects of professionalism. Almost every teacher and subject organization has a code of ethics or a statement on teacher rights and responsibilities. In general, you might say that a teacher has a right to be treated as a professional, with the respect and confidence that goes with the title. You have the right to determine the best ways to teach your students; to be free of undue pressures from parents, administration, and other teachers; and to participate in the development of curriculum and selection of textbooks and materials.

On the other hand, you also have responsibilities.

1. You are responsible for providing the best possible learning experiences for every student in your classroom. You cannot be selective, teaching only those you like or those who learn easily. Every student is teachable and your duty is to teach.

During a new teachers' meeting, the building principal explains and discusses your professional rights and responsibilities.

2. Teach everything that is required. This is most clearly applicable in the self-contained classroom. You cannot neglect any subject just because you consider it unimportant or you do not like it. You were hired to teach everything.

3. Continue your education to remain competent. You need to attend workshops, take courses, and read outside materials if you are to remain current.

4. Provide a positive role model. The students and the community look to you as an example. Your dress, manners, moral conduct, attitude, values, and personal conduct are always being observed and oftentimes imitated by the people you serve.

5. You are part of the teaching team and are obligated to help the school run smoothly, provide leadership when needed, help new or weaker teachers to grow, and participate in school functions.

6. Observe confidentiality. You will have access to records and sensitive information. This information is to be shared only with those who *need or are entitled* to know. Discussing grades or family history with a special teacher, counselor, or principal in an effort to develop an appropriate plan of action is acceptable. Telling a parent or student about another student's private data is not acceptable.

7. Avoid idle gossip about students. If you discuss a child with another teacher in a positive way, seeking help for that student, you are acting in a professional manner. If you discuss a student in a negative way, labeling or degrading him or her, you are not acting in a professional manner.

In summation, you must be a professional person if you expect to be treated as one. Ethical behavior is a must. Do the best you can and cause no harm.

Teacher Accountability

Parents want the best for their children and are becoming more insistent on good teaching. Table 8.1 shows five types of teacher accountability. One way they can improve the quality of instruction is by having their legislatures or certifying agencies institute teacher testing programs.

You may find that you must take and pass a state examination to get into the teacher education program, and another before you can be certified. Other states are requiring teachers to take and pass examinations to maintain their certification. One of the more notable examples of this is the TECAT (Texas Examination of Current Administrators and Teachers) exam given in Texas since 1986. Every teacher, regardless of tenure, number of years teaching, and college degrees, is required to take the exam. A retake is offered to those who fail the exam, but failure to pass the exam results in revocation of certification and subsequent loss of job. All new teachers, from in

Table 8.1 A Ladder of Teacher Accountability

ACCOUNTABILITY	TO WHOM	RESULTS
Personal	Self	Self-satisfaction
Instructional	Students	Students are learning
Confidential	Parents	Positive role model
Professional	Administrators	Contributing team member
Ethical	The Community	A competent professional

state or out of state, must take and pass the TECAT exam before they can teach in Texas. Many other states are adopting similar policies. If you plan to teach, plan on testing to prove your competence.

Another way that parents are assessing instruction is by the standardized test scores of students. It may not be a completely fair way to determine if you have taught or not, but it does give an indication of which teachers are doing a good job and which ones are not. Consistent low achievement by your students would seem to indicate poor performance on your part.

In summation, you must be a professional teacher if you are to be treated as one. Ethical behavior and accountability are required at all times.

Changing Jobs

Many teachers go to work in a school they like, teaching a grade level they enjoy, and remain there for their entire career. But many do not. Teachers change jobs for reasons such as better opportunities, spouse relocation, change of grade level, or to try something new or different. If you want to change jobs, there are three types of changes to be considered: job change within the same school or school system, moving to another school within the state, and moving to a different state.

Within the Building or System: This is usually a very simple matter handled by the principal when the change is within the building. There are three factors that are considered before changes are made.

1. *Need:* If you want to change but there is no vacancy where you want to go, there can be no change. You many want to teach third-grade or eleventh-grade English, but if those jobs are filled then you have to wait until a vacancy occurs. There may also be other factors that prevent the change.

2. *Qualifications:* Are you qualified for the job and do you have the necessary certification? When you graduate and receive state certification, your certification states specifically which grade levels and subjects you can teach. Elementary certification usually allows you to teach all subjects in a self-

Sometimes a teacher may want to relocate.

contained classroom for grades kindergarten to 8. Many states allow you to teach only your majors and minors in a departmentalized program.

Secondary teachers can usually teach in grades 8 to 12, but only in their majors and minors. Other areas such as special education, speech and hearing therapy, counselors, and administrators each have their own certification. If you wish to move into one of these positions, you must do extra work to obtain the proper certification.

Qualifications for the positions are also important. Many schools take the position that *certified* does not always mean *qualified*. For example, a person who has certification but has never taught in an area would not be given preference over a person who has been teaching in that area.

3. *Seniority:* Teachers who have been in the system longest are usually given preference when openings occur. Exceptions are administrative positions where different rules apply and, as stated above, when qualifications override seniority. As a new teacher, you may not be able to change jobs within the system as readily as a teacher who has seniority.

Within the State: You may want to leave your job and move to another school system in the state. Your certification is valid anywhere within the state, but you may encounter other problems. First, you must find a job. This is the same as when you looked for your first job. You will write letters, send resumés, and hopefully get an interview. Your experience may help in this process or it may not. Second, you may experience a change in pay. You may find that your new position may be in a system that pays less or will not give you credit on the pay scale for all of your past experience. You may also loose your tenure status.

In Another State: Moving to another state requires that you meet the certification standards of that state. Most states have reciprocity agreements that allow the certification from one state to be valid in another. If you move to a state that does not have reciprocity, then your transcript must be evaluated against that state's standards. This may mean additional coursework before you can teach in that state. Some states have other requirements that must be met in addition to possessing a valid teaching certificate. You may be required to take a teaching exam like the Texas TECAT, or a course in state history or government.

   If you are planning to teach out of state, get your home state certification through your university before you leave the state. Then contact the state educational agency of the new state for a listing of requirements. If you are interviewing, you can usually find out what you need to do from your interviewer. If the school is genuinely interested in you, they will help you meet the requirements.

Obtaining a Master's Degree

It is to your advantage to continue your education after you graduate. How you will do this may depend on your state requirements as well as your own personal needs. As stated earlier in this chapter, states are getting away from permanent certification and are making continuing certification dependent on continuing postgraduate work.

   You may be required to complete a master's degree, or you may be able to complete the necessary work to obtain the degree while fulfilling continuing education requirements. You may want to obtain a master's degree as a prelude to or as a part of certification in counseling or administration. You may even want to go on to a doctoral program. Many schools have a pay-incentive program that is indexed to additional hours of graduate work with an extra step for the completion of the master's degree.

   A final reason for completing a master's degree is for personal satisfaction. You may want it because it provides you with a sense of accomplishment.

   On the other hand, you may not want to get an advanced degree because it is not important to you. Perhaps you feel the additional coursework and expense are not worth your effort. The continuing education work that you do will be selected for reasons other than the dictates of a degree plan. You may want to wait until you are employed and perhaps even have tenure before you get an advanced degree. The decision to pursue a master's degree is really a very personal choice that you will make after you complete your undergraduate work and actually begin teaching.

■ Summary

In this chapter we have explored some of the questions that are often asked about the future. It is never too early to look ahead because selecting your career is a long-term decision. Becoming a teacher is only the first step; being a teacher is your life's work.

■ The Workshop

Activitiy I

Invite a principal to the class to discuss the hiring of new teachers. Ask those questions that need to be asked. Be sure that you join in the discussion. This is an opportunity to find out what is important to an administrator. If it is not possible to bring in a speaker, then you should try to go to a school and interview a principal.

Activity II

Investigate the professional organizations that are available to you as a student. You may want to join some of them for the experience as well as to have them on your resumé. First, look at the local chapters of the Student National Education Association (SNEA), the Student Council of Exceptional Children (SCEC), and any others. Now look at some of the student memberships for organizations such as NSTA, NCSS, ICR, and others. It might be feasible for you to attend a state conference of one or more of these organizations.

■ Questions and Thoughts

1. I speak fluent French. Is it necessary to take all the course requirements to obtain the foreign language minor? Can I take a test that will exempt me from a course?

2. Pursuing the master's degree requires a financial and a personal commitment. A master's degree is usually not required to maintain the teaching certificate. However, the advanced degree is an asset for a variety of professional activities that may be available to you later in your professional career.

3. What are the certification requirements for middle-school and junior high school teachers?

4 What are the advantages and disadvantages of teaching in a private school or academy? Some topics to consider are caliber of students, achievement, parental support, pay scales, benefits, morale, satisfaction, and security.

■ Readings and References

Eison, J. (1990, Winter). "Confidence in the Classroom: Ten Maxims for New Teachers." *College Teaching, 38:* 21–25.

Jandura, R. M., and Burke, P. J. (1989). "Differentiated Career Opportunities for Teachers." *Phi Delta Kappan Fastbacks, 287:* 7–26.

Lent, J. (1990, January). "Welcoming the 1990's: The Decade of the Teacher." *The Instructor, 99:* 25.

Nunnally, M. (1989, May). "Teacher Testing, Georgia Style." *Science Teacher, 56:* 30–32.

Stanley, S. J., and Popham, W. J. (Eds.). (1988). *Teacher Evaluation: Six Prescriptions for Success.* Alexandria, VA: Association for Supervision and Curriculum Development.

The Times Educational Supplement, 3810 (July 1989): 22.

■ ■ ■ **Chapter Nine**

Social Issues Affecting the Teaching Profession

■ Definitions

Abuse: A general understanding of abuse is any physical, emotional, sexual, or material condition that puts the child in immediate danger.

Accountability: This is the posture of accepting and being responsible for specific and implied professional duties.

At Risk: Students are at risk of failing to achieve academic goals when factors such as poverty, homelessness, low self-esteem, abuse, or significant emotional or behavioral problems are present.

Family Stress: Conditions such as poverty, unemployment, chemical abuse, divorce or separation, health problems, and other factors cause and contribute to family stress.

Mobility: The practice of moving from place to place, in part due to personal and economic conditions. Mobility can be a positive or a negative characteristic from a socioeconomic point of view.

Multiculturalism: This is the state or condition of incorporating numerous cultures into one pluralistic society.

■ Focus Questions

1. Why should the social issues of the day be of concern? How will they affect your classroom performance?

2. Who reports suspected child abuse? What happens if you do not report it? What can you do about it?

3. What is the difference between an abused child and a neglected child?

4. Why is multicultural education important? Who are multicultural students? What do you do with them?

5. What is *accountability*? Are you accountable, and if so, to whom and for what?

■ Introduction

Teachers of the 1990s and the beginning of the twenty-first century face many professional and personal challenges. The professional preparation of teachers (i.e., the college courses, student teaching, seminars, workshops, and other academic preparations) are integral components of quality teacher training programs. These things prepare teachers for classroom instructional responsibilities.

It would be pleasant if every teacher could begin professional service in an ideal classroom, school, or community. It is common for new teachers to visualize a classroom with energetic, bright students who eagerly await a totally positive educational experience. There are a number of social conditions and situations that make this idealized version of education an unrealistic one for some teachers and students. College and university teacher training programs prepare you for academic responsibilities, but what prepares you for the social issues, problems, challenges, and situations you will probably face as a teaching professional?

Teachers and professional organizations share a growing concern for the social issues that are affecting our students, their families, our schools, and our communities. They are equally concerned about how these issues and situations affect such things as funding policies, legislation, curriculum decisions, consolidation, test scores, teacher evaluation, and one's ability to cope on a daily basis. The news media regularly conduct white-paper investigations into the sociology of change in our society and its many effects on the family, particularly the traditional nuclear family of a mother, a father, and two or three children.

Social issues such as mobility, demographics, multicultural education, accountability, changing communities, child abuse, and neglect are some of the serious concerns shared by teachers and other professionals. Why are they so vitally concerned? They are concerned because the sociological changes that affect society in general also affect families and ultimately affect the students in our classrooms. The behaviors, attitudes, and potential academic problems teachers must deal with are manifestations of various social situations.

As a new teacher, you should be aware of some of the social issues affecting the teaching profession. This chapter will introduce you to some issues. It is not a complete course on the sociology of the twenty-first century; it serves as an informational tool, not a bandwagon.

■ ■ ■

Child Abuse and Neglect:
The School Component

It is generally agreed that today's families are under pressure from a number of sources: economic conditions, job insecurity, emotional and personal stresses, mobility, divorce and separation, the necessity for both parents to work outside the home, and many other factors. The popular image of the ideal family is one of nurturing, love, safety and intimacy (Brezina, Selengut, and Weyer, 1990, p. 253). Having a good, happy family life is the goal of most people. The numerous stresses that families endure make this ideal happy family a remote or distant possibility for many adults and their children.

Family stress manifests itself in a variety of ways; one of them is child abuse and neglect. Gelles and Strauss (1988) suggest that abusive behavior toward children is not just the action of "evil persons," but is a reaction or result of modern family structures and organizational patterns. Child abuse denotes significant harmful or life-threatening actions against children. Abusive behaviors toward children could include such things as sexual abuse, physical abuse (beatings, burns), uninhabitable living conditions, withhold-

■ Short Shot

Teachers become aware of child abuse by personal observation and direct reporting. In cases of sexual abuse, the student victim may explicitly tell the teacher what is happening, or implicitly tell the situation with leading questions such as, "Is it wrong/bad if . . . ," "What should I do if . . . ," or other statements that lead you to believe that sexual abuse may be or is probably occurring.

A student who is seeking help from an abusive situation may answer your direct question affirmatively. In such a case, you must take action immediately. A simple reassuring statement such as "I will get help" is sufficient for the time being. You are not a counselor or a psychologist, so don't attempt to counsel, analyze, investigate, or interfere in other ways.

The student's safety may be at risk, so you must respect confidentiality while you follow the procedures established by state law. It is vitally important that teachers know the correct procedures for reporting possible sexual abuse cases to the proper authorities. A minimal responsibility for most states could be: (1) verbally report the incident to the building principal and (2) make a written statement and give it to the building principal (or other designated school representative) and copy it to the police student liaison officer, sheriff, and child protection official. When the report is received, the case in handled by these officials.

ing food or medical care, or other severe conditions that place the child in immediate physical danger.

It is common for teachers to expect students to come to class mentally and physically ready to learn. Part of this readiness includes physical aspects such as getting a good night's rest, having a nutritious breakfast, being clean and dressed properly for the weather, and/or other conditions. The psychological or mental readiness includes coming to class with a positive attitude, a willingness and capability to concentrate and perform academic duties, and being free from undue stress and worry so that learning can be the top priority during school hours. A student coming to class with all of these characteristics has a definite advantage. However, there are greater numbers of students coming to class severely lacking in one or more of these areas.

Identifying Abused Children

Neglected or abused children are not difficult to identify in the classroom situation. Some very obvious clues would be visible bruises, welts, cuts, or cigarette burns or scars on the arms, legs, or head. These visible clues must be reported to the proper authorities at once, probably the building principal, the police or county sheriff, and the child protection agency (see Figure 9.1).

OBSERVE	RECORD	REPORT	ACTION
What do you see or hear?	Write specific details	Make an oral report	Officials investigate
Actions Reactions Be alert	Keep a log Record dates	Submit a written report	Families receive assistance Educational program adaptations

Figure 9.1   **Reporting Child Abuse: A Process Chart**

Behavioral clues become equally apparent to experienced professionals. Some of these include a dramatic decrease in academic performance, social withdrawal or clinging behavior (younger children), acting-out toward others, avoidance, verbal abuse, self-abuse, other antisocial behaviors.

Students who are neglected show some of the same behaviors although they may not be as severe. Neglect or abuse may be manifested by listlessness or unusual lack of energy (young children putting their heads down on the desk for long periods, staring into space, crying, showing little or no interest in play, etc.), being consistently unclean and/or improperly dressed, being hungry, showing few or no emotional reactions, being uncommunicative with adults or peers, and doing little or no schoolwork.

Neglected and abused children are at risk for failure to succeed in school. The abusive or neglectful situation in the home precludes a joyful, successful school day. Worry, stress, fear, and a negative self-image are large barriers for students to overcome and free their minds for academic learning. The school community has an obligation to report these situations and to do everything possible to access the appropriate social services for the family.

Know the Laws

In the state of Minnesota, statute 626.566 states:

> The reporting of suspected neglect, physical or sexual abuse of children in the home, school and community setting is required by the following professionals or their delegates: educators, dentists, doctors, foster parents, group home day care personnel, nurses, pharmacists, police, psychiatrists, psychiatric/clinical social workers, psychologists, social workers. . . .
>
> The public policy of this state is to protect children whose health or welfare may be jeopardized through physical abuse, neglect, or sexual abuse; to strengthen the family and make the home, school and community safe for children by promoting responsible child care in all settings; and to provide when

necessary, a safe temporary or permanent environment for physically or sexu-
ally abused children. . . .

Any person required by this act to report suspected abuse or neglect, who
willfully fails to do so, shall be guilty of a misdemeanor.

In Minnesota, reportable child abuse can be any of the following: physical
abuse, emotional abuse, material abuse, sexual abuse, or neglect. Almost all
of the other states have similar laws, and you are expected to know and
abide by them.

The Support System

Social services are available through city or county government sources, as
well as through private or church-related resources. A number of school systems have programs for students in families undergoing change (death, divorce, chemical abuse, abandonment); these programs are directed or supervised by licensed school counselors or psychologists. It is important to encourage parents to enroll their children in such programs at the earliest possible moment. Counseling and self-help groups will not eliminate the negative
situation overnight, but they may offer a temporary safety zone where students can regroup and start to function more successfully in the academic
atmosphere.

After the necessary reports have been filed and the appropriate processes are underway, the teacher must continue his or her primary responsibility, which is to teach and instruct. If the student is not removed from the

*Teachers and case workers
must work together to
protect children.*

▪ **Short Shot**_____

Child abuse and neglect are not pleasant topics of conversation for teachers, administrators, parents, neighbors, or police officials. Pleasant or unpleasant, teachers are required by law to report any and all suspected or affirmed cases of abuse.

Being aware of possible abuse is not pleasant, and neither is following the law and actually making the report. But it must be done. You are the professional and certain responsibilities are vested on you by the public sector. You will probably feel very upset, worried, anxious, and even fearful if you ever encounter an abusive situation. It is not easy; there is no question about it. Reporting abuse requires courage, commitment, and, yes, even love. Do you love this student enough to do what the law and common decency demand? Are you part of the problem (covering it up, ignoring it) or are you part of the solution (trying to get help for the student and the family)? The choice is yours.

home, and this is usually the case, he or she will probably be in class the next day. The teacher must be professional and conduct class(es) as usual, providing continuity of program for everyone. The school and classroom may be the safest, most comfortable place for this student to be at the time, so it is important that the academic situation be as normal as possible.

All students need reassurance, encouragement, and support in times of stress and uncertainty; this is especially so for abused or neglected students. A sudden or dramatic improvement in academic achievement will probably not happen, but the teacher must establish some achievable goals for the student.

A cooperative planning session with the student can result in some realistic goals. The student must know that the teacher expects him or her to do classwork and, perhaps more importantly, that the teacher has every confidence that he or she *can be successful.* The confidence and support of the teacher is very important at this time. Some adaptations or adjustments in assignments and class requirements may or may not be necessary to give the student the all-important feeling of success and accomplishment.

At-Risk Students: The New Challenge

Slavin and Madden (1989) define *a student at risk* as "one who is in danger of failing to complete his or her education with an adequate level of skills" (p. 4). Using this broad definition, at-risk students could include those with significant social and emotional problems, students in poverty, students with developmental skills that are significantly below average, students with chronic attendance problems, students in abusive families, and students who fail to progress for whatever reason. Students are at risk when they are unable to achieve academic and social goals at a rate that is consistent with their peers.

Effects and Characteristics

Some local, state, and federally funded programs have attempted to identify and remediate students who are at risk of academic failure. These early intervention programs propose to provide the necessary skills at the earliest possible moment to help students achieve; Project Head Start is a well-known example of an early intervention program. Some students are at risk before they even enter kindergarten, and some programs are geared specifically to address the academic, social, and behavioral deficiencies of three-, four-, and five-year-old children.

Students of all ages can be at risk of failing to succeed in a traditional school environment. Primary-aged children receive supplementary tutoring or instruction with programs such as Chapter I. The emphasis of many early intervention programs is to strengthen reading and math skills, because so much emphasis is placed on success in these two areas as being the benchmark of academic success.

The problem of high school dropouts is another matter of concern to parents, teachers, administrators, law enforcement officials, and potential employers. Students with poor achievement, adjustment and behavior problems, low self-esteem, and family problems are definitely at risk, not only of physically dropping out of school but of dropping out emotionally. They are at risk of being unable to lead a satisfying life outside of school as an adult, in addition to being poorly equipped to obtain satisfying employment and to maintain it over a period of years.

Academic Accommodations

Teachers, parents, administrators, school boards, and other concerned citizens realize the importance of identifying and servicing high school students who are at risk. School restructuring, new and innovative program models, differentiated staffing, curriculum differentiation, and other experimental and innovative ideas are being researched and implemented, not only to keep the at-risk students in school until graduation but to provide the support system they need.

A germane curriculum is an important criteria for a number of at-risk students. Many of them ask: Why do I need another English class (or history, or math); how can it possibly help me? I want to work in retail sales. These types of questions can be answered in a direct, job-relevant manner when the curriculum is geared toward various student needs and requirements. It seems logical that if students are already at risk of failing and dropping out of a traditional junior or senior high school situation, continuing in the *same environment* will probably not encourage success. Clearly, a different educational structure is needed to provide the academic and social skills these individuals require to remain in the system and experience success.

What are some of the changes being made to accommodate at-risk students? New programs include a variety of things, such as cooperative learning; peer coaching; flex-time; work study; new curriculum; a committed, dedicated, specially trained teaching staff; much smaller class size; more individual instruction from the teacher(s); self-help groups; different school culture; and other changes characteristic of model programs.

Schools and programs for at-risk students of all ages require a committed student population (the students must recommit themselves to achieve success), a competent and committed staff, and a supportive community. The school community must recognize and accept some responsibility for providing an appropriate school experience for the students who perhaps are the most needy.

Servicing at-risk students is not always a popular responsibility; special programs, facilities, and staff are very expensive to provide. However, when these students develop a positive self-image, experience success, establish some immediate goals, and develop appropriate life skills, they have a better chance of becoming productive, successful adults and community members.

Multicultural Education

The concept of multicultural education is not new; the concept and the factual implementation in our educational system, kindergarten through the university level, have been realities for a number of years. Initially, multicultural education consisted of a token unit, probably in the social studies curriculum, introducing some random facts or concepts on black Americans. Generally speaking, multicultural education did not include material on Native Americans, Mexican Americans, Asian Americans, or other cultural groups. Certainly, instruction and materials did not exist in abundance across the curriculum.

A Definition

What is *multicultural education?* Is there a definitive statement that includes the various features of several cultural groups? The prefix *multi* denotes much or many; the noun *culture* means the training, development, and re-

■ People in Education

J. P. Guilford

J. P. Guilford is an important contemporary theoretician. He identified the domains of intelligence as being figural, symbolic, semantic, and behavioral. His Structure of Intellect (SOI) model suggests 120 cognitive abilities and is used widely in identifying gifted children. The SOI is a composite of mental abilities, and provides a basis for discussion and instructional planning for mentally superior children.

finement of the mind, morals, and taste. A colloquial definition could combine these two things: Multicultural education is the training and development of the mind and morals of many (groups).

In the Classroom

Teaching students and preparing them to meet the various challenges and realities of the next decade and beyond is the mandate of all new and experienced teachers. It is not practical to expect to enter your first teaching assignment and teach, reinforce, or affirm only those cultural tenets from your own personal background.

A typical teacher can expect to have students from a variety of backgrounds (Black, Caucasian, Mexican, Native American, Asian, Arabic, etc.) in the classroom. All of these students have the right to learn and participate in educational activities related to their particular cultural heritage. Multicultural education provides the means to accomplish this goal; it provides students with the necessary skills to function in a variety of social and cultural situations.

The trend is to teach multicultural issues across the curriculum; in other words, to infuse it into every curriculum area (reading, social studies, language arts, music, art, and others). It is not sufficient to teach a unit or an isolated lesson on mideastern culture and then claim to have fulfilled the requirement for teaching multicultural issues. Curriculum handbooks specifically state the multicultural strand as well as lists of appropriate instructional materials for students and teachers. Publishing houses produce a variety of updated materials that are specifically designed for elementary and secondary students.

The scope and sequence of multicultural education includes a variety of topics. Some of them are language, history, literature, music, politics, family life, ethics, customs, values, mores, art, education, and demographics. The philosophy of this curriculum is that no particular culture is inherently superior, better, or worse than any other. Each culture is important and valuable to our emerging American society.

A Matter of Language

A teacher may encounter a multicultural reality at any moment. For instance, a non-English-speaking family moves into the community and registers their children in the local elementary or high school. An hour later, or perhaps the next morning, the student is a member of your class. He or she may speak no English at all or, at best, a few social phrases. Regardless of the language fluency, the student is here now and you must teach him or her.

This scenario is not just a remote possibility. *Teacher Magazine* (1990) reports that 15 percent of our students use a native language that is not English (see Figure 9.2). Special funds are available to hire ESL (English as a Second Language) or LES (Limited English Speaking) teachers, but they are usually part of the support staff and provide supplemental instruction.

The language barrier presents an immediate challenge and professional opportunity. The teacher must begin to communicate with the student immediately and encourage the other students to do the same. Non-English-speaking students begin to learn English almost immediately by being with other students and adults who are modeling it; they use both verbal and nonverbal cues to communicate with peers.

The educational implications for teachers include an awareness of cultural taboos (i.e., particular gestures or movements), immersing the student into various language activities and experiences, providing a comfortable educational environment, setting reasonable curriculum and/or behavioral-social goals, and seeking ways to ensure academic success for the student.

Educating All Students

It is a strong probability that aspects of multicultural education will be included in the professional responsibilities of most new teachers. These responsibilities may include direct instruction of non-English-speaking students, teaching required textbook material, or serving on a multicultural education task force or curriculum committee.

Whatever the role happens to be, some strategies for addressing multicultural issues are helpful and necessary. Methods, strategies, and procedures are suggested and outlined in textbooks, instructional materials, curriculum guides, workshops, seminars, and advanced coursework. Recommendations and guidelines for implementing and teaching multicultural education are frequently available from the various state departments of education and other professional groups. Teachers are advised to participate in advanced training to increase their instructional expertise in this area.

Number of K–12 students in public schools: **40,896,000**
K–8: **29,366,000** 9–12: **11,530,000**
in private and parochial schools, K–12: **4,955,771**

Proportion of children who come from a family living in poverty: **1 in 4**
Percentage of the poor population who are children: **40**

Proportion of children who live with a single parent—
usually a working mother: **1 in 3**
Percentage of black children who come from single-parent families: **50**
Of Hispanic children: **25** Of white children: **16**

Percentage of children born to teenage mothers: **14**
Percentage of students who will become teenage parents themselves: **15**
Percentage of children born to unmarried mothers: **23**
Percentage who will be born to parents who divorce before the child is 18: **40**
Percentage who will be born to parents of whom one will die before
the child reaches 18: **2**
Number of children who live with neither parent: **1.9 million**

Percentage who have a physical or mental handicap: **16**

Percentage of students whose native language is not English: **15**
Percentage who have poorly educated, even illiterate, parents: **10**

Percentage who are latchkey children with no one to greet them
when they come home from school: **30**

Percentage of student enrollment that will be minority by 2010: **38**
By 2020: **48**
Number of the 25-largest school districts with nonwhite majorities: **25**
Proportion of states with public school enrollments that
are more than 25 percent nonwhite: **Half**
Percentage of students who are minority in:
Hawaii: **77** New Mexico: **57** Mississippi: **58** Texas: **49**
California: **46** South Carolina: **45** Louisiana: **43** Maryland: **40**
Alabama: **38** Arizona: **38** Florida: **35** Delaware: **32**
New York: **32** New Jersey: **31**
Percentage of American children who live in California, Florida, Illinois, Michigan,
New Jersey, New York, Ohio, Pennsylvania, and Texas: **50**

Number of children who have no health-insurance coverage: **12 million**
Daily number of teenage girls who give birth to their *third* child: **40**
Proportion of students who will probably not finish school: **1 in 4**
Of whites: **1 in 10** Of Blacks: **3 in 10**
Of Hispanics: **4 in 10** Of Native Americans: **5 in 10**
Percentage of high school seniors who have used illegal drugs: **54**
Proportion of seniors who drink alcohol *daily:* **1 in 20**
Percentage of seniors who began using alcohol prior to high school: **56**
Number of boys who carried handguns to school at least once in 1987: **270,000**
Who did so each day: **135,000**
Who have access to handguns: **8.7 million**

Figure 9.2 Who You Will Teach
Source: Teacher Magazine, April 1990, p. 39

■ **People in Education**

Frank Williams

Frank Williams is associated with research in the identification and measurement of creative abilities. He developed the Model for Implementing Cognitive-Affective Behaviors in the Classroom. This model emphasizes three dimensions: curriculum (subject matter content), teacher behavior (strategies for teaching), and pupil behaviors (cognitive/affective). It extends the scope of both cognitive and affective learning.

Williams proposes that students must learn not only cognitive material but also the thinking and feeling skills, and there are specific ways for teachers to teach them. His expertise also includes education for gifted students.

In addition to an obvious multicultural situation, such as a foreign-speaking student in the classroom, there are a number of other conditions and situations that concern teachers. Providing a quality educational experience that prepares students for higher education, immediate employment, and a fulfilling satisfying life as an adult is the goal of teachers, administrators, and the community at large. It is an honorable goal and we constantly strive to make it an achievable goal.

Are we successful in our efforts? *Teacher Magazine* (1990, p. 39) indicates that one in four students will probably not finish high school (one in ten of white students and three in ten of black students). This is an alarming projection. Whether you teach third grade or secondary English grammar, it is difficult to survey your classes and not silently ask yourself: Which one of these students will not finish school?

A Changing Student Population

Some 50 percent of the states have public school enrollments that are more than 25 percent non-white (*Teacher Magazine,* 1990, p.39). With percentages such as these, the multicultural issue is paramount. How can we more adequately address the cultural needs of students? What is the *culture* of our public schools? Do cultural issues enhance or detract from the students' ability to be successful in the schools as they are presently designed and/or managed? The culture of schools and its relationship to student achievement and teacher performance is a topic that bears further investigation (see Figure 9.3).

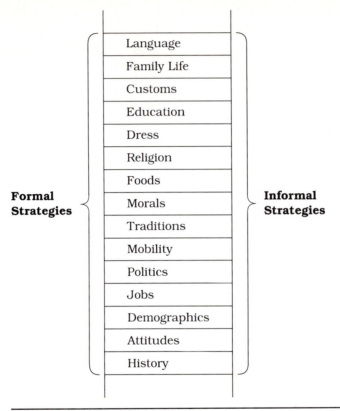

Figure 9.3 A Multicultural Program: Topics to Consider

Three additional statistics of note are: (1) 50 percent of black children come from single-parent families, (2) 10 percent of students have poorly educated or illiterate parents, and (3) 38 percent of the student enrollment will be minority (students of color) by the year 2010, and by the year 2020 it will be 48 percent, if predictions are realized (*Teacher Magazine,* 1990, p. 39).

What are the implications of these predictions for the school system? It seems clear that the number of minority students is increasing and they are coming from single-parent situations. Some practical, everyday concerns of teachers include such things as:

1. The school system's ability to meet the needs of minority students from various backgrounds.
2. Individual teacher's academic preparation to teach multicultural issues.
3. The school community's readiness to accept and accommodate a variety of cultural groups.
4. The school's and the community's process of changing from a primarily white system to a diverse multicultural community.

5. The changing standards, goals, objectives, evaluation and management processes, and outcomes.
6. The roles and expectations of teachers and administrators.
7. The traditional role of the school: What is it? Is it appropriate for the changing student population? Can change occur fast enough to meet society's needs?
8. The dynamics of change regarding traditional teacher-student-parent expectations (i.e., student responsibility, parent involvement, care and nurturing, homework, discipline, support, respect, behavior, family values, preparation for school learning, and others).

The challenge for teachers is to make every effort to provide an adequate educational experience for students from *all* cultural and ethnic groups. The publishers of educational materials are including multicultural strands in many curriculum areas. It is important that this information is included and used in textbooks, filmstrips, trade books, and other supplementary materials. It is equally important that teachers reeducate themselves to teach the material at a high level of competence.

Teaching multicultural issues with the attitude of Do I have to teach this? sends clear, *unsupportive* messages to students. Teachers must make every effort to develop a positive, enthusiastic teaching style and attitude toward incorporating multicultural education into their teaching repertoire.

Accountability: Who Is Responsible?

A perceptive adult can hardly read a magazine, journal, or newspaper without finding an article challenging the education community on the matter of accountability. Why are we seeing so much press coverage, numerous debates, discussions, and reports on the issue of professional accountability? Some probable contributing factors are the increasing costs of education, low standardized test scores, the number of students with significant academic and behavior problems, increased demands for more and better instructional materials, as well as other social problems concerning children and youth.

School is where young people are grouped together for the large part of the day. Parents and the community look to the schools and the educational setting to solve many situations and problems associated with school-aged young people.

Teachers Are Accountable

Accountability issues frequently revolve around persistent questions such as, Are we getting our money's worth? and Are schools and the teachers really doing the job? Professional teachers certainly are accountable for many responsibilities, personal and academic. Good teachers are not threatened or intimidated by accountability; they go to work and do what they are hired to do, which is to teach students. They are accountable to themselves as professionals, to administrators and school boards as responsible employees, to parents and the community as educators, and to their students as persons primarily responsible for their formal education. On any given day, observers can see teachers in classrooms teaching the required curriculum to their classes. Their greatest concern is that students will learn what they need to know to become happy, productive adults when they leave the school setting.

Measuring accountability by such means as test scores is very unfair, tenuous, and unreliable. Comparing the test scores of a high-achieving group with those of a group of Chapter I students is hardly equitable. Who actually taught the most and/or worked the hardest—the teacher of the high group or the teacher of the low group?

The whole issue of formal testing to measure students' achievement and/or learning is very controversial. Some students take tests better than others. A student's reading ability is an important factor in his or her total test scores. An individual test actually measures and ranks one's performance on the particular day the test is administered. In actuality, the particular student could conceivably do significantly better (or not as well) taking the exact same battery of tests the very next day. The student factor in the test scores controversy is very flexible.

Using a teacher's *effort* as a synonym for *accountability* is also loaded with divergent elements, such as teaching time, performance and ability levels of the students, behavioral problems, absenteeism, the number of mainstreamed special education students in the class, the quality and availability of age-appropriate instructional materials, and numerous other factors that have some effect on overall class performance.

Conscientious teachers make every effort to teach all the things that are required and mandated by the local school district as well as the particular state department of education. They are accountable for teaching a large amount of material in addition to meeting the numerous personal and social needs of the students. It is not professional to "teach the test" (i.e., teach the test ahead of time, give clues or hints to specific test questions, or other such practices that would give students an unfair advantage over another person's class). Doing this in any form is clearly unacceptable. The teaching profession generally opposes the use of student test scores to measure or assure accountability.

The general public expects teachers to teach students the academics; this certainly is a reasonable, achievable expectation. Teachers attend a college or university for four or five years of professional training to obtain a license to teach specific areas of the curriculum. They have special talents and abilities in certain areas and they want to teach and share them with others. Teachers welcome academic accountability.

The Community Is Accountable

There is a prevailing sentiment that educational accountability is somehow directly related to the amount of money the local school district and/or the state and federal government allocates to education. There is no question that significant amounts of money are required to operate and manage schools. The school community wants to provide the best education for its students that it can reasonably afford. It is unfortunate that a cadre of people and media propose the idea that they will provide the funding and we (the school and the teachers) are responsible for the educating.

This singular attitude toward the financing and the delivery of services in education is unfortunate and even damaging for everyone concerned. It proposes and promotes an adversarial relationship between the community and school personnel. It seems to delegate the inclusive responsibility for educating students to teachers and others who work in the educational system. Consider the proposition: Everyone is accountable. Is this reasonable, practical, and feasible?

The community at large is accountable both directly and indirectly. The community provides direct support to the school by allocating the necessary funds to conduct effective programs. Direct support includes a positive, supportive attitude and philosophy of education. The community is supportive when direct interest in student achievement is evidenced by attendance and news coverage of school events.

Indirect community support is also vitally important. This includes such things as providing the necessary social services that enable parents to do their job well, maintaining a safe community, keeping housing up to standards and codes, and to be advocates for good education. The community becomes accountable when it maintains an atmosphere where education and effective schools can flourish.

Administrators Are Accountable

Administrators and other school officials must be accountable. Management responsibilities, such as fiscal accountability, employing and retaining only the best faculty and staff personnel, providing the tools and materials everyone requires to perform their duties, effective and responsible strategic planning, adapting a proactive attitude, responding to particular community circumstances, and other important jobs, comprise an accountable administration.

Parents Are Accountable

An effective, productive school has accountable parents. Good parents do many things to assure a successful educational experience for their children. They provide a safe, secure, pleasant home and family life; accept responsibility for providing proper medical care and nutritious meals; and provide proper clothing, emotional support and nurturing, guidance, and many other things. Whatever the ages of their children, responsible parents are available for the support and encouragement their children need to be successful. Responsible, accountable parents are an invaluable resource for successful accountable schools.

Students Are Accountable

Is it reasonable to expect students themselves to be accountable? Can kindergartners be accountable? And are secondary students accountable for their actions and their learning? An effective school system promotes the philosophy that all students are held accountable for academic tasks. Simply stated, students must attend class regularly, be attentive, do the assignments, and give an honest effort to do their best.

It is irresponsible for a school or individual teachers to expect or accept less. Making exceptions or excuses only gives students a clear (if nonverbal) message that school in general or specific assignments aren't really that important. If the total school experience is important to everyone in the system, from the superintendent to the custodial staff, it will be important to the students. Total cooperation and support are necessary for this philosophy to be realized. Telling all students, straightforward, what is expected of them can be very effective when it is followed by consistency.

Accountability is everyone's responsibility. The sharing of responsibilities makes each person's objectives more readily achievable. When parents and the community provide an adequate support system, students are more receptive to the efforts of teachers (and others) to educate them. Coming to school ready to learn cannot be overemphasized. Accountability is both a responsibility and a reward for all persons involved.

■ Summary

Being a teacher in the years to come is an exciting prospect. Technological advancements, school reforms, new student populations, new curriculum innovations, and many other things contribute to a variety of professional challenges. In addition to the exciting, uplifting experiences you will enjoy, there are some issues that may not be so pleasant. These, too, must be accepted, endured, and hopefully solved.

Teaching is not a static experience, as there are always situations that must be faced and problems that must be addressed. Some of the issues discussed in this chapter will probably be a part of your professional experience at some time. As a teacher, you are in a position to be a proactive person to solve a problem, make a decision, or work to improve a situation that affects students. Teachers make many decisions every day. Are you ready to make those crucial decisions that can make school a better place for students to be?

■ The Workshop

Activity I

In small groups, discuss the characteristics of at-risk students. Are there differences between at-risk elementary and secondary students? If so, what are they? Define the responsibilities parents and the school have to these students.

Activity II

Go to the university library and read at least five articles on effective schools. What are the significant characteristics of effective schools? Keep these things in mind so you can be aware of them when you begin your clinical experiences and interview for a teaching position.

■ Questions and Thoughts

1. How are teachers and administrators protected from countersuits when they report child abuse? Are teachers protected in any way by their professional associations?

2. What are the recommendations for teachers regarding touching students (i.e., pats on the back, holding a child's hand, physically restraining an out-of-control student)? Is age appropriateness a factor?

3. Can a teacher be sued for filing a child abuse report in good faith that later proves to be unsubstantiated?

4. Are teachers required to teach multicultural issues in schools where there are no minorities?

■ Readings and References

Brezina, P. B., Selengut, C., and Weyer, R. A. (1990). *Seeing Society: Perspectives on Social Life*. Boston: Allyn and Bacon.

Cahoon, P. (1989, February). "Ambassadors: Models for At-Risk Students." *Educational Leadership*: 64.

Cuban, L. (1989, February). "At Risk Students: What Teachers and Principals Can Do." *Educational Leadership, 46*: 29–32.

Gelles, R. J., and Strauss, M. P. (1988). *Intimate Violence*. New York: Simon and Schuster.

Gonzalez, M. L. (1990, June). "School + Home = Program for Educating Homeless Students." *Phi Delta Kappan, 71:* 785–791.

Reed, S., and Sautter, R. C. (1990, June). "Kappan Special Report—Children of Poverty: The Status of 12 Million Young Americans." *Phi Delta Kappan, 71:* K1–K12.

Slavin, R., and Madden, N. A. (1989, February). "What Works for Students at Risk: A Research Synthesis." *Educational Leadership, 46:* 4–13.

Teacher Magazine. (1990, April). "Who You Will Teach."

Wehlage, G. G., Rutter, R. A., and Turnbaugh, A. (1987, March). "A Program Model for At-Risk High School Students." *Educational Leadership, 45:* 70–73.

■ ■ ■ **Chapter Ten**

The Real World

■ Focus Questions

1. We will be discussing various real-life classroom circumstances. Have you ever been in any of these or similar situations? What did you do? What did the teacher do?

2. Is the real classroom always on task and conducive to learning? Can you think of ways to make a learning situation out of these events?

3. In your classroom observations, what are some real-life situations that you encountered? How did the teacher handle them?

■ Introduction

This chapter consists of various reality situations. These are real situations that occur in some classrooms. You might want to start a discussion of known incidents and the resolution of the incident. These situations are included to give you a look at the real world. There are a lot more possibilities than these few, and not all will occur in your classroom, but some will.

A scenario is given, followed by a discussion of either what might occur, what you might do, or some implications of the event. Remember that the discussions are only one of many possibilities. You should try to write your own thoughts about the event described. The real answer to a real situation is what *you* will do if it happens to *you*.

■ ■ ■

Reality Situations

SCENARIO 1

You are visiting a sixth-grade classroom to fulfill course requirements. The teacher is called to the office and you are left alone with the class. An adult enters the room and announces, "I'm here to take Josh to the doctor."

Discussion: At this point, you are not a teacher, a student teacher, or a verified school district employee. A reasonable reaction would be to smile and say, "Fine." However, as an observer, you cannot possibly know all the various home and family situations surrounding each student. Release of such information is confidential. Consider these factors:

1. You don't know if this adult is really the parent.
2. The adult may be known to the student and he may appear willing to go.
3. A "release from school with mother or father only" permission may be in the student's records.
4. Does this adult have a signed release from the office (this procedure is required in many areas)?

5. Illegal removing of children from school does occur during custody and divorce cases.

To protect yourself, escort the adult to the office for check-out procedures or call on the intercom for the principal to assist you. Do not enter into a confrontation. Remember, if this is indeed a legitimate situation, the parent will respect you for your professionalism.

SCENARIO 2
The student-teaching period is a very important part of the teacher education program. It is exciting to contemplate being in a classroom and having the opportunity to teach. The university supervisor, the principal, your advisor, and your instructors all want this to be a very positive, rewarding experience. A portion of their professional responsibility is to prepare you for successful student teaching. Rarely do situations arise that seriously impair a student teaching experience. Some examples of a serious impairment to student teaching could include any of these:

1. *Threats*
2. *Sexual harassment*
3. *Lack of supervision from the supervising teacher*
4. *Unresolvable personality conflicts*
5. *Any other serious matter*

Serious problems seldom develop during student teaching.

Discussion: When these events occur, it is a serious matter for the student-teaching coordinator, the principal, the supervising teacher, and the student teacher. The working relationship of the university and the school district (or the individual building) is at risk and the matter must be handled very professionally. Serious situations must be brought to the attention of the coordinator immediately. If they cannot be reasonably resolved, it may be necessary to remove the student teacher and reassign him or her to a more productive situation.

SCENARIO 3

It is agreed that new teachers need supervision and assistance the first year of professional service. They are not expected to know everything; even experienced teachers need to have questions answered or particular matters clarified. Asking pertinent questions is not an indication of weakness; rather, it indicates a desire to learn and to grow. Mr. Sanchez is teaching second grade. He did not student teach in this grade level, as he intended to teach the sixth grade. He is floundering in the teaching of reading with an innovative reading series. He needs to get on track before the situation is out of control. What can he do?

Discussion: This teacher must take action at once. An immediate resource would be the reading curriculum committee chairperson or building representative. This person can provide both materials and instructional practices recommendations, as well as suggestions for a peer-coaching relationship. Observing a fellow teacher use the new program can be very beneficial. A secondary resource is the building principal. He or she can provide sequential direct observations and recommendations for more successful teaching.

Where do teachers get answers to their questions? How can they receive professional assistance? There are available resources in the school itself as well as outside sources. Here is a brief list of some needs and resources.

Needs	*Resources*
Certifications or license	The local continuing education committee; the State Board of Teaching
Mainstreaming a special-education student	The case manager; the special education teacher or director
Conflict resolution	The principal
Teaching materials	The librarian; the IMC director
Contractual matters	The bargaining unit representative (the president or grievance committee chairperson)
Curriculum requirements	The curriculum handbook; the grade or department chairperson; the principal

Curriculum information	The specific curriculum chairman at the State Department
Courses and workshops	Local colleges or other school districts; staff development coordinators
Facilities problems	The custodian
Classroom discipline	The principal
Everyday minor nuisances	A friend

This brief list gives suggestions for who to contact when certain needs arise. Going to the principal is not always necessary or advisable. Contacting the most direct source is usually a better idea.

SCENARIO 4
Truancy is a problem at both the secondary and elementary levels. Secondary students can skip school and slip through the system rather easily. Some contributing factors are:

1. *They can report for home room in the morning and then leave the premises.*
2. *If the attendance clerk calls the home, they can respond "I'm sick" (the parents aren't always spoken to on the phone).*
3. *It may take several hours or days to contact the parents at home or at work.*
4. *Unfortunately, society regards skipping school as a normal acceptable rite of adolescence (i.e., "a few days won't matter").*
5. *Teens are more capable of taking care of themselves; there are fewer checks and balances.*
6. *The system frequently is not prepared to force students to be in class.*

As professionals, teachers and administrators must confront truancy as an important issue. Parents need to be informed if their child is not in attendance at school.

Discussion: If there is no truancy policy for the school, one must be established in the best interest of the students. If one is there, it must be enforced by everyone, not just some of the staff members. Every teacher must report absences and be sure they are checked. The attendance clerk does the phoning and receives a response, but there is a point when the professionals must step in. Teachers are responsible for the education of students, and they can't teach Jim or Nancy if they aren't in class.

Catching truancy as soon as possible is very important. A parent-teacher-student conference should be scheduled at the earliest moment. Once again, do you (and the parents) care enough to intervene and get this student into class? Some steps to follow are:

1. Check with the attendance clerk.
2. Contact the parents at once; they may or may not be aware of the situation.
3. Arrange a three-way conference; be part of the solution, not part of the problem.
4. Get assistance from the counselor.
5. Notify the principal or other authorities.

SCENARIO 5

There are many nonacademic duties that are required of secondary teachers. After-hours responsibilities can be considerable. Football, basketball, track, concert band, choir, debate, yearbook, theater, and many other activities are part of the secondary experience and require the services of certified teachers. These are usually paid positions on the B-schedule of the master contract. The school community and administrators expect faculty members to attend school-related functions.

It is the second week of the fall quarter. The building principal announces, "Remember, the PTA Open House is next Tuesday evening from 7:00 to 9:00. We hope to see you all there." What is your reaction and responsibility? Tuesday is your bowling night.

Discussion: Teaching is hard work. After teaching a full day, teachers are tired. It is a fact of life that teachers must devote a certain amount of their private time engaged in school-related functions. An attitude of "I'm teaching and fulfilling my contractual duties from 8:00 until 3:30; evenings are my private time" is unrealistic. Professional responsibilities (as specifically stated in the master contract) and expectations (possibly unwritten, taken for granted) must be honored. In some schools, faculty attendance is assigned on a rotational basis. Attendance at school functions is good public relations and it establishes teachers as a viable part of the community. Plan to make these events a part of your life.

New teachers are advised not to schedule personal activities until they are apprised of the professional responsibilities associated with their new job. The school calendar of events is probably available from the principal or district offices. Attendance at school-related events is an important part of your job.

SCENARIO 6

You are the new teacher and your first assignment is a first-grade class. Typically there will be several bouts with the stomach flu during the year. On a particular day, little Suzie becomes ill and begins vomiting profusely. (Young children do not always admit they are feeling sick!) The class reacts loudly in various ways. Some typical reactions are shrieks, several youngsters informing you simultaneously "Teacher, Suzie's sick!", others are already moving their desks or chairs out of the way, and another child will volunteer "Shall I go get the custodian?" With all of this confusion, what can you do to recover the situation?

Discussion: As the teacher, you must act quickly; you have a sick child who needs you. If there is a sink in the room, take her there immediately or bring the wastebasket to her desk until the vomiting stops. This is better than trying to escort her down the hall to the health services office. If you do this, the problem will be in the hallway, too.

Verbally reassure and calm the other children. When Suzie is finished, call the office for the custodian to come and clean the room, and ask the nurse or health services aide to come and get Suzie. Take the class into the hall to wait, or direct them to one side of the room. It is important to accompany very sick youngsters to the office or the lavatory; do not send them alone, as they may faint on the way and injure themselves. When the room is ready, reconvene your teaching. Do not dwell on the incident.

SCENARIO 7

Generally speaking, kids like school. They like their teachers, their classmates, and most school activities. Occasionally, a student may enjoy school so much that he or she does not want to go home at dismissal time. The issue of students staying after school is a concern of many teachers and principals for various reasons. Kristen is a third-grader who frequently wants to stay after school. She has a variety of academic and social needs. Should the teacher allow her to remain after school?

Discussion: Without establishing a complete case study for this child, it is probable that what she really needs is more attention from this significant adult role model. Staying after school gives Kristen the undivided attention of the teacher, which in turn helps her feel more secure in personal relationships and (hopefully) be more successful in academic performance. These surely are positive outcomes.

The insightful teacher could work toward these outcomes during the school day by:

1. A concentrated effort to give her more rewards
2. Reinforcing her successes
3. Encouraging more positive peer relationships
4. Encouraging participation in organized after-school activities/classes
5. Working closely with the parents

6. Assigning her various classroom duties (cleaning boards, straightening book shelves)
7. In severe cases, investigating the possibility of abuse or neglect

New teachers usually feel honored when a student asks to stay after school. Teachers enjoy their students and frequently wish they had more time to relate to their students on a one-to-one basis. Although this is surely an honorable request, there are some serious issues to address in permitting students to remain after class:

1. The period after dismissal until the end of the duty day is designated preparation time.
2. This time is used for faculty and/or curriculum meetings.
3. Colleagues and parents need to see teachers for professional reasons.
4. Teachers are called out of the room for phone calls and other reasons.
5. The matter of liability is critical.
6. The relationship of the teacher with this particular student and the rest of the class needs to be examined carefully.

There are a number of other factors that can be added to this list. Many are strong positives and others are serious negatives. Teachers view this matter very critically. New teachers are advised to follow school district policy very carefully.

SCENARIO 8
One of the most difficult, heart-rendering experiences for teachers to manage is a child with school phobia (a very severe reaction to school). This condition manifests itself in many ways. Some typical behaviors are refusal to leave the house in the morning, refusal to get on the school bus, severe temper tantrums, crying or screaming, faking illnesses, or running away.

The parents of Mark, a school-phobic child, frequently bring him to school in a hysterical, out-of-control condition right to your classroom door. The other children are entering the room witnessing this extreme behavior. What can you do?

Discussion: Reassure the parents and the child that everything will be fine. It may be necessary to solicit help from another teacher or the principal to release the child from the parent. Tell the parents to leave at once; the longer they stay, the more difficult it becomes for the child to make the separation and for you to establish control. Leaving under these circumstances is very difficult for parents, but it must be done.

Once the child realizes he cannot "work a deal" to go back home, it is amazing how quickly the hysteria subsides. In a matter of minutes he will hang up his coat, sit down, and be more ready to start the day. It is essential that the parents and the teacher be calm, firm, and consistent at all times. A school-phobic child should be referred to the school counselor.

SCENARIO 9

Statistics indicate that half of the nation's teachers will leave the profession in the next five or six years, largely due to retirements. These vacancies are filled by new teachers and others returning to the profession after leaves of absence. There could easily be one new teacher on the faculty, and that person may be you! How do new teachers cope?

Discussion: At first, new teachers feel somewhat overwhelmed by the teaching expertise and educational level of other faculty members. However, as the first few weeks slip by (and they do go quickly!), the new teacher soon realizes that she or he is a bona fide member of the faculty with all of the routine rights and responsibilities. Establishing personal friendships and professional relationships is very important; they remain for a lifetime.

New teachers serve on various committees throughout the year and are expected to fulfill specific duties and speak freely. Differences of opinion are natural, and you can be assertive without being obnoxious. It is not necessary to pattern yourself after any other teacher. You are a professional and must make decisions regarding your students and your teaching. Follow-

Will you be his replacement?

ing established guidelines and practices as stated in the policies manual is necessary.

Generally speaking, experienced faculty members are very happy to have new teachers join the faculty. As professionals, they will do many things to help you adjust to the job and the community. It is not necessary to feel all alone. Chatting in the hall after dismissal is encouraged in many schools to share ideas and successes. Some districts are starting new teacher support groups that meet monthly to share ideas, solve common problems, and socialize. Being a new teacher lasts for only one year—so.enjoy the experience!

SCENARIO 10

There is no question that we live in a highly mobile society. Families move to different locations for a variety of reasons: employment opportunities, home ownership, personal reasons, lower rents, better educational opportunities for their children (real or perceived), or as an adventure or change. When families move, it affects the school population of two systems: the school that loses students and the school that enrolls them.

Some schools have populations that are more mobile than others. The mobility factor of a particular school or district can change rather quickly due to the housing situation, jobs, and other socioeconomic conditions.

A second-grade teacher in a large Midwestern school system had a 50 percent turnover in her classroom during one school term. Why is this a matter of concern?

Discussion: Teaching in a changing community can be very disconcerting for teachers. At the beginning of the school term, you establish your long-range goals for the class as well as a number of individual goals for particular students. Classes begin and everything appears to be progressing smoothly; perhaps you have identified one or two students that may require support services and you begin the paperwork to initiate the process. Then you receive notice from the office that the family is moving. Will this student be identified in the new school? Will he or she receive needed services? Teachers are concerned about this issue.

It is a challenge when new students enroll in class. The teacher must get acquainted with the new student and his or her parents. Transfer records must be studied and examined, but what if they don't arrive for several days or weeks? The teacher must somehow determine the instructional level of the new student and make arrangements to include those special needs into her short-term and long-range plans. Helping the new student adapt to the new class and the new school is an important responsibility for the teacher. A student with a severe behavior problem can disrupt the classroom atmosphere rather quickly. If two or three new students have learning disabilities, that situation requires more accommodation and planning.

Teaching every student who appears in the class is a major responsibility of all teachers, and most professionals cheerfully accept this. Teachers are human beings with feelings and emotions, and both of these are affected by the number of changes that occur during the course of the school year. Teachers become attached to their students as they watch them grow, mature, and learn. It is difficult to say good-bye when students must move; the high performers, the student with a learning disability, the abused or neglected student—each one takes a part of you with him or her when leaving your class. You think about them and often wonder how they are doing. Multiply these factors five, six, or ten times, and you may begin to understand why student mobility is a concern of teachers.

■ Summary

These reality situations do not, by any stretch of the imagination, represent all of the real-world problems that you will face. There will be serious situations, funny situations, emotional situations, frustrating situations, and a lot of routine situations. But teaching will never be boring. You will laugh and you will cry over your students, but the memories of all of the smiles and tears from your days as a teacher will make you glad you chose teaching as a profession.

■ The Workshop

Activity I

Discuss the scenarios given in this chapter. Which discussions do you agree with? What are your disagreements?

Activity II

Relate a scenario that has happened to you in school. How was it resolved? How would you have handled it? What is the worst thing you remember happening in your school career?

Activity III

In a small group, do a brainstorming activity and generate a list of some other situations that might happen in a classroom. For each situation you identify, decide on two or three practical solutions. Discuss as a large group when you are finished. Use the following chart to help you record. Be sure to use situations for both elementary and secondary classrooms.

A Chart for Recording Classroom Situations

Situations	Solutions
1.	1.
	2.
	3.
2.	1.
	2.
	3.
3.	1.
	2.
	3.
4.	1.
	2.
	3.
5.	1.
	2.
	3.

■ Questions and Thoughts

1. What are the contributing factors related to school phobia?
2. Do the police take action in cases of truancy?
3. Are repeated moves during the academic year harmful to students? Why or why not? Which ages are the most affected by changing schools? The least affected?
4. Is it appropriate to ask a teacher you know to supervise you for student teaching?

■ Readings and References

Brezina, P., Selengut, C., and Weyer, R. (1990). *Seeing Society: Perspectives on Social Life*. Boston: Allyn and Bacon.

Educational Leadership, 46, no. 3 (November 1988).

Educational Leadership, 46, no. 5 (February 1989).

Phi Delta Kappan, 71, no. 10 (June 1990).

Phi Delta Kappan, 72, no. 2 (October 1990).

Stanley, S. J., and Popham, W. J. (1988). *Teacher Evaluation: Six Prescriptions for Success*. Alexandria, VA: Association for Supervision and Curriculum Development.

Tiedt, P., and Tiedt, I. (1990). *Multicultural Teaching*. Boston: Allyn and Bacon.

■ ■ ■ Name Index ────────────────

B
Bloom, Benjamin, 19
Brezina, P. B., 193
Bruner, Jerome, 161

C
Canter, Lee, 85

D
Dechant, Emerald V.,
        126
Dunn, Kenneth, 54
Dunn, Rita, 54

F
Felton, Debbie, 27
Flanders, Ned, 169

G
Gagne, Robert, 88
Gallagher, James J., 41
Gelles, R. J., 193
Guilford, J. P., 200

H
Hunter, Madeline, 4, 22

J
Johnson, David W., 96
Johnson, Roger T., 96

K
Kolb, David, 30

L
Lehmann, Irwin J., 119
Liebowitz, Marian, 41

M
McCarthy, Bernice, 30
Madden, N. A., 197
Mager, Robert, 88
Mehrens, William A.,
        119
Montessori, Maria, 45

P
Papert, Seymour, 128
Pavlov, Ivan, 60
Piaget, Jean, 7, 128

R
Renzulli, Joseph, 148
Rowe, Mary Budd,
        110

S
Selengut, C, 193
Shanker, Albert, 179
Skinner, B. F., 68
Slavin, Robert E., 92,
        197
Sodeman, Judy, 16
Strauss, M. P., 193

T
Tyler, Ralph, 88

W
Wadsworth, Barry J., 7
Weyer, R. A., 193
Whitehouse, Karen, 4
Williams, Frank E., 40, 203

■ ■ ■ Subject Index _____

A

Abuse, 192–197
   definition, 192
   verbal, 71, 85
Accountability, 8, 21, 31, 176,
      184–187, 192, 205–208
   of administrators, 21, 32, 207
   of the community, 207
   definition, 176, 192
   ladder of, 185
   of parents, 207
   of students, 208
   of teachers, 184–185, 205–207
Accreditation, 156, 170
Administrators, 8, 15–17, 88,
      205–209
   accountability of, 207
Admission(s):
   to teacher education, 143–145
   to university, 141–143
Affective learning, 108
American Federation of Teachers
      (AFT), 179–180
Art teacher, 123
Assertive Discipline programs
      (Canter), 85
Assistant superintendent, role of,
      20–21
Association for Supervision and
      Curriculum Development, 67
At risk, 197–199
   academic accommodations,
      198
   activities, 49, 209

   articles on, 209–210
   characteristics, 195
   definition, 36, 192
   teacher, 174
Attitude of teacher, 89–90, 91–92
Auditory mode of learning, 60

B

Behavior:
   article, 174
   behaviorist(s), 68
   classroom control, 64–66
   definition, 52
   EBD, 55, 131
   ethical behavior of teacher, 8–9,
      184
   GLD, 127-129
   observation guide, 48
   school phobia, 218
   stage development, 7
   student, 83–88
   teacher, 91–92
   teacher interviews, 159
Behaviorism (Pavlov), 60
Board of Education, 19–20
Boston University–Chelsea Public
      Schools Project, 42
Brain dominance, 57
Bulletin boards, 93–94

C

Carnegie Forum's Task Force on
      Teaching as a Profession, 43
Carnegie Foundation, 42

Cause-and-effect model (Hunter), 22
Certificate and certification:
  continuing, 178–179
  maintaining, 178
  National Teacher Certification, 42–43
  obtaining, 142, 146, 177
  provisional, 156
  special licensing, 108
  steps toward, 144, 176–179
Chamber of Commerce's Business Education Partnerships, 14
Changing jobs, 185–187
Chapter I, 39
  definition, 2
  early intervention, 36–37
Child study team, 21
Children, enjoying/liking, 109–115
Circles of Learning: Cooperation in the Classroom, 96
Civil Rights Act of 1964, 31
Class control, 24, 92
  and behavior, 64–66, 83, 91
  components, 65–66
Classroom arrangement, 63, 95
Classroom management, 52, 61–64, 70, 92, 93
Classroom visitation, purpose of, 81–82
Clinical experience, 2, 5, 6, 146, 153, 170
Code of Ethics, 8–9
Cognitive domain (Bloom), 19
College experience, 4–6, 139–152
Commitment to teaching, 4, 6–8, 10, 113, 120, 122, 124, 132
  private and public school project, 42, 43
Communication disorders, 130
Community:
  accountability of, 207
  as a resource, 15–19

Community resource persons, 14
Computer(s) in education, 13–14, 95, 128, 170
  Papert, 128
Conditions of teaching, 11
  elementary, 167–169
  mobility, 162, 168, 185–187
  responsibilities, 168, 170, 183–184
  rewards, 27, 129, 168–171, 172
  secondary, 169–172
Consolidation, 176, 193
Continuing education, 2, 52, 176, 178, 187
Continuing Education Units (CEUs), 176, 178
Contracts, 78
  language of, 54–55
Control management (*See* Class control)
Cooperative learning, 78
Coordinator(s), 21–23, 29
Coursework, 140, 168
Curriculum, definition of, 36
Curriculum committee, 52
Curriculum coordinators, role of, 21–23
Cyclic pattern of teaching and learning, 10–11

D

Departmentalized classroom, 56, 156
Direct experiences with children, 116–118
Director of special education, role of, 23
Discipline, 64–66, 83
Discovery learning (Bruner), 161
Display areas, 93–94
Due process, 176

E

Early childhood, 37, 45, 167
Early intervention, 36, 37, 130, 198
  at risk, 198
  definition, 8
  early childhood/special
    education, 45
Educational Cooperative Service
  Units, 44
Educational legislation, 30–31, 32
Educational psychologist, 52
Educational research, 66–69
*Educator's Self-Teaching Guide to
  Individualizing Instruc-
  tional Programs*, 54
Elementary education, 167–169
  decision to teach, 115–125,
    134–135
  special characteristics, 11–12,
    37–39
Elementary and Secondary
  Education Act, 31, 39
Emotional Behavior Disorder
  (EBD), 131–132
Employers, 81, 157–159, 182
Endorsement, 45, 156
English as a Second Language (ESL)
  (LES), 45, 150, 201
Enrichment Triad Model, 148
Environment, classroom, 93–97
Ethics, 6, 33, 97, 106, 180, 183
  definition, 8
  NEA Code of, 8–9
Evaluation of teachers, 24
Expectations of the profession, 6–8
Experiences, school-related,
  116–118, 145, 160–161,
  164–166
Expository teaching, 52
Extracurricular activities, 163–166

F

Field experience, 79–81, 104
First year of teaching, 118

Foreign language programs, 44
4MAT System (McCarthy), 30
*4MAT System: Teaching to Learn-
  ing Styles with Right/Left
  Mode Techniques*, 30
Funding, 36

G

General education courses, 138,
  140
General learning disabled (GLD),
  55, 127–129
Gifted students, 40–41
Grade-point ratio (GPA), 6,
  141, 144, 146, 160, 161,
  177

H

Head Start, 37, 39, 198
High School for the Engineering
  Professions, 41
Holmes Group Consortium, 44–45

I

Incidental teaching, 52
Instructional assistants, 23
Instructional Materials Center, 2, 27
Instructional objectives (Mager), 88
Interest inventories, 118–119
Intervention, 56, 198
Interview(ing), 157, 159, 161

J

Jobs, teaching, 157, 159, 161, 162,
  168, 172, 185–186

L

Language-delayed students, 130
Law(s), 30–31, 39, 176, 194,
  195–196
  education, 30–31
  federal, 30–31, 39, 55, 126
  PL 94–142, 30, 55, 126
  state, 31, 40, 195

Learning modalities, 59–61
Learning process, 103
*Learning Together and Alone:
    Cooperation, Competition,
    and Individualization,* 96
Left brain, right brain, 30, 57–59,
    64, 108
Licensing, 2
Limited English Speaking, 45, 201

M
Magnet schools, 41–42
Mainstream(ing), 15, 36, 108, 126,
    127, 128
Major(s), 80, 121, 123, 138, 142,
    143, 144, 150–152, 159–160,
    167
Managing to Teach, 142
Mandated programs, 36
Marketability, 164
Master's degree, 187–188
Middle school, 46–47
*Mindstorms: Children, Computers,
    and Powerful Ideas,* 128
Minor(s), 80, 138, 142, 143, 144,
    150–152, 159–160, 167
Mobility, changing jobs, 168, 185
    to another state, 187
    in the building, 170, 185
    in state, 186
Mobility of families, 193, 220,
    221
Modalities of learning, 59–61, 72,
    73
Model for Implementing Cognitive-
    Affective Behaviors in the
    Classroom (Williams), 203
Montessori programs, 45
Multiculture, multiculturalism, 43,
    165, 192, 199–205
    in the classroom, 200
    definition, 43, 192, 199
    and language, 44, 45, 201
Music teacher, 123–124

N
National Board for Professional
    Teaching Standards, 42–43
National Council of Accreditation
    for Teacher Education
    (NCATE), 156, 170
National Defense Education Act, 31
National Education Association
    (NEA), 8–9, 179–180
National Teacher Certification,
    42–43
Neglect, 193–197
New teachers, 6, 7, 68, 182, 186,
    193
    assistance for, 22, 24
Nontraditional students, 2
Nursery school, 46, 48

O
Observing, observations:
    checklist(s), 48, 99–102
    classrooms, 81–97, 111, 117, 129
    physical environment, 93–97
    rationale, 81
    role of observer, 82
    teachers, 61, 79–80
Open enrollment, 40
Open school, 47
Operant conditioning (Skinner),
    68
Organizational patterns, 17–30
Organizational skills, 92

P
Parents, 11, 15–17, 27–29, 193,
    207–208
Personality surveys, 118–119
Phi Delta Kappa, 67
Physical education, adaptive, 55
Physical education teacher,
    121–123
Physical environment, 93–97
Physically handicapped students,
    126–127

*Piaget's Theory of Cognitive
    Development*, 7
Pilot program, 52
Portfolio, 68, 145, 156, 164,
    166
Practical Approaches to Individu-
    alizing Instruction, 54
Preparing Instructional Objectives,
    88
Principal(s), 23–26
Profession of teaching, 3–33, 37, 81,
    115
    definition, 3
    entrance into, 4, 115, 141
    expectations, 6, 90
Professional organizations, 4, 7–8,
    179–182
    membership in, 4, 181–182
    subject matter, 180–181
    teacher, 179–180
Professional rights and
    responsibilities, 183–184
Programs in education, 36–49, 52
    Boston University project, 42, 49
    discussion of, 37–38
    foreign language, 44
    for gifted, 40
    limited English, 45
    magnet schools, 41
    multicultural, 43
Public Law 94–142, 23, 30, 39,
    126
Public relations and teacher, 27

R
Reading specialist(s), 23–24,
    130–131
Research, 36–38, 53, 66–69, 96
    informal example of, 67
    need for, 66
    reading list, 68–69
Retirees as resources, 14
Revolving Door Model (Renzulli),
    148

S
Scales for Rating the Behavioral
    Characteristics of Superior
    Students, 148
School organization, 3, 17–30
    board of education, 19
    community, 18
    coordinators, 21
    director of special education,
        23
    organizational chart, 18
    parents, students, 29
    principals, 23
    student support team, 21
    teachers, 26
School-related experiences,
    116–118
Schools for creative and performing
    arts, 40
Seatwork, 86
    definition of, 78
Secondary education, 17, 37,
    39–41, 43–44, 80, 109,
    169–172, 186
    decision to teach, 115–125,
        134–135
    special characteristics, 11–12,
        113
Self-contained classroom(s), 56, 95,
    120, 156, 168, 184, 186
Seniority, 54, 186
Social services, 196–197
Social-interaction model (Flanders),
    169
Special education, 30, 45, 87, 108,
    126–132, 148, 149, 160, 186
    director of, 23
    Emotional Behavior Disorder
        (EBD), 131–132
    General Learning Disabled
        (GLD), 127–129
    law(s), 30, 108, 126–127
    physically handicapped, 23, 55
    speech/language, 21, 45, 55

Specialists, 120–125
    art, 123
    music, 124–125
    physical education, 121–123
Speech-delayed students, 130
Speech-language teacher, 21, 45,
        130, 170, 186
Staff development, 52
State Department of Education, 2,
        206
State-development theory (Piaget),
        7
Structure of Intellect (Guilford),
        200
Student management team, 25
Student population, 203–205
Student support services team, 21
Student teaching, 5, 6, 29, 37,
        79–81, 117, 146–149, 170
Students, 29
    accountability, 208
    behaviors, 83–88
    characteristics, 29, 112
    role in school, 29
Subject organizations, 180–181
Substitute teaching, 172
Superintendent, 20
    assistant, 20–21
    role and responsibilities, 20–21
Supervising teacher, 138
Support systems, 21, 31, 46, 56,
        171, 196

T
Tactile-kinesthetic mode of
        learning, 60
Taxonomy of Educational
        Objectives, The, 19
Teacher:
    accountability of, 205–206
    behavior, 90–92
    candidate, 2
    characteristics, 113, 119,
        134–135

license, 2, 42
    observing, 88–93
    responsibilities, 25, 57
    role, 11, 26–29
    and self-esteem of students,
        28
Teacher assistant (TA), 27
Teacher Credentialing Office, 4–5
Teacher Magazine, 201, 202, 203,
        204
Teacher organizations, 179–180
Teaching, 2–15
    definition, 9–10
    expository, 11, 52, 60, 62, 64, 95
    incidental, 52, 53
    and learning process, 103
    playing games, 113–115
    as a profession, 3–8
Teaching the Gifted Child, 41
Teaching Makes a Difference,
        142
Teaching positions, availability of,
        157–159, 162–163
Teaching Students Through Their
        Individual Learning Styles:
        A Practical Appraoch, 54
Technology in education, 13, 14,
        128, 170 (See also
        Computer(s) in education)
Tenure, 24, 30, 182–183
    definition, 2, 182
Traffic flow in classroom, 95–97
Title I, 39

U
Undergraduate curriculum
        requirements, 139–140
University:
    advisor, 5, 29, 119, 138, 141,
        142–144, 151, 165, 177
    coordinator, 80, 88, 97, 119,
        146–149
    faculty, 5, 138
    requirements, 141–149

V

Visual mode of learning, 59–60
Vocabulary in teaching profession,
    53–56
Voluntary Open Enrollment
    Program, 40

W

Work habits, 86–87
Working conditions, 93